ALL EYES EAST

ALL EYES EAST

LESSONS FROM THE FRONT LINES OF MARKETING TO CHINA'S YOUTH

MARY BERGSTROM

First published in 2012 by
PALGRAVE MACMILLAN®
in the United States—a division of St. Martin's Press LLC,
175 Fifth Avenue, New York, NY 10010.

Where this book is distributed in the UK, Europe and the rest of the world,
this is by Palgrave Macmillan, a division of Macmillan Publishers Limited,
registered in England, company number 785998, of Houndmills,
Basingstoke, Hampshire RG21 6XS.

Palgrave Macmillan is the global academic imprint of the above companies
and has companies and representatives throughout the world.

Palgrave® and Macmillan® are registered trademarks in the United States,
the United Kingdom, Europe and other countries.

ISBN: 978–0–230–12062–4

Library of Congress Cataloging-in-Publication Data

Bergstrom, Mary.
    All eyes East : lessons from the front lines of marketing to
China's youth / by Mary Bergstrom.
      p. cm.
    ISBN 978–0–230–12062–4 (hardcover)
      1. Youth—China—Attitudes. 2. Youth—China—Social conditions—
21st century. 3. Youth—China—Economic conditions—21st century.
    4. Intergenerational relations—China. 5. Marketing—China. I. Title.

HQ799.C5B47 2012
305.2350951—dc23   2011039718

A catalogue record of the book is available from the British Library.

Design by Newgen Imaging Systems (P) Ltd., Chennai, India.

First edition: March 2012

10 9 8 7 6 5 4 3 2 1

Printed in the United States of America.

For my dream team:
Jonathan, Scarlett, Haile, and Prudence

CONTENTS

FIGURES

FOREWORD

I FIRST CAME TO CHINA 25 YEARS AGO. Given the country's long history, this seems in some ways like the blink of an eye; in other ways, however, it is the equivalent of a geological era. China is changing to such an unprecedented degree that sometimes it is hard to appreciate the profound implications of this transformation, both for China and for the wider world.

Yet for any business seeking to prosper in the global market, and anyone who wants to discern the contours of tomorrow, understanding China is crucial. That is one good reason to read *All Eyes East*. Mary Bergstrom knows this subject intimately, and her book explains how China's young people are reshaping the world's business landscape in groundbreaking ways:

- *Digital technology*. China has the largest base of Internet users worldwide—bigger than the total population of the United States—and its numbers are growing by 15% a year.
- *Cell phones*. With roughly 1 billion subscribers, China is the world's biggest mobile phone market, and about one-third of all subscribers use their phones to access the Internet.
- *Automobiles*. China recently overtook the United States to become the world's biggest market for family cars, and some analysts say that its domestic luxury car market will more than double in the coming years.
- *Tourism*. Within a few years China is expected to become the world's largest tourist market, with approximately 130 million travelers venturing abroad annually.
- *Consumer goods*. Many analysts believe China will become the second-largest consumer market in the world within three years, with enough purchasing power to buy 14% of the world's products.

- *Luxury goods.* China already buys one-quarter of the world's luxury goods, and is predicted by some to grow by 25% annually over the next five years.

DRIVING FORCES AND KEY PLAYERS

For these and many other reasons, all eyes are indeed facing east, and Mary Bergstrom's book reveals many of the forces driving China's remarkable transformation. Naturally these forces include rising living standards and spending power, but they also encompass society's rapidly changing attitudes about what is acceptable and what is desirable. Take, for example, China's recently developed consciousness about environmental issues, or its exploding market for luxury goods. When I first arrived in China in the mid-1980s, the very concept of luxury was frowned upon politically. When clients such as Dior, Hennessy, and Louis Vuitton wanted to launch products in China, I had to work with them to develop a new vocabulary for these products.

Today it is a different world, one with profound implications for many different groups:

- *Women.* Said by Mao Zedong to hold up half the sky, women have been newly empowered by economic and demographic factors. Globally, they control an estimated two-thirds of the world's discretionary consumer spending, and their contribution to household incomes has risen steadily over the past few decades. What will China (and the world) look like as women's spending power and social influence continue to rise?
- *Entrepreneurs.* Recent research shows that 54% of Chinese adults under age 30 plan to open their own businesses, while 44% of those born in the 1960s and 1970s harbor similar aspirations. These hopefuls include the so-called "second generation" of wealthy Chinese youth seeking, among other things, to rebrand themselves as entrepreneurs rather than simply the privileged elite.
- *Consumers.* Only a generation ago, the choice of products available in China was quite limited, and people accepted whatever was available. Today, consumer activism has become a watchword, especially among the younger demographic. This activist trend, combined with the rapid adoption of social media, means that consumer-facing companies in

China must stay on their toes—a development with huge significance for consumer brands.

- *Chinese companies.* An innovator for 5000 years, China will soon produce some of the world's strongest and most original global companies. As they seek market share both domestically and overseas, these companies will need to communicate differently than in the past, using digital technologies that are a radical departure from tradition both in their speed and in their unprecedented openness. Until quite recently, the notions of branding, marketing, and strategic communications were alien concepts in China, but as its global stature grows, the issues its companies are called upon to manage are becoming increasingly complex.

All Eyes East focuses on Chinese youth, a demographic cohort that will play a vital role in the world's most rapidly aging country. But the book looks beyond that demographic to analyze the implications of a rapidly evolving social landscape in the world's most influential emerging market. Read it to understand the opportunities available and to avoid the pitfalls of failing to grasp the key forces shaping this newly ascendant power. Above all, read it to understand the most fascinating and important societal transformation of our time.

SERGE DUMONT
Vice Chairman, Omnicom Group Inc.

ACKNOWLEDGMENTS

I WROTE THIS BOOK TO ENCOURAGE PEOPLE AS WELL as brands to look beyond the surface to learn something meaningful and moving from pioneering young Chinese. This book is an expression of gratitude for all of the experiences and relationships I have had living in China. It has been a rare privilege to develop and learn from a diverse network of trendspotters, youth experts, and partners.

I could not have written this book alone. I thank all of the excellent interviewees—academics, tastemakers, youth, marketing mavens, journalists, and creators—who have lent their experience and insights to this book (be they explicitly referenced or not). Even though my name graces the cover, the journey has been a true group effort. Special acknowledgment is due to my good friend Rebecca Catching for her constant encouragement and superb editing. I would also like to give express credit to Toni Young and Jiang Xinyi, key members of my staff who have provided committed research and thoughtful analysis. Lastly, all of my research mentioned in the book is the work of our team. I congratulate and appreciate the collaboration.

INTRODUCTION

> With too many dreams which are just adults' hypotheses and too many expectations which gradually become desperation, I am just afraid that my destiny has already been written by society. I know where I should go; but whatever happens, I won't have the right to say it out loud.
>
> —From preface to Su Zizi's "Diary"

SU ZIZI WAS BORN WHEN SHE FIRST UNDRESSED AND stepped naked in front of the camera. In the beginning, other photographers directed her from behind the lens, but as she gained confidence in her own point of view, Su stopped being a model and became an artist herself. Su did not intend to use her body to force debate; rather, her foray into modeling was a byproduct of simple financial need. She came from a poor family, and in order to chip in on the costs of her education, Su disrobed for modeling gigs that paid 500 RMB a session.[1] She did not take the work lightly. For a nice college girl, it meant stepping far outside the frame. By mainstream standards, nude modeling was a debased, low-level occupation that had unsavory implications. College students, on the other hand, were held in high estimation for their ascension up the ladder—but were considered to have little sexual experience or awareness. As the first college student to publicize her own work as a nude model, Su broke ground and posed unsettling questions about new values involving sexuality, gender, and success in China. The personal liability of her choice to defy society's concepts did not escape her. Su acknowledged the gravity of her transgression by adopting an alternate identity (Su Zizi is not her real name) and kept her job a secret from her parents.

Her first exhibit of nude images, *Who Am I*, took place at Renmin University where the 19-year-old was enrolled as a sophomore. The next show, *Age of Kidnapped Dreams*, assumed grander proportions: eighteen nude photographs and a 5-minute video were shown at a gallery in Beijing's prestigious 798 art district.[2] For the opening, Su literally offered herself up as a canvas, encouraging visitors to paint their own words on her flesh.[3] With each step, Su pushed forward with her transformation from average girl trying to make it in the city to social provocateur. Her daring was uncomfortable and as such, she incited both admiration and anger. Still, in less than a year after her first college show, Su had already published three books about her life and was writing and directing a short film to tell the story of her generation.

Su's work put her on the fringe of society, but she did not ascend to this position in a vacuum. Her role as revolutionary was enabled by important changes in her environment. In this way, Su's story is the story of all modern Chinese youth. Her story would be impossible to understand without first recognizing the classification of generations that pushes youth into feuding camps based on the decade in which they were born. Born in the 1990s, Su was more open-minded than previous generations about expressing her own ideas about sexuality and forcing a response. Her willingness to stray from the mainstream represented new personal and political frontiers for China and, although she speaks as an individual, Su represents scores of others like her. As youth develop confidence in their own points of view, they build increasingly vibrant subcultures that represent a shift away from the mainstream. It is because of these alternative tribes that Su was able to find the necessary support to enable her choice to become a provocateur.

After having witnessed the heartache of the generation before her working to keep up with just-out-of-reach consumption imperatives, Su became disillusioned with normal roads to success and determined instead to forge her own path. Like Su, the next wave of Chinese workers sees a profession as a means of obtaining personal satisfaction, not just a salary.

It is difficult to imagine another point in China's history when a 19-year-old girl from a disadvantaged background could have risen to fame as an avant-garde artist. The mix of China's gender imbalance and rapid modernization opened the doors for this young woman, an unlikely protagonist, to walk through and exercise her girl power. In another time, Su's looks might not have warranted a position as a model at all. Attractive, but not in a traditional way, Su's placement in front of the lens represents youth's expanding ideas about new beauty codes – and the idea of difference in general.

Both on and offline, youth like Su are speaking up and finding a space for their opinions to matter. Their ability to mobilize in small groups is helping to spread social activism in the mainland and consequently reshaping what has been a monologue into a conversation. As they gain confidence in their own expression, millions of Su's peers are expanding their scope to re-imagine themselves and the world around them.

Throughout her story, Su took advantage of opportunities to explore and expand her identity. She asked questions about who she was and what she stood for—and invited others to do the same. For young Chinese, the notion of a constantly evolving identity and a redefinition of Chineseness is central to determining the next phase of youth culture. The narrative is far from over.

Su's story has particular value for brands that hope to tap into this young and influential market. Recognizing the impact of Su (and others pioneers hard at work establishing a new paradigm for youth in China) is a critical mission. She is part of a wave of young vanguard Chinese who are determining what they can and should be. Neither their parents nor their international peers have experienced the same degree of opportunity (or enormous expectation) as the first generation to emerge from the world's greatest economic miracle.

This book is based on my own experiences on the ground in the mainland, and it tells the story of Chinese youth as I have come to understand it. It incorporates work that my research team has conducted: rich ethnographies that involve peering into closets, witnessing online communities, and digging into the difference between what is stated and what is real. It channels voices from true culture creators, average kids, and everyone in between. To complement my own experience and present the market from other angles, I have called upon experts from brands, academia, marketing agencies, and the media to bring examples to life and provide critical analysis.

It is my hope that reading this book will enable you to stand confidently on the front lines. By opening new doors of understanding and empathy, connecting with youth will be less formidable and more rewarding. By creating a closer relationship, more relevant products and marketing can benefit companies and consumers.

CHAPTER 1

The New (R)evolutionaries: The Post-70s, Post-80s, and Post-90s Generations

> Post-50s and post-60s get money, post-70s get girls, and post-80s only get pressures.
>
> —Han Han, novelist and China's most
> popular blogger, born in 1982[1]

I REMEMBER THE EXCITEMENT I FELT DODGING treacherous Shanghai traffic on my way to meet a potential senior research manager. Let's call her "Maggie." On paper, Maggie had everything I was looking for—she seemed like someone who would be curious enough to dive deeply for understanding and organized enough to make sure her efforts led to insights. I nodded at most of her answers, until she got to the part about working with others.

She would be happy to work with people from her own generation (those born in the 1980s) and even with the previous generation, but Maggie was quick to communicate a clear bias against those born less than a decade after her. "I don't know if I could work with a post-90s," she lamented, "they are too wild." When I asked her to expound on her judgment, her assertion was unshaken—despite an admitted lack of first-hand experience. Supported by rumors she had read online and anecdotes from her same-generation peers,

Maggie had determined that youth just a few years her junior were too different to work with.

What struck me was her confidence in making a declaration that was not based on any personal connection. This was especially surprising for someone whose work depended on unbiased research and analysis. And yet, it wasn't surprising. Even the media was making sweeping assumptions about people based on the decade in which they were born. Youth in the mainland were being pitted against each other, sometimes based on as little as five years' difference in age. The generations were not playing nice.

In China, each decade presumably brings a new change in mind-set. Until recently, the Chinese named generations in sequence, from the first generation (pre-1949) through the fifth generation (post-1989). In the post-Mao mainland, the country's race to modernity has created very different childhoods for each generation, inextricably melding youth with the opportunities, expressions, and motivations of their decade. Today, generations are more linked with a moment in time than they are with each other. As such, they are named after the decade in which a person is born: the post-1970s, the post-1980s, and the post-1990s.

But there are no hard or fast rules for defining generations. For example, the United States uses demographics to help create segments. Gen X (generally defined as those born in the late 1960s to early 1980s) was originally called the Baby Bust generation, for its low birth rate, as compared to the large Baby Boomer generation that preceded it. Generation Y, or the Next Generation, followed, and its members have been nicknamed the Echo Boomers, or the Millennials, again in reference to the group's size compared to the Baby Boomers. This structuring (Baby Boomers, Gen X, Gen Y) is used in many countries, including Russia, the Czech Republic, South Africa and Brazil.[2]

Other countries take a different approach to defining a generation. In lieu of following demographic shifts, some countries mark new generations when they experience influential events or critical changes in their population's mind-set and behavior. Japan refers to its young generations as the Post-Bubble Generation; the Shinjinrui Junior Generation, also known as Generation Z; and the Yutori. India defines new generations when critical shifts in outlook occur (i.e., the Traditional Generation; the Nontraditional Generation; and the most recent, least self-reflective, most globally compatible Gen Y).

Although China has marked its generations every decade, gaps arise even in this abbreviated time frame. In my research, I have witnessed critical shifts in attitudes in audiences with as little as three to five years' age difference. I have also noted that, while they self-identify with the decade in which they were born, some youth feel and act more aligned to another generation. Grasping the character of these generations is critical to understanding Chinese youth and to resonating with target audiences. It also serves as a poignant example of how fast-moving influences have accelerated divisions.

Generational labels in China are not just descriptive, they are also deeply personal. Unlike their Gen X and Gen Y counterparts in the United States, Chinese use generations to establish strict boundaries. These labels align individuals with a specific and universally understood group, a movement that is larger and more powerful than any single individual. In this vernacular, Chinese youth are commonly identified—and perhaps most importantly, identify themselves—by the decade in which they were born. For example, someone born in 1976 would be referred to as a post-70s, while his cousin born in 1987 would be a post-80s, and his neighbor born in 1994 would be a post-90s. These descriptors connote categories with very specific personalities. The statement, "She is a post-90s" says just as much about the "she" in question as it does about the post-90s as a category.

FROM FRIEND TO FOE

The year 2008 was a turning point in many ways for youth in China—it was jam-packed with events that caused them to reevaluate their position in their communities and in the world. At the end of 2008, I conducted a study of the changing attitudes and behaviors of trendsetting youth for an advertising agency that services a variety of youth-focused brands. In a year that included the Olympics, the sex scandal of pop superstar Edison, and confrontations with foreign powers over Tibetan independence, respondents revealed that the most important event of the year was the Sichuan earthquake.

As the nation rallied resources to support earthquake victims, an unexpected star emerged: Chinese youth. The earthquake initiated a groundswell of activism—young people donating time and money, organizing, and participating in relief efforts. All eyes were on China's only children as they took initiative for the first time to contribute to society.

Before the quake, the post-80s generation was described as Little Emperors, and was reputed to be self-serving and individualistic. In the wake of the earthquake, more than six thousand volunteers arrived on-site to help victims recover; 80 percent of these volunteers were reported to be members of the post-80s clan. Beyond the volume of volunteers, the selfless quality of their commitment was also unexpected; the media hailed the post-80s' willingness to sleep on the street and bring their own rations in order to help with the relief effort.[3] Many youth even transported volunteers and supplies in their own cars because they did not trust official aid networks to deliver. The post-80s showed they could think and act beyond themselves, and caused the country to rethink negative stereotypes. At the same time, their actions further amplified how and why the generations perceived themselves to be not only different but also separate from each other. A line was being drawn in terms of responsibility and nonconformism.

In contrast to the spotlight on the post-80s, the earthquake cast a shadow on the post-90s. Video clips of the post-90s, seemingly unaware of the earthquake, and screenshots of their blog posts portrayed them as less than patriotic. Compared to the post-80s' enthusiastic volunteerism, the post-90s seemed uncaring and ill informed. In this important time of need, the post-80s rose to the top and pushed the post-90s down.

Xiao Yun, a pretty girl claiming to be a post-90s from Sichuan, exemplified her generation's contentious reputation. After the quake, Xiao Yun posted more than a hundred scantily clad photos of herself online with the stated mission of raising money for Sichuan relief. The photos, which drew more than 1 million views, also attracted controversy and further drew the lines between the generations.

While some criticized her for such a sexy public display, Xiao Yun and her supporters—exhibiting typical post-90s individualism versus post-80s mass orientation—argued that it was her right to express herself.

BROADCASTING TO THE GENERATIONS

The reputation of each generation has been spread virally and fine-tuned using videos, charts, and jokes to boil them down to their essence. The result is more than just casual, sloppy slang; these concepts have been given a platform for widespread acceptance. Stereotypes brewed in youth's internal distribution loops have percolated up into the mainstream media and made their way into official, state-run headlines.

The mainstream media has capitalized on the country's generation fixation, leveraging differences to create entertainment that exploits and explains the gap. Airing on Shanghai's Arts and Humanities television channel, *Speak Out* allows the audience to tackle current events and new societal developments. Besides its subject matter, the show draws eager viewers keen to compare generational viewpoints. The program identifies audience members by their generation, name-tagging participants simply by decade (the post-40s through the post-90s). For *Speak Out*, labeling a speaker by generation is all that is needed to help viewers understand and categorize his or her point of view. One episode banged away at the idea of couples from different social and economic backgrounds getting married. While more traditional-minded speakers argued that an unequal footing leads to struggle and unhappiness, others claimed that backgrounds matter less in modern times. A post-50s male suggested that the obsession with a good match was the result of mothers butting into their child's welfare. He warned that the practice was out of date and that it hampered parents' relations with their children. A post-70s female creative planner felt strongly that people's social standing could be changed quickly in modern China, and thus it was an antiquated means of judging a person's quality. A male post-80s playwright waxed poetic, "This is not a pig farm, and we are not looking for a qualified pig to generate the best piglet."

Another television program focused on generations airs on Hunan Satellite TV. The first program to use a number as its name is *8090*, squarely targets post-80s and post-90s viewers. The weekly program allows youth to voice their personal problems and gain exposure to different perspectives. Episodes tackle issues germane to youth trying to find their way, including whether girlfriends should financially support their boyfriends, and what a woman who found herself pregnant and married to a cheating spouse should do. The show's 12-person observation team, called 8899, is composed of television hosts, students, white-collar workers, and experts from various fields.

While shows like these create a dialogue, they also highlight the chasms between youth in China, often leading to bad blood. At first, the post-70s fretted over the post-80s' lack of responsibility, then the post-80s insulted the post-90s, only to have the post-90s fire back. In China, each group expresses a general sentiment of superiority but with very different reasoning. The post-70s see themselves as China's responsible old guard, the post-80s perceive themselves to be the shiny face of new China, and the post-90s are confident enough in the system to create breaks from it. The media both illustrates and exploits these stereotypes to explain differences and enable generalizations.

THE GLOVES COME ON(LINE)

Despite obvious differences between the post-70s and their younger peers, it is really the battle between the post-80s and the post-90s that has captured the attention of the nation. The start of the altercation predates the earthquake by a few short months and has been attributed to a seemingly benign bout of name-calling.[4] When a group of post-80s created and uploaded a treatise against the post-90s to a video-sharing site, post-90s "netizens" (the term used to describe Chinese Internet citizens) responded in kind. Taunt forth, taunt back. A video battle was born.

The first offense, titled "On the Non-Mainstream," was a video created by youth in the style of an official China Central Television (CCTV) news broadcast and uploaded to a video sharing site.[5]

The mock program, titled "Super News," at first seemed real. The creators maintained high production values, employing a motion graphic title sequence and dubbing over real newscasters' commentaries with their own dialogue. The topic of the newscast was the problems of the post-90s. A fictitious professor was the featured expert—the bag covering his head, with a face drawn in black ink, tipped viewers off to the spoof.

Reviewing a collage of sexy, silly images that the post-90s uploaded of themselves, the professor criticized the generation's unique online vocabulary (officially called Martian language) and their hallmark big-eyed, pucker-lipped, Photoshopped self-portraits. The professor griped that these photos featuring exaggerated big eyes and puckered lips made the post-90s "look like monkeys." His overall analysis that the generation was "stupid" was followed by a montage of post-80s mocking the post-90s for their style, language, and public displays of sexuality.

This taunt prompted a comeback from the opposing side. Titled "Response from a Non-Mainstream Beauty," the video shows a post-90s girl tapping away at her pink PSP (PlayStation Portable gaming device). Her hair is held purposefully in a messy side bun, her makeup and expressions exaggerated in allegiance to her generation's unique style. In the background is her computer, a collection of pink toys, and other trappings associated with a girl following China's cult of cute.

Throughout her single-shot, ten-minute monologue against the post-80s, she continues to multitask with her PSP. She rants that the post-80s are jealous of the post-90s' comfortable and glamorous life and boasts that she has friends with Hummers, living in big houses in Pudong (a recently developed, swanky area in Shanghai). She warns the post-80s that her generation is coming up and taking over. She closes her speech by contorting her face into some highly adorable, puffed-cheek expressions augmented with hand signals to the audience. While not exactly fighting words by most standards, this exchange prompted a snowstorm of video insults from both sides. The post-80s point the finger at the post-90s for acting outside of the norms, and the post-90s point back that the norms are old news.

GENERATIONAL SNAPSHOTS

To understand the generations, it is useful to look at them individually, but a comparative analysis provides some context for the changes between each generation. Generations have evolved on a sliding scale: the post-70s are traditionalists, the post-80s are more conservative leaders, and the post-90s are linked with nonconformism. The evolution in attitudes and behaviors can be seen across many areas. James Farrer, director of the Institute of Comparative Culture at Sophia University and author of *Opening Up: Youth Sex Culture and Market Reform in Shanghai*,[6] has been studying the sexual evolution in Chinese society for 20 years. His analysis shows that each generation's beliefs about sex have been linked to the social and economic times they have lived through. As Farrer notes, "Of all the generations, the post-80s experience the biggest generation gap. The post-90s is much more likely to have parents that are liberal. They also are the first generation to grow up with extreme differences in wealth, and they're very aware of that. They are also the first to grow up where China is a rich country—and without that sort of anxiety and hunger that everybody in China used to have, that need to join the big world out there. The post-80s still feel like they need to catch up, but there is a sort of smugness in the youngest generation [the post-90s]."[7] The generations demonstrate an evolution in attitudes and behaviors that starts with the last generation to have a memory of a pre-open China, the post-70s.

THE POST-70S: GROUP-ORIENTED TRADITIONALISTS

Coming of age when China was still considered to be a poor country reinforced the post-70s' group thinking as a means of survival. Over 220 million strong, growing up surrounded by grandparents, parents, and siblings, the post-70s were raised with a strong work ethic and were oriented to improve living conditions for the whole family. Brought up during the transition from the Cultural Revolution, the post-70s grew up in an era when the government was easing its responsibility for providing clothing, food, housing, and occupations.

The post-70s were raised with values that today seem distant from those of the more individualistic post-80s and post-90s. The post-70s grew up with fewer opportunities than subsequent generations to exercise their own choices; expectations of a life separate from the group had not yet taken root during their childhoods. As a result, research today points to the post-70s being more conscientious workers and more apt to consider the impact of their actions on others. The post-70s' considerations for the group and their long-term outlook (saving for the future and revering the past) are ancient history for the post-80s and post-90s, who are preoccupied with instant gratification.

In the process of segmenting young consumers for a client, I asked respondents to help pinpoint and compare generational profiles. Each interview was conducted individually and in-person to enable a deeper understanding of how and why attitudes had been formed. I have used these respondents' self-assigned foreign names when possible, as it is a meaningful personal choice and a common practice among youth to choose an alternate name that they will use both socially and professionally. This phenomenon itself generated a book called *In China, My Name Is* by Valerie Blanco and Ellen Feberwee.[8] Young Chinese commonly choose English and Japanese first names, but also may name themselves after objects or make up their own moniker. Some of the most memorable names I have come across include Killer, Attila, NATO Bomb, Rfu, and Swear, but they also trend in cycles. For example, as I write this, we have a solid base of trendsetters who go by Apple.

In this study, we find that youth are confident in their opinions about other generations and generally agree on a set of common characteristics that define them. The post-80s and post-90s perceive the post-70s as "traditional," "conservative," and "steady." Post-70s youth are seen as more sensitive to others and more likely to act as a member of the group than as the star.

> "They are graceful and harmonious with a steady attitude. They treat people in a more generous way than the post-80s."—Coey, Shenzhen, a post-90s (research conducted by The Bergstrom Group, 2009)

The post-70s are perceived to be the more methodical generation: more likely to think things through, plan actions, and default to organization over chaos. More adept at long-term planning than their younger peers, they are recognized as the last generation to value financial responsibility and save, instead of spend.

> "They are older than us by a generation, so they still hold some old ideas. They think they should save all the money they earn [in case something goes wrong]. So what's the point of earning money? Post-80s and post-90s will spend their money and then try to make more money."—Hunter, Shanghai, a post-80s (research conducted by The Bergstrom Group, 2009)

Unique in "thinking before they leap" about others, the past, and the future, the post-70s are seen as more conscious of the bigger picture. Another key differentiator between the generations is the post-70s' use of technology as a tool for information rather than pure entertainment. In the eyes of the post-80s and post-90s, these traits contribute to negative feelings that the post-70s are unable to live in the moment, that they are out of touch, and unwilling to learn new ways of doing things.

THE POST-80S: STATUS-MINDED LEADERS

At 223 million strong, the post-80s are the first to be born into China's new era of market reforms and opening up. Raised as single children under the one-child policy, the post-80s are the first generation to command the attention of six adults (two parents and four grandparents). Growing up, everywhere they looked, the post-80s were in the spotlight. As new academic and professional doors opened, the post-80s were the first to walk through them. As new products, brands, and experiences became available, the post-80s were the first to experiment and report back to the group. Accustomed to receiving the lion's share of financial and emotional attention from their families, the post-80s were brought up with a sense of entitlement—and an expectant audience.

New China's first generation has been termed the Strawberry Generation (good looking, but easily bruised), Little Emperors (treated like royalty), and the Me Generation (lacking consideration for others). Motivated by high family expectations, the post-80s wielded their power to develop new notions of success and status. They introduced the notion of personal luxury, and imported individualism from abroad to define their own hybrid value system. The post-80s' aspirations seem more similar to the post-90s' rebellion, but their actions descend directly from the post-70s' group values.

The post-80s are now in a pivotal position. Armed with their own incomes and a newly polished image, the post-80s are frequent stars of the mainstream media. Accomplished in their own right, six of the top ten Chinese celebrities named by *Forbes Magazine* in 2010 are post-80s—including uber-pop superstar Zhou Jielun (Jay Chou), who is Taiwanese but rules the mainland's pop scene (#2); basketball impresario Yao Ming (#4); Chinese actress turned Hollywood star Zhang Ziyi (#5); Taiwanese folk-popper Cai Yilin (Jolin Tsai) (#7); Olympic hurdler Liu Xiang (#9); and "it" actress Fan Bingbing (#10).

While society largely fretted over the Strawberry Generation's superficiality and foreign-minded character before 2008, its reputation changed dramatically after the Sichuan earthquake. Their newfound selfless behavior in helping quake victims gave them new standing as responsible patriots. Still, in describing the post-80s, the post-70s and post-90s are keen to point a finger at the generation's materialism, consumerism, and fixation on work despite often lacking experience.

> "The post-80s always think they are mature enough, but actually, they lack experience. In this rapidly developing society, they're stressed and worry about jobs. One of my friends has been job hunting, but keeps losing out because he doesn't have any experience. My friends who are post-80s always complain about how difficult it is to find a job, and seem very depressed."—Kerry, Shenzhen, a post-90s (research conducted by The Bergstrom Group, 2009)

The post-70s and post-90s are not the only ones to question the post-80s' real capabilities. The post-80s themselves are increasingly aware of the advantages—and weaknesses—of their unique position.

> "We know what we want. We have a good education because we are the only child in the family. Sometimes, though, parents will spoil us, which leads us to be selfish."—Joey, Shanghai, a post-80s (research conducted by The Bergstrom Group, 2009)

The post-80s stand between the other two generations: the post-70s see the post-80s as too frivolous, while the post-90s see the post-80s as too serious.

Figure 1.1 Post-80s and post-90s youth wearing T-shirts proclaiming the values of their generations. Photo by Leena Zhou

POST-90S: REBELLIOUS INDIVIDUALISTS

Numbering over 200 million, the post-90s are the second generation of only children and the first to be born into an already open and established society. From the post-90s' point of view, China has always been a superpower. In their lifetimes, the economy and China's status in the world have grown steadily; a constant flow of new brands, new technologies, and new experiences is par for the course for post-90s.

Raised by the post-70s, the post-90s are more confident than the post-80s and prize speaking up and acting out in ways that were previously unheard of in China. Along with more liberal home lives, the post-90s have been shaped by access to sophisticated technologies and exposure to a wider net of influences that have reshaped what the post-90s believe to be possible. With constant online access, the post-90s have been raised to expect nonstop connection and change.

Many have criticized this generation for growing up without hardship and introducing negative elements like public displays of sexuality and violence to society. The generation has been dubbed them the Jelly Generation (colorful but lacking substance).

Coming of age as China reinvents itself from manufacturer to innovator, the post-90s are more confident and eager to leave their independent mark. As change agents who draw outside the lines, the post-90s see the world that the post-80s created as out of date. The opinions of others matter less to the post-90s, who have established a powerful insularity by introducing non-mainstream subcultures to China. By adopting new, smaller subcultures, the post-90s have drawn a wider boundary for behavior. Casual sex? OK. Skipping college? Possibly. For the post-90s, the world has shifted from black or white, yes or no, to a big bag of possibilities. Not intimidated by taking their own path, the post-90s have earned a reputation for rebellion that can often test society's patience. Their attitudes and behaviors put pressure on society's notions of public versus private, and personal expression versus group responsibility. By uploading videos of their own amateur sex scenes and of physical bullying in school, the post-90s are creating a new dialogue about morality.

The post-90s are described in more neutral terms like "unconventional" and "carefree," but are also tethered to more a negative reputation that rests on the post-90s' notoriety for going against the grain. Many resent the post-90s' attention-grabbing antics and technology-amped lifestyle. The Jelly Generation is perceived to be on a mission to redefine itself, taking China along for the ride—whether it wants to go or not.

> "Post-90s are bastards. They are looking for too much stimulation, and they are way too crazy, too open-minded."—Lexie, Shanghai, a post-80s (research conducted by The Bergstrom Group, 2009)

Not intimidated by others' judgments, the post-90s have defended their rights to express their individuality and are proud of being unique.

> "People know post-90s to be self-centered and independent, but we are excellent—having our own thoughts and creative spirit."—Yurica, Shanghai, a post-90s (research conducted by The Bergstrom Group, 2009)

Although the relationship between the post-80s generation and their parents represents arguably the most significant generation gap of our times, the feud between the post-80s and the post-90s has captured the spotlight.

RETHINKING WHO I AM AND WHAT I CAN DO

The generations of youth in China are different in two fundamental ways: one is in how they think about their relationships, and the other is in how they express themselves. In terms of relationships, the post-70s represent one end of the spectrum, identifying and behaving as part of the larger group. As the first generation of only children, the post-80s upset the hierarchy and established themselves as group leaders. Finally, the post-90s have disconnected further to develop and attach themselves to their own subgroups. As new generations have taken the stage, they have shifted their relationships with the group—evolving in action from survival to expression, in identity from members to individuals.

As each generation has altered its relations with the collective, its members have developed their own identity as separate from the group. In attitudes and actions, each generation has created its own legacy. The evolution maps as follows: the post-70s represented a more traditional point of view, while the post-80s ushered in a new mainstream and the post-90s bucked this mainstream to foster their own non-mainstream.

THE ECONOMIC BACKDROP

In many ways, the evolution of the generations in China can be charted alongside China's economic development. The 1970s was a building decade for China as it strived to recoup self-sufficiency at the close of the Cultural Revolution. The 1980s was the debut decade for China to take its place in the world by reinstating international trade. In the 1990s, China began taking a pivotal position and outshining other leading nations in production and consumption. Growing up in these times helped to form the generations' attitudes and behaviors.

The post-70s came of age watching China fight its way up and out of poverty. They witnessed a reinvention of values and tactics that allowed the nation to double its gross domestic product (GDP) between 1981 and 1990. By introducing elements of capitalism, the government was able to boost productivity by incentivizing production above and beyond state quotas. As communal farms were dismantled, farmers were able to sell—and make a profit—from their work.

Opportunities also began to migrate back to the cities from their Mao-appointed post in the countryside. As China engaged in new trade relationships, an open-door policy encouraged foreign investment. The first Special Economic Zone (SEZ) was established along the coastal city of Shenzhen and given special permissions in order to enable easy trade. In 1985, tariffs were lowered to further stimulate trade, and by 1989, almost 22,000 joint ventures had been established in China. Among these early entrants were 952 American firms, including the iconic consumer brands Chrysler and Coca-Cola.

The post-80s was brought up during the next stage of China's development, after the fight for the survival that the post-70s experienced. The post-80s came of age as China rose to become an economic superpower, with new ways to increase wealth and new options for spending it. As leaders in their families, the post-80s were the first to follow new career and consumption paths influenced by the outside world. Empowered by Deng Xiaoping's accelerated market reforms to create a "socialist market economy," the Shanghai Stock Exchange was reopened in 1990.[9] In 2001, China formalized its status as a world power by gaining membership to the World Trade Organization (WTO).[10] The post-80s witnessed the expansion of the nation's borders and influence with the return of Hong Kong in 1997 and Macao in 1999.

When the post-80s entered the work force, they saw new doors open and private interests become increasingly powerful. While the post-70s experienced the state as all-pervasive, the post-80s were exposed to new "office worker" dreams in private enterprises that demanded increased productivity but provided higher salaries. By the mid-1990s, the private sector outperformed the state sector's share of GDP for the first time.

The post-90s saw China emerge as not only a global player but also a world leader, and the post-90s mind-set is greatly shaped by these victories. When they were growing up between 1990 and 2004, the post-90s witnessed annual economic growth of 10 percent per year. At the same time, the iron-rice-bowl mentality, or the idea that the work unit is the provider of all services and that jobs are for life, was beginning to disappear due to the decommissioning and privatization of state-owned enterprises, which decreased by 48 percent between 2001 and 2004. China's exports surpassed those of Japan in 2003, making China the world's third largest exporter after the United States and Germany.[11] It also became a major tourist destination, hosting the Olympics in 2008 and the World Expo in 2010. And also in 2010, China marked its miraculous growth by becoming the world's second-largest growth economy. These coming-of-age moments for China offered further validation for the post-90s.

As each generation grows up, their values and tastes shift. A chart that floated across online communities demonstrated how each generation would celebrate Christmas, highlighting the differences between the post-70s, post-80s, and post-90s. It showed the post-70s enjoying themselves, going to a traditional, upscale Chinese restaurant, followed by watching a movie. The gift they hoped to receive was a Cadillac equipped with an On Star system. The post-80s, on the other hand, preferred to eat at a popular buffet-style restaurant and then pop over to a club called Babyface to party. For gifts, Swarovski and Louis Vuitton topped their list. Last, the post-90s set out to meet friends at McDonald's and play video games. The presents they asked for included Red Bull and Durex condoms. Even in this brief example, we can see how the post-70s are reputed to be more traditional and focused on family, how the post-80s are perceived as white-collar status seekers, and how the post-90s are viewed as fast kids on a mission to push the limits.

EVOLVING VALUES

Mirroring China's shift from producer to consumer, its consumption landscape demonstrates an evolution in youth values. Leveraging consumption to tell their own stories, young Chinese have increasingly looked at brands as a vehicle for the expression of new status. Understanding the era each generation grew up in is important to mapping their expectations and assumptions going forward.

The post-70s were traditionalists, following a group path, eager to belong and not stand out. They could still imagine China as a poor country with rural roots—consumers had few means to buy products and only a few domestic brands to choose from. In an era of limited expendable income and few options on the market, notions of choice and status were meaningless. Spending during the post-70s era was a family affair; products were evaluated primarily on their price and functionality.

The post-80s changed all that. With their parents earning more and with no sibling competition, the post-80s had more spending power than the post-70s ever imagined. Their needs drove the majority of the family's spending, propelling this generation to become an important sector of the economy. Shopping for status, the post-80s and their eager-to-please parents redefined the concept of basic needs—not only food, clothing, and shelter but versions of each that would inspire envy and acceptance.

The nation became obsessed with spending on these Little Emperors. China Market Research Group (CMR) estimated that spending by (or on) the post-80s accounts for 20 percent of the country's total spending. Average monthly expenses for raising the post-80s kids amounted to 39 percent to 52 percent of the average household's total expenditures.[12] Parents were anxious for their prodigies to get ahead and were willing to spend to ensure their child's future—funding tuition for newly privatized schools and tutoring to help their child keep pace with the competition. The average cost of raising a post-80s child from birth to high school graduation was estimated to total 490,000 RMB, but many netizens priced the cost at more than 1 million RMB.

For the first time, Chinese youth considered the question: "How do I represent myself with the things I buy?" Armed with income from two parents and four grandparents, the post-80s were able to experiment with consumption as a means of personal expression and identity building. As new brands and whole new categories of goods became available, the post-80s were at the forefront of testing and reporting back their findings in person to their families and online to their friends. Consumption became a form of social capital, and the post-80s were eager not only to lead but also not to be left behind.

The post-80s collected information, constantly researching and making new choices and rejiggering brand hierarchies. For marketers, this generation was irresistible and insatiable—always eager to try the next thing and rarely willing to buy the same brand twice. With new options popping up all the time, repeat purchases and brand loyalty seemed out of date.

THE CHOICE OF A NEW GENERATION

When KFC entered the market, it offered a unique avenue for retail tourism, taking what once was a simple transaction and infusing it with new, exotic value. For the cost of a meal, diners could get a taste of Americana. With this new meaning, and contrary to its reputation in the United States, KFC became a place to see and be seen in the mainland. When McDonald's followed in 1990, consumers were offered a choice of American restaurants.[13] Not only were foreign brands in a battle against old competitors from their home turf, new competitors started crowding the market from other countries and China itself. Kungfu is a local-born Chinese fast food chain that came to life in 1994, touting images that have a noticeable resemblance to Bruce Lee in the chain's visual identity. The menu is a health-conscious fusion of Chinese flavors, including egg custard with preserved pork, steamed chicken and mushrooms, and fish ball noodle soup. Their slogan ("Steamed is more nutritious") takes a jab at the fried competition, emphasizing that steam cooking is healthier.

Inevitably, domestic brands entered into every category. Competition started edging into Nike's territory when the Chinese sportswear brands Li Ning and Anta were established in 1990 and 1994, respectively. More competition followed across every category, and youth were eager to exercise their newfound power of choice—confounding companies that were striving to build brand loyalty.

CURATING THE NEW NON-MAINSTREAM

Just as the post-80s led China into a new mainstream marked by choice and status, the post-90s took the post-80s' individualistic spirit to a new extreme. Born into a society that had already accepted the notion of youth as leaders, the post-90s imported a new level of daring to go against societal norms and create a new non-mainstream.

Along with prizing the hunt for options and fostering the new value of individualized style, the post-90s were raised in an era that took previously private behavior public. As an outcome of their increased wealth, access to information, and individualism, the post-90s were more comfortable with public exhibition (including sex, violence, and dissent) than preceding generations. Online and on the streets, the post-90s are strutting fresh ideas in the face of old ones. While the post-80s drove the notion of status and consumption, the post-90s provided a public relations campaign for rebellion.

VERY EROTIC, VERY VIOLENT

When the post-90s entered middle school and high school, free and personal expression online was a given. The first free blog hosting service (BlogCN) had been around since 2002, providing a platform to invent Internet celebrities and to broadcast shock topics to push at China's moral boundaries. The legacy of the post-90s may be its carrying sex away from the realm of taboo and into the public sphere. Despite the country's conservative policies and traditions regarding premarital relations, some post-90s have taken it upon themselves to reinvent values associated with sexuality. By uploading videos of their (often public) encounters, the post-90s have forced the issue of premarital sex among youth. These scandals come in a variety of flavors, usually with a "gate" clipped on at the end—for example, "Breast Groping Gate," "Pants Stripping Gate," and even the not particularly sexy sounding, location-based scandal "Dongguan Technical School 3P Gate."

Earlier generations frown on the post-90s' exhibitionism, while the post-90s argue that sex is a natural part of life that does not merit shame. In this same vein, a post-90s going by the pseudonym Su Zizi drew attention for displaying artsy photos of herself in the buff. The photo exhibit, called "Who Am I," was displayed at her school, Beijing's Renmin University of China, in 2010.[14] In a video aptly titled "Nude Model Su Zizi," Su explains that her exhibition poses questions about privacy, the definition of an artist, and taboos relating to sex and nudity. Says Su, "The exhibition is my homework, and I am not afraid of expressing myself this way. I think people need to get rid of their burdens and, by being naked, they can know themselves better."[15] Su's work is provocative not only because she is physically naked but because she allows herself to be emotionally exposed as well, a trait more commonly associated with her generation than with previous groups.

While the post-80s hid their feelings of depression, anxiety, and disenfranchisement, the post-90s were willing to shout them to the world. Besides the topic of sex, the headlines that follow this generation often include violent acts such as suicide and bullying. In committing—and distributing—violence online, the post-90s have taken China aback. With these outward expressions of frustration and unrest, this generation has been an easy scapegoat for what many see as China's moral decline.

BFF'ing the Internet

The evolution of the post-90s is indistinguishable from the rise of the Internet and its role in evolving youth's communication and expression. The post-70s largely received one-way communication from others. The Chinese Communist Party, their families—everyone was an authority figure, and the generation had few outlets to call their own. The Internet and all of its possibilities did not exist when the post-70s were growing up. Today, having always been a part of a communications network rather than the center, the post-70s largely look online for its functional benefits. Online behavior for them is largely driven by external relationships (work, spouse, parents, and kids).

The post-80s, on the other hand, witnessed the introduction of the Internet. Growing up, the post-80s were cornered by societal pressures; their access to new experiences and consumption power came at a high price for these Little Emperors. Schools and parents created a competitive environment with a narrow margin for deviation from the norm. Their failure or success was a reflection on the family. Burdened by constant comparison and supervision, the post-80s grew up under a microscope. With little time to themselves outside of structured school and family agendas, the post-80s had few opportunities to express or experiment with independence.

An animated short by young artist Wang Chengzhi sums up the generation's anxiety and feelings of constant pressure. In the animated film, a child runs away from his scolding parents and teachers, but finds no outlet. The clip ends with the words "We are always running, but we can't escape."[16]

Under constant surveillance and feeling the pressure to perform, the post-80s welcomed the Internet like a breath of fresh air. For the post-80s, growing up as the only child at home and, as adults, working long, hard hours with very little time to themselves, the online realm became a 24/7-whenever-they-want-it, there-when-they-need-it best friend. Finally able to express and share on their time schedule, this generation relied on the Internet for self-exploration and building community.

THE INTERNET AS VILLAIN

The next generation would take the post-80s' interpretation of the Internet as an anonymous personal space and turn it upside down. Distinct from the post-80s' relationship with a closeted virtual life, the post-90s took the Internet from confidant to outspoken doppelgänger. They flexed their digital muscle to broadcast messages that would test definitions of public and private, acceptable and obscene.

As netizens grew in number and power, concern mounted that fans were turning into junkies, that the influence of the Internet was becoming negative—and powerful. Links between violence, moral decline, and the Internet were widely publicized to help the government build a case against the increasing power of digital deities. In 2008, the China Youth Association for Network Development issued a report claiming that 70 percent of crimes committed by juveniles were "induced by Internet addiction." The following year, there were an estimated tens of millions of young Internet addicts in China (nearly double the figure from 2005). Whether or not these numbers are fair representations is debatable. What is clear is the government's positioning of the Internet as a threat to the status quo.

To combat the digital revolution, the Chinese government established numerous measures with the intent of monitoring connection, location, activity, and content. To curtail youths' digital connection, Internet addiction camps were set up to rehabilitate "addicts" and Internet cafés were closely monitored. Hoping to force players to come up for air, the government initiated time limits on games. After three consecutive hours of play, Massively Multiplayer Online Role-Playing Games (MMORPG) players were penalized with reduced abilities. Continuing to play to a five-hour mark further decreased a player's power.

To curb the influence of gaming activity, the government instituted the real name system, requiring players to enter their government-issued ID number to play online games. Unsurprisingly, notoriously smart and dedicated netizens found a way around the rule, developing transformer programs to allow gamers to hide their real identity and continue playing after state-determined end times.

In 2009, it was proposed that content control software called Green Dam Youth Escort be loaded onto all new personal computers sold in the mainland. The software was a censorship vehicle, reportedly aimed at stamping out the spread of pornography. And while a much more serious conversation erupted about politically motivated monitoring and citizen rights, netizens had a good laugh at the software's impracticality. Targeting sexual terms (*huang* means "pornographic," but also "yellow" in Chinese) and using image recognition of large patches of skin color regions in online images proved more comical than threatening. The software tagged promotional pictures for *Garfield: A Tale of Two Kitties* and flesh-colored pork dishes as pornography. In response, netizens created their own jab at the software, a manga-style character dressed in green named Green Dam Girl.

When all else fails, the Great Firewall is assumed to be a deterrent to accessing state-disapproved content. But in reality, any young person with a personal computer has the ability—and likely also knows how—to download his or her own free Virtual Private Network (VPN). For the powers that be, policing Chinese youth online is a sophisticated game of cat and mouse; for young Chinese, being online is a necessary entitlement, critical to their social and emotional health.

MARKETING TO THE GENERATIONS

The trick, of course, to marketing to these generations is understanding what motivates them: what makes them feel confident, what causes them stress, and what nuanced lifestyle details they connect with. Because intergenerational relationships are more adversarial in China than other countries, companies need to tread lightly. Each generation offers its own opportunities and traps.

CHEVROLET CRUZE EMPATHIZES WITH THE POST-80s

As consumer audiences and competitors have become more sophisticated, brands have shifted focus from broadcasting big to targeting

Figure 1.2   Chevy Cruz's Old Boys video draws on post-80s' memories of Michael Jackson

small. Understanding the generations is a critical part of this strategy. Joan Ren, executive deputy director of Marketing and Distribution Department, and deputy general director of Chevrolet Sales and Marketing Department of Shanghai General Motors (GM), makes an apt comparison: "They say America is a nation of nations. In China, it is a market of markets."[17] GM's product line reflects the need to diversify to meet the increasingly splintered market. Buick, GM's first brand sold in the mainland, had been very successful, but with such a large territory and multiple consumer groups to cover, there was a danger of stretching Buick's value too thin. To keep pace, the portfolio now includes Cadillac for luxury, Buick for premium, and Chevrolet for mainstream consumers. To prepare for a faster-paced, more demanding future car market, GM is also cooperating with the Pan Asia Technical Automotive Center (PATAC), the first Sino-foreign automotive engineering and design joint venture in China.

The car market in China is dynamic and is evolving at lightning speed. GM estimates that new car buyers tend to be young (25–35 years old) and new to the category (85 percent of purchases are made by first-time buyers). Although they may have less direct experience, young car enthusiasts are extremely well informed about their options. Leveraging a plethora of official and user-generated sites and communities online, young buyers often know as much as the salespeople about the vehicles on the floor. Not limited to one brand, however, they are versed in foreign as well as domestic product lines and often know more about future models than cohorts in other countries. With domestic models that offer a good price-performance value, GM knew that Chevrolet had to make an emotional connection to compete.

To create a bond with this young power group, Chevrolet initiated a campaign that would help identify and inspire their target. The brand looked online to connect with young consumers, yet was wary of campaigns that would click—but not connect. As Ren cautions, "Reaching doesn't mean admiration. You can get a lot of clicks but that doesn't ensure good admiration for your brand—or that it will be shared to [social] circles."[18]

Chevrolet took an ambitious long-term approach to leveraging online tools. Teaming with the video-sharing site Youku and China Film Group, the trio set out to make a statement. Ren explains, "When we had the opportunity to work with China Film Group and Youku, we all believed that whatever we did for this target, admiration was number one. Number two, we wanted to arouse a dialogue within our target group without a commercially motivated, one-way formation."[19]

The three partners launched a short film series called "Bright Eleven," allowing eleven young filmmakers to create ten works that would be publicized and broadcast online on Youku. Young creatives were given the directive to use whatever means they felt would best express their talents, and were not required to showcase the brand or product. The brand was not looking to create a commercial; rather, it was hoping to associate itself with a creative spark.

The goal was to serve the audience by building a cultural totem that would serve as an iconic reference point to anchor the generation. As Ren explains, "In China, every generation has had its own iconic films. Unfortunately, this generation doesn't have very strong iconic films to brand the generation...our ambition is that maybe 5 or 10 years from now when people think about this generation, these ten movies can be a good summary."[20] The concept was not to have one film that would capture a generic youth's imagination; it was to empower ten different voices to speak in their own unique vocabulary. The resulting body of work is sophisticated and diverse—and targeted straight at a powerful segment of car buyers. Notes Ren, "If you put the ten movies together, [it serves as a summary] of how this generation is living and working, in cities and in different conditions."[21]

Although many post-80s may appear mainstream, their internal worlds are more multidimensional than is assumed. Ren points out, "You can tend to be very mainstream but in your heart, you can be a different you. Every 24 hours, you may only have 20 minutes to show your extravagant ways...these people are more multidimensional, much more sophisticated than what society frames their personalities [to be]."[22] Ren's point is important in that it underscores both youth's use of the Internet as a means of critical self-expression and the difference in public and private identification of personality.

This tension between crafting an external appearance to meet societal expectations while holding a more intimate personality inside is a hallmark of the post-80s. The film *Old Boys* tells the story of two school friends and their childhood dreams of grandeur that turn into an acceptance of mediocre adulthoods. Like many of their same-generation peers, the characters idolize Michael Jackson. In school, they study dance and music, skills that help them defeat the school bully (who is outfitted in a red leather suit à la Michael Jackson in the infamous "Thriller" video, while the hero is dressed in black and white à la Michael Jackson in the "Billie Jean" video). The fight is resolved by dance. Not only does the hero defeat the villain, but he magnanimously teaches his challenger some hot, new moves. The hero is haloed in light, and projects an ethereal feeling of freedom and power.

But as the two friends grow into men, they abandon their dreams for real life: one becomes a barber, one a wedding emcee. Life feels average and predictable until a chance encounter encourages these "old boys" to try out for a new television talent show and rekindle their dreams. The old boys (the eldest in the competition) do not win; they are slighted by competitors from the flashier post-90s.

But before being voted out of the competition, their televised ballad lamenting unrealized dreams brings viewers across China to tears. In tone, story line, detail and emotion, *Old Boys* hit a home run for Chevrolet's relationship with the post-80s. The car is not the star, but rather it is the post-80s themselves, a generation that feels both physically on stage and emotionally waiting in the wings.

The film's creators made specific choices to enable this deep connection. The use of Michael Jackson as a cultural anchor linked the film with the post-80s generation. As Ren describes, "If you are a post-80s, your memory still holds some old things.... When you mention a particular old song, story or name, [post-80s] still can echo with you.... [For] post-90s, you talk about music, songs, some last generation big events, and they may not have any concept of that at all."[23] The choice to connect with one generation over another was conscious; the brand knew that a general appeal would not leave a meaningful impression. To resonate with the post-80s, Chevrolet demonstrated that it knew who they were and how to inspire them.

LI NING MAKES A CHANGE

The domestic footwear brand Li Ning recognized Chinese youth's shift in focus and repositioned the company from "Anything Is Possible" to "Make The Change." A distinct move away from the idealism of the previous slogan, the new tag line was personally motivating and inspiring within the confines of what society would accept. Unlike the cowboy nature of "Anything Is Possible," "Make the Change" encouraged youth to continue to embrace change. The ethos was meant to help young consumers, leaders in the next stage of development, stay the course to realize their personal dreams—as well as those of the nation. Frank Chen, chief marketing officer of Li Ning, expounds on the meaning behind the repositioning, "Over the last 20 years, change has been *the* buzz word for China.... We needed to capture what consumers were feeling. We said to them if you stop changing, [China's evolution] will stop and we want to be the brand that grows with you."[24] Chen's point of view speaks to the national imperative for evolution; there is no expectation or advantage to stick with what has worked in the past.

Like all sports brands, Li Ning must continuously mine younger fans of the brand to stay relevant. As post-90s consumers have moved into the spotlight, the brand has had to seek new meaning with younger consumers. While the post-70s and post-80s remember the brand's founder bringing home China's first Olympic gold medal in 1984, the moment is ancient history for the post-90s. For Li Ning, the challenge is to go beyond what the brand meant in the past in order to create new associations. As Chen explains, "The post-90s know who he [Li Ning] is, but they did not experience the moment [when he won China's first Olympic gold medal in 1984] so that affinity isn't there for the younger consumers. We need to build Li Ning's own image off of what the brand represents and not what the founder represents."[25] As consumers continue to evolve, brands must discover the next vehicles to express their core values and create resonance.

Evolving from "dare to think" to "dare to say" and "dare to do," the battle cries of each generation are unique and tell a specific story. The post-70s dared to think differently, the post-80s went a step further to speaking out, and now the post-90s have dared to live and act outside the norm. By embracing a "dare to do" mantra, Li Ning's initial expressions of the "Make the Change" campaign were targeted to the post-90s. Copy that read "Post-90s Li Ning" overtly linked the message with the generation, and the expressions were implicitly targeted as well. Television spots showing a dark, artistic montage of athletes from around the world talking about their personal goals and not wanting to be judged by others was meant to resonate with a generation in search of independence and redemption.

Unfortunately, because of the competition between generations, taking a stance that visibly emphasized the post-90s risked alienating post-70s and post-80s customers. After the repositioning, Li Ning's Baidu forum saw some members shaking their fists that the brand never truly cared about their generation. In their estimation, Li Ning had served them a double whammy: the brand had aligned with a generation they thought little of, and their own generations had not been addressed. They felt that the Chinese sports brand—*their brand*—had offended and damaged them personally.

"My first feeling [after seeing the ad] was heartbreak, which then turned into shame. Li Ning deeply hurt the innocent post-80s consumers. Last year, I spent 300 RMB to buy a pair of Li Ning sport pants. To afford them, I had to have instant noodles for dinner for a week.... Now, how can post-80s go out wearing these products?"—GG, a post-80s

"Even though I only wear Adidas and Nike shoes, I insist on buying a pair of Li Ning to support the national brand. Every time I go abroad, I wear Li Ning to show foreigners that we Chinese trust Li Ning. But after seeing the 'Post-90s Li-Ning' campaign, I will not support the brand anymore."—Yihao, a post-80s

Li Ning learned the lesson quickly and moved "Make The Change" away from an anthem dedicated to the post-90s to a campaign that had resonance for youth across generations. As Chen clarifies, "There was a disconnect between the positioning and the creative expression of that positioning. To successfully target youth, a brand can be perceived as youthful if the tone and manner of the communication stirs their emotions, not by simply telling them you are their brand. They will tell you if you are post-90s or not—not you telling them."[26] Li Ning learned a valuable lesson in subtlety and in creating a message with implied (not explicit) meaning.

For brands, targeting the generations can be a trap. Overtly communicating with post-80s can mean seeming out of touch with post-90s, while tapping into post-90s can mean alienating post-80s. To define a long-term vision, brands need to be careful to understand but not follow the generations' definitions of themselves, for they are sure to change.

LOOKING BACK

Lightning-fast social and economic development has created stark generation gaps between decades. The post-70s holds a totem of responsibility, while the post-80s see themselves as the stewards of a new China. The post-90s, having grown up in an era of constant growth, see their role as disruptors. While youth primarily identify with the decade into which they were born, some also feel and exhibit alignment with other generations (these jumps can happen in under five years). While youth and the media expound on these differences, marketers need to be careful about overtly targeting one generation at the expense of another. Each generation sees itself as separate—and superior.

LOOKING FORWARD

This chapter is meant to help you think more deeply about connecting to youth. How could the information be leveraged in these scenarios?

1. How can a brand demonstrate empathy without alienating generational rivals?
2. How can a campaign target specific generations without overshadowing the core brand message?
3. How can companies create iconic creative that will give generations a sense of unity and legacy?

CHAPTER 2

PROGRESS: MAPPING NEW ROADS TO SUCCESS

> You may not always succeed even if you work hard, but you will fail if you give up.[1]
> —Yao Ming, former NBA basketball player, born in 1980

LOOKING AT TRENDS IN START-UP BUSINESSES, I interviewed a group of young entrepreneurs for a client to better understand their motivations and direction. One young man who piqued my interest was Lifu, a hip-hop aficionado born in 1989 who had turned his love of dance into a studio called Speed Control. But he wasn't content to stop at teaching youth in Shenzhen how to bust a move. He wanted to translate the brand into merchandise that could be sold all over the mainland—and possibly the world. He was looking at different products, including street gear and towels, that could help him carry the feeling of bold expression that students experienced to an outside audience. Despite not having a formal business education and being a relatively low-profile personality, Lifu was confident. There weren't many examples of other dance studios branching into branded merchandise, but Lifu was knowledgeable about the channels for creating, marketing, selling, and distributing. After all, he had navigated online communities all of his life to stay in touch with friends, dive deeper into his interests, and buy difficult-to-find items.

Lifu is just one example of a young entrepreneur following the trend of turning personal interests into a brand. While Taobao (a Chinese site similar to eBay) founder Jack Ma is a larger-than-life figure who inspires admiration, motivated youth also reference examples from their own generations. Although these young dreamers may be small-time now, their experiences are inspiring a distinct movement away from traditional career paths.

YOUNG ENTREPRENEURIAL VISION

Increasingly disillusioned with what traditional employers offer and confident in asserting themselves, many youth are charting new roads to become their own boss. In 2010, the Kelly Global Workforce Index found that more than half (54 percent) of surveyed adults under age 30 had plans to open their own business. These hopefuls from the post-80s generation are helping to pioneer entrepreneurship in China, even more so than their older comrades. The same survey found that 44 percent of people born in the 1960s and 1970s

Figure 2.1 A young entrepreneur in Shenzhen builds his dance studio brand. Photo by Feng Lei (Ayu)

desired to own their own businesses, and 39 percent of those born in the 1950s had similar aspirations.[2] This burst of upstart enthusiasm has come after a long hiatus that started in 1949 and lasted until the 1980s. Although the Chinese Communist Party only officially recognized private entrepreneurs in 1988, the idea has moved quickly from the margins to the mainstream.

Youth may not have a personal history of entrepreneurship (most do not have family relations who have been their own bosses), but increasingly they are finding role models to inform and inspire their choices. While Bill Gates was the de facto idol for aspiring entrepreneurs just a few years ago, young Chinese are now looking closer to home for mentors.

THE POWER OF PRIVILEGE

While they are distinct from the average Chinese, rich second-generation youth are also looking at entrepreneurial roles in commercial and philanthropic endeavors as a means of revising what power will look and behave like in China's next act. These second-generation players, called *guan er dai* if their parents are government officials, or *fu er dai* if they hail from super-rich families, are able to carve out new access and privilege thanks to their parents' efforts and connections.

Although empowered by birth, China's rich second generation have suffered a mixed reception due to the wealth gap. Once revered, China's affluent youth now find that inherited position and power are no longer enough. Many hope to prove themselves beyond their parents' accomplishments and become known for their own independent contributions. Their aspirations are a true testament of society's reevaluation of pedigree, a symbol that the past is not as important as the future. In a joint survey conducted by two nonprofit organizations (the Shanghai Youth Homeland Civil Society Organization Service Center and the Relay China Youth Elite Association), respondents voiced their discontent with being labeled as the rich second generation.[3] Hoping to craft their own reputation independent of the family's bank account, they aim to be seen as pioneers and contributors. They hope to rebrand themselves as the second generation from entrepreneurial—not just rich or official—families.

CHARTING A NEW VALUES MAP

Youth are poised to spark a new conversation about the meaning of success in China. Fast-paced economic development and being the only child in the family have forced young Chinese into the spotlight, competing against each other to meet society's increasingly high expectations for them as students, workers, and finally as consumers. But as inflation has tipped to outpace salary increases, the benefits of sticking to the prescribed program have weakened and caused youth to take a second, critical look at what constitutes success. In this analysis, they are rebalancing ideas about how they want to live, work, and consume. In this quest, young Chinese are reversing trends and inventing surprising new ones to help them move closer to an integrated, satisfying, and sustainable lifestyle.

Along the way, young Chinese are inviting and even daring employers and consumer brands to take the journey with them. But even as employers struggle to find management strategies that will be effective for post-80s workers, the post-90s are coming up fast and presenting a fresh round of challenges.

THE CHINESE LENS

The first step in understanding Chinese youth as workers is to appreciate what makes them unique. In "Reckoning with China's Gen Y," Nandani Lynton, adjunct professor of Management at China Europe International Business School (CEIBS) and Kirsten Høgh Thøgersen, professor of Psychology at Sun Yat-Sen University, posit, "Traditional Chinese values focus on family, relationships, achievement, endurance, and sacrifice of self for the group. They also include the ideal of the golden mean or harmony, and hierarchy as the basis for social structure and interaction."[4] The article claims that China's young workers, while modernizing, are not Westernizing and that these traditional attributes still inform their motivations and have an impact on their behavior.

Tom Doctoroff, CEO of North Asia at J. Walter Thompson (JWT) and author of *Billions: Selling to the New Chinese Consumer* and *What Chinese Want*,[5] sees this same trajectory from a consumer perspective. Doctoroff asserts, "The Chinese consumer is becoming modern, becoming international, but not becoming Western. The evolution of the Chinese consumer is happening very, very rapidly but the superstructure on which it rests is not."[6] While young Chinese may be adopting superficial traits similar to their international contemporaries, their values and motivations both as workers and consumers remain rooted in a distinctly Chinese context. Adopting surface cues keeps them up-to-date in a general, modern youth vernacular, but the distinctly Chinese foundation from which they see themselves and the world is not so easily transformed.

TWO DISTINCT WAYS OF SEEING THE WORLD

Although the country's modernization seems unstoppable, the notion of Chinese society following in Western footsteps seems highly unlikely. Researchers at Massachusetts Institute of Technology (MIT) (building on previous research, including Richard E. Nisbett's book *The Geography of Thought: How Asians and Westerners Think Differently...and Why*) claim that Westerners and East Asians exhibit different neurological patterns when making judgments about the same scenarios.[7] Specifically, these scholars theorize that Westerners are less adept at recognizing interdependence, while East Asians have more difficulty recognizing independent objects. This means that if an image or a scenario is unveiled to a Westerner and an East Asian, the two individuals will perceive fundamentally different stories.[8] These researchers posit that Westerners tend to focus on central objects, paying little mind to their surroundings or supporting figures. East Asians, on the other hand, view the totality of the scene. The central assertion is that Westerners tend to pick up more detail, whereas East Asians are more attuned to understanding interdependent relationships. One way to understand these findings is to think of Westerners as cameras with a good zoom lens, whereas East Asians could be likened to cameras equipped to take better panoramic pictures.[9]

This difference in perspective may help to explain why Chinese are assumed to have a more deeply holistic view of work, life, and consumption. As Lynton and Thøgersen suggest in their 2009 research, "Chinese strength, on the other hand, comes primarily from immersing the self in the collective and using the energy of the group. Chinese begin with a view of life, work and community that is far more integrated than that of Westerners."[10] This analysis asserts that Chinese do not segment an image or concept into parts; instead, they seek balance to make a whole. In this integrated point of view, one critical goal is to balance individual desires with external expectations.

COMPARING AUTONOMY

Growing up without siblings, Chinese youth are accustomed to always being on center stage. Every move is family fodder open for debate: which school to attend, which career path to follow, which job to take, and when to look for a new one are all decisions for the group. This relationship that integrates family and work is much more intimate than it is in the West and even other East Asian countries. A survey comparing high school students' ambitions found that Americans were the most independent: 90.3 percent reported being able to make decisions about their future, including deciding which school to attend, without their parents' interference. Korean students reported the second highest level of independence at 77.5 percent; the Japanese followed at 61.1 percent; and Chinese came in as the least autonomous, with 43.5 percent reporting the ability to choose their own school.[11]

This level of connection with the family is understandable. For Chinese parents, having children follow a path with an established economic outcome has its own meaning. Because China lacks a mature and comprehensive social security system, parents are often financially dependent on their children's future earnings to support them when they retire. Socially speaking, a child who succeeds reflects well upon the parents and provides a key source of pride and acceptance from the parents' peer group. Alternately, a child who does poorly may cause embarrassing exclusion and a sense of failure for the whole family.

From a Western perspective, it is hard to overstate the impact of the family in China. Children are important to their families, and families are similarly vital for youth. This codependent dynamic often complicates how youth recognize success and support.

In her research analyzing young Chinese professionals and comparing them to peers around the world, Lynton has identified distinct Chinese attributes and paradoxical relationships. In a 2010 study she conducted of young Chinese professionals, 98 percent of respondents ranked family as extremely important. However, only 11 percent of Chinese respondents noted family as a main source of inspiration.[12] It would seem that, for Chinese young people, while family is a top priority, the relationship is associated more with pressure to meet expectations, continue the family's upward mobility, and care for elders than with a source of personal pleasure.

In this study, when asked what would make their life better, respondents ranked having a better personality first and spending more time with their families last. This result can be seen as a symbol of young Chinese changing the rules of the game. By aspiring to a better personality, they are looking to define for themselves a more individually relevant notion of success. The study suggests that youth recognize and regret that, in the rush to get ahead, their personal development has suffered.

Elucidating Chinese youth's unique relationship with family, Lynton states, "To Chinese, family is so important but also family is a bit of a burden because you are going to have to take good care of them."[13] In stark contrast to the Western family's relegated spot in the background, a Chinese family's position is front and center for youth.

Notions of interrelatedness and prioritizing the group are ever-present pillars of how Chinese youth understand the world and how they plot their course towards the future. Lynton asserts that Chinese youth, while becoming more modern, are not constructing and aligning new values in a vacuum; they are doing so with respect to the balance and parameters of existing relationships.

IMPORTING THE WHITE COLLAR

In 1977, the National Higher Education Entrance Examination (otherwise known as the *gao kao*) was reinstituted after a ten-year hiatus during the Cultural Revolution. The exam marked a renewed investment in education for the country and a new benchmark for success in society. With it came a tide of hierarchical accomplishment and competition, sweeping up parents and their only children, who were clambering to avoid being left behind.

The renewed value of formal education went hand in hand with new employment opportunities; the 1980s opened new work/life paths for youth to explore and conquer. To make room for a more diversified economy, the state relaxed its role as sole provider and opened doors for private enterprises to be established. Previously, the state—as the primary employer—determined workers' location, function, and mobility. As compensation, workers could expect that the state would provide housing, rations, and security. The path was predictable with a clear progression and with equal and understood compensation at each level.

With new schools and employers on the scene, Chinese experienced a greater degree of autonomy and were able to decide for themselves what course of action to take in their lives. Their decisions—and the repercussions of their choices—were no longer tied to the state.

In 1979, Beijing installed Foreign Enterprise Service Group Company (FESCO) to help foreign companies establish operations in China. As new enterprises moved into the mainland, gates opened for the first generation of white-collar employees. In the 1980s, the term "white-collar" became synonymous with working for foreign companies, a glamorous and privileged post.

Those rare individuals who could speak a second language were initiated first into a foreign work culture. Especially in demand were so-called "sea turtles"—those who were born in China, had lived or worked abroad, and then returned to China. Hung Huang, now a famous publisher, entrepreneur, and pioneering personality in China, was one of the first to return home to reap the benefits of her experience in the United States. In 1985, when she came back to the mainland, Hung was hired by an American company and reportedly earned a salary of 800 USD a month, an unbelievable sum compared to the average graduate's monthly pay of 56 RMB.[14] With earning (and spending) power far superior to the average Chinese, a new icon of social mobility emerged: the white-collar office worker.

With this kind of contemporary folklore, it is no surprise that, when the first English recruiting ad was placed in 1988, interviewers were overwhelmed with applicants eager to get in on the cash and culture boom. In stark contrast to the equalized salaries of the Cultural Revolution just a decade or so earlier, staff in foreign companies were reported to earn five to ten times as much as state employees.[15] The white-collar dream was highly alluring in an era when production and consumption were being established as core social values.

SPENDING TOMORROW'S MONEY TODAY

New values fueled by increased disposable income allowed youth to be the first in line to experience the recently imported consumption-driven lifestyle. Having grown up in an era of economic expansion, youth assumed that their personal incomes would continue to rise as well. With little concern for being laid off or preparing for the worst, saving became less relevant. This attitude, combined with high disposable income enabled by living with parents into adulthood, allowed youth to direct most of their earnings to consumable goods and services. This new culture of consumption gave way to youth's reputation of "spending tomorrow's money today." Instead of following previous generations' lead in hedging bets by saving for the future, youth ushered in the idea of immediate retail gratification. The value of earning to consume was reflected in the media's portrayal of an office-worker lifestyle.

OFFICE DREAMS

The office worker ideal made its way into Chinese pop culture in 1990 with the dramatic television series *Gong Guan Xiao Jie*

Figure 2.2 A look typical of the office lady style of the mid-1980s. Photo by Yang Zhengyu

(PR Lady). When the show debuted, its overall viewership was estimated at a staggering 90.9 percent, demonstrating the country's curiosity to peek behind the scenes of the white-collar revolution. By watching the series, viewers were exposed to new work and consumer lifestyle choices and caught a glimpse of the emerging class of "chuppies" (Chinese yuppies). The show's hook was part entertainment, part modernization guide. In the series, colleagues shared trials and tribulations on their way to the top in the rapidly urbanizing southern city of Guangzhou. The first episode showed two professionals sitting in a café discussing a possible move to Canada as Western classical music played in the background. Characters used their self-appointed English names and key English terms to reveal an openness and connection to the outside world.

Young people were impressed by what they saw and eager to stay on track, hoping to become chuppies themselves one day. With high salaries and a new social mobility, youth imagined an exciting future. They were eager to don Western-style suits, gossip with coworkers about office politics, and dream of someday becoming a manager. But the real payoff would come in the form of a salary that would make their parents proud, impress their friends, and provide them with a ticket into a new world.

The best-selling book *A Story of Lala's Promotion* was originally penned in 2007 by Li Ke as a novel, but was adopted as a popular and informative "how-to" guide.[16] From her position in the human resources department of a Fortune 500 company, the author provided a first-hand account of how to work and live as a white-collar employee in a foreign environment. When the three-installment book series was adapted for television, the "how-to" aspect of the story was scaled back and the entertainment factor was pumped up. To enhance the story's appeal to television audiences, the love interest became a prominent part of the story line, and foreign brands made guest appearances. Product placement was a great way to connect brands to a glamorous vision that was focused on upward mobility and pioneering consumption.

In one memorable scene, after completing a difficult task, Lala retreats up to the company's rooftop to enjoy a cup of Maxwell House coffee (in the background is a well-placed billboard for the brand). The blue cups featured in the series, with the coffee manufacturer's logo, are unusually large for China and available for purchase on Taobao: "As seen on TV, in *A Story of Lala's Promotion!*" The cups allowed fans their own smaller-scale token of a white-collar memory.

When the movie version was released in 2010, it further elevated the consumption story line within the main plot. Product placements by Lipton, Nokia, and Lenovo were par for the course in this romantic comedy. But unlike its predecessors, the movie upped the ante to put luxury brands on the big screen too, in a leading role. With famed *Sex and the City* style guru Patricia Fields consulting on costumes, luxury brands were highlighted as the new wardrobe of success.

Typical of Chinese youth's reputation for "spending tomorrow's money today," Lala's buying sprees increase with her salary, and she releases her frustrations by a credit card-enabled shopping extravaganza. Even happy dates with her hunky boyfriend are retail-minded, set against the backdrop of Beijing's high-end mega mall, Sanlitun Village. Happy or sad, a good trip to the store seems to be just what the doctor ordered for Lala.

The success of the formula aligning brands with office workers' high-power spending has led to a series of branded entertainment properties eager to capitalize on association. White collar-targeted entertainment properties like *Ugly Betty* (in Chinese, it is referred to as "Ugly Wudi") has been co-opted as a television series by personal care brand Dove and "Unbeatable" is a made-for-the-web branded series presented by Unilever's Clear shampoo. The film *Color Me Love* won Apple the award for Best Product Placement in a Foreign Film, from Brandchannel in its 2010 annual Brandcameo Product Placement Awards. At this stage, Chinese audiences have seemed open-minded towards branded entertainment and more tolerant of overt marketing than Westerners. Consumption isn't a dirty word; rather, it's a commonly accepted social value.

ANT TRIBES

Popularization of the office worker fantasy has equated the idea of being an urban white-collar employee with being on the road to happiness. This notion has enticed young dreamers to pack up life in smaller towns to take their shot at success in the big city. Ninety million of the estimated 150 million migrant workers who travel from smaller cities in search of better opportunities are young Chinese under 30.[17] This mass relocation is more than a physical change of address, however; these migrants are reimagining themselves and their futures. They are shifting their scope from being up-and-comers in the communities they were born into, to chasing the ultimate prize in the nation's highest profile capital cities.

While at home these migrants were seen as local stars, they are often initially shoved down to the bottom of the heap when they move away. The term "ants," coined by sociologists, refers to migrants who live on the outskirts of urban centers—squeezed together in tight, inexpensive housing in the hopes of transitioning to something better. The phenomenon was a result of a boom in college graduates, set loose in the same direction to hunt their fortunes. When they arrive in the country's most promising opportunity hubs, bright-eyed youth are confronted with the challenge of rising real estate prices and less-than-adequate salaries. To afford the transition from rural up-and-comer to big-city success story, youth crowd together to cut costs, with two or three people sometimes sharing a ten-square-meter room.

Roughly calculated, this phenomenon affects approximately one million migrants in major cities—there are an estimated one hundred thousand in Beijing alone. One area, Tangjialing, was said to house three thousand residents before the arrival of the ants. Two years later, Tangjialing had reportedly accumulated fifty thousand residents.[18] Lian Si, a postdoctoral fellow at Peking University wrote a book titled *Ant Tribe* and then its follow-up,[19] *Ant Tribe II*,[20] detailing life inside the movement.[21]

Although most of these ants suffer an initial shock, they are largely willing to pay the price to make the transition. In a 2008 survey, the China Youth Research Centre declared that 56 percent of migrants under 30 years old planned to buy property and settle in their adopted cities.[22] While simple math would suggest that not all of these migrants will succeed, it is a testament to Chinese youth's optimism and individualism that so many try.

LESSONS FROM THE FACTORY FLOOR

The dream of making it big in China is not reserved only for white-collar college graduates. In 2010, the Shenzhen-based tech factory Foxconn suffered a rash of tragedies when over a dozen (mostly successful) suicide attempts were made by 18- to 24-year-old factory workers. (Although not an anomaly in the context of other factories in China, the news was a high-profile wake-up call.)[23] Foxconn is a 60 billion USD manufacturer filling orders for the likes of Dell, Hewlett-Packard (HP), and Apple, employing roughly one million employees across several campuses. When the news broke at Foxconn, the media jumped.

The outbreak shed a harsh light on worker conditions in Chinese factories and illustrated the human price of low-cost manufacturing. One suicide victim had racked up 286 working hours in one month, about three times the legal limit. His efforts had yielded small rewards. Even after accounting for overtime pay, his salary came to approximately one USD an hour.[24] The *New York Times* uncovered a series of other hostile working conditions including verbal abuse, military-style drills, and mandated self-criticisms. But this part of the story is hardly new.

The true revelation in the Foxconn suicides is the contradiction between the last generation of workers and the current one. China's reputation as a manufacturing powerhouse was built on the backs of the first wave of migrant workers. These pioneers came from the countryside prepared to sacrifice long hours of back-breaking labor to help support their families back home. There were few other options. But this single-minded motivation was not passed down to the second wave. Even if they were not equipped to take advantage, youth saw other options that made factory work highly unsatisfying. This distinction between the old and the new worker has caused companies to realize that reevaluating human resources is a mission critical to realizing long-term business strategies.

Raised as only children, today's young workers believe that they have the opportunity to achieve (and to some extent are entitled to) a better life than their parents' generation. Unlike the first migrants, the second wave dares to dream of a better life —not just for their families but for themselves. They do not want to wait to realize this life in the future; they want it now. Youth today have witnessed a modern mobility in China and have changed their ideas about what is possible. They have seen overnight celebrities and highly unlikely heroes soar past their expected station. Blue-collar youth have seen distinct models emerge from nothing, and they want a taste of that expanded potential for themselves.

From the factory floor to the boss's office, youth are seeking something more fulfilling, more aspirational, and even more personal than what has been offered in the past. Even at Foxconn, the workers nicknamed the warehouse trolleys their "BMWs," in the hopes of one day trading them in for a real one of their own. Despite coming from a small town and working in a factory, one suicide victim dreamed of becoming a model. Sociologists explain the epidemic of suicide by pointing out that youth today are more educated, more aware of their rights, and less willing to suffer or "eat bitterness" than their predecessors. Because young people's possibility map has been redrawn, the era of a simple salary exchange for a simple job is over.

THE STRESS OF THE NEW IDEAL

For those who did make it into the inner office sanctum, young white-collars were the first to be exposed to the drawbacks of trying to become a one-man success story. One of the primary deficiencies of these early entrants was coping skills. Chinese youth, although driven to achieve, had been given little guidance in how to manage pressure. Even when compared to other East Asian cohorts, Chinese students reported feeling the most stressed out. The results of a 2010 survey, conducted by the China Youth and Children Research Center in conjunction with the Japan Youth Research Institute, the South Korea Youth Development Institute, and Idea Resource Systems, showed that almost 86.6 percent of Chinese youth polled felt heavy pressure from all sides: schools and parents, as well as competition from peers, and even themselves.[25]

Beyond the surface appeal of the shiny new office environment, having to adapt to unfamiliar expectations was stress-inducing for most Chinese. Research on white-collar work pressures that was released by the Horizon Research Consultancy Group (Horizon Group) in 2003 showed that two-thirds of office worker respondents demonstrated psychological fatigue brought on by the demands of the workplace. Primary stressors included "too many things to do in a short time" and "having to force myself to keep up with new technology and field developments."[26] Youth felt stress in their daily environment and began to question where this unfamiliar path was leading.

HITTING THE GLASS CEILING

The appeal of the exotic office worker dream has begun to fade as youth experience stress adapting and question their ability to move forward in a foreign enterprise. In the early white-collar stages, companies coveted employees with inside knowledge and outside experience. Employers hoped that employees would be able to cross communicate, adding value to on-the-ground operations and serving as a liaison for company headquarters. This led to a corporate bias to lure foreigners, sea turtles, and Chinese from Hong Kong and Taiwan into positions of power. As a result, mainlanders who had not studied or worked outside the Middle Kingdom acutely felt the glass ceiling in foreign organizations. In 2011, Booz & Co. conducted a study that underlined this dynamic. The study estimated that only one-third of Western multinational companies' (MNC) China operations were led by mainland-born CEOs. Young workers plainly see this cap—and they do not like it.[27] More comfortable expressing themselves passively, employees take their complaints to their peers before their supervisors. For example, young employees in a global marketing organization added "no future" to their instant messaging (IM) signatures to share their dissatisfaction.

Foreign enterprises have suffered a backlash of negative perceptions since the office worker dream was born. The impression now is that life for a mainlander in a foreign environment can be unstable, stressful, and counterintuitive. In my research, youth often complain of a distinct lack of work/life balance and personal connection to foreign employers. Looking to the future, these professionals perceive limited potential for growth in foreign enterprises, which compounds their low level of commitment.

RETURN TO THE IRON RICE BOWL

In comparing research on students' preferred employer types from 2007 to 2010, it is clear that the employer-employee relationship is changing. In earlier studies, graduates favored foreign-funded enterprises; they topped the list of employer types at 30 percent in 2007, but dropped to less than half that number (14.5 percent) in 2010. This decline in popularity can partly be explained by the financial crisis. Sino-foreign joint ventures also experienced a drop in favor but with a less drastic decline, from 26.2 percent in 2007[28] to 19.5 percent in 2010.[29]

Disillusioned by the exotic foreign office, youth are reassessing their values and opening alternate doors that may offer more opportunity with less risk. Increasingly prioritizing stability and mobility, youth have returned to Chinese companies and even employment with the state (the so-called "iron rice bowl"), an option that fell out of favor at the peak of the white-collar revolution. As testament to youth's return to stable employment, China's 2011 national public servant exam attracted roughly 1.41 million applicants.[30] Like many redirects in China, this swimming back into the stream has occurred on a larger-than-life scale; one community organizer position reportedly lured 4,700 applicants.[31]

OVERDOSING ON WHITE-COLLAR DREAMS

Whether an employee works in a foreign or a Chinese company, the office dream is being tarnished. As the number of graduates has tipped to outnumber opportunities, the notion of salaried office workers being at the top of the food chain has been put to the test. Difficulty finding suitable employment has caused a mini-panic among students. At the same time that they are coming to grips with the lack of opportunities for China's mammoth supply of degreed applicants, youth are also becoming distraught that the wages for these positions may not equal the effort.

Adding fuel to the fire, the Chinese Academy of Social Sciences' Institute of Population and Labor Economics reported in 2010 that salaries for new college graduates had in some cases dipped below laborers' earnings.[32] This occurred because, while wages for laborers had steadily increased since 2003, college graduates' incomes remained largely stagnant despite inflation and increased competition.[33] This realization forced would-be college students to question the benefit of higher education and to come up dubious.

UNLICENSED ABILITY

Scandals involving people in positions of power climbing to the top with dodgy credentials have further pushed youth to reckon with the value of an education. In 2010, when Tang Jun, the former president of Microsoft China and Shanda Interactive Entertainment, was accused of falsifying his academic credentials and even patents, the discussion about the importance of education heated up. The debate wagered, "Can someone's accomplishments be less if his degree is fake?" The outing of such a highly respected, accomplished individual left many with an uncertain perspective.

Doubt about the benefits of a college degree and the increasing numbers of role models who succeed despite not sticking to the recipe for success have led young Chinese to investigate new directions. In some cases, youth are changing course midstream, even before they move beyond high school. The Ministry of Education stated that eighty thousand students in Shandong province had abandoned preparing for college entrance exams in 2009 due to increasing apprehension about finding work after graduation.[34] These youth were disillusioned; the dream that had been sold to the previous generation had seemingly been tarnished.

THE WEALTH GAP VARIANCE

In 2006, an associate professor from Beijing University posted to his blog that his salary of 4,768 RMB (evidenced by his pay slip) did not cover his living expenses. This newly public accounting prompted other workers to post their earnings and many more to see, compare, and analyze the situation. The phenomenon, dubbed "online salary exposure" attracted a following. According to a joint survey by *China Youth Daily*, China Youth Daily's Social Research Center, and Sina, the phenomenon refined people's thinking about the wealth imbalance: 49.7 percent believed that it clarified salaries, while 45.1 percent thought the phenomenon helped people get a better understanding of their own social status.[35]

As China's wealth divide became more prominent, online salary exposure provided proof of the disparity. This open forum gained so much attention because it was the first of its kind. Previously, people had limited knowledge about how much others earned. This made it difficult for them to discern their standing relative to their peers and to know how much better (or worse) people in other cities and occupations were faring. Prior to online salary exposure, youth were surrounded by reminders of the spending divide but had no way of making a personal, numbers-based connection to the wealth gap.

During the Cultural Revolution era, workers hardly had to deal with social imbalances. There was no mystery; their compensation was standardized, provided by the state, and based on years of service. But in the 1980s, it became clear that some people were living up to Deng Xiaoping's adage that "to get rich is glorious," while others plainly were not. But Deng had predicted this. When opening economies in the coastal cities, he qualified the call to action with, "Let some people get rich first." What Deng neglected to mention, of course, is that wealth quickly creates a divide between the haves and the have-nots.

FALSE PRIVILEGE

By the year 1998, 20,000 foreign enterprises had registered in Shanghai, and by 2005, another 120,000 companies had joined the ranks.[36] As more employers entered the ring, the status and benefits associated with foreign offices diminished. For those who pursued an arduous academic track to gain membership to an exclusive club, the shift was disappointing. When laborers' salaries leveled out with those of white-collar workers, the bubble burst. Late entrant office workers came to refer to themselves as "fake white-collars."[37]

But office workers aren't the only ones to feel the pinch. Today, the term "working poor" is used to describe the inadequacy of salaries to meet the rising cost of living in general. In a survey conducted by *China Youth Daily* and New.qq.com, 75 percent of online respondents considered themselves to be working poor.[38]

NEW CONSUMPTION PATHS

A few global brands have recognized this shift in attitude and leveraged new messaging to keep pace with consumers' changing points of view. Christine Xu, the vice president of national marketing for McDonald's, outlines the brand's consumer-led approach: "[We always think] how can we resonate with youth and how can we show that our brand has a role in facilitating their aspirations? . . . We always think 'why do we matter to Chinese consumers and what can we do for them?' "[39]

Xu explains how the McDonald's brand integrated this ethos into its communications, saying, "The 'Zero Burden' campaign is to promote our grilled chicken platform. When we talk about that product, we need to think about how we can elevate that product into a more emotional communication."[40] The emotional connection in this case is tied to the post-80s' feelings of being overwhelmed. Since opening up, Chinese society has embraced a very materialistic view of prestige. When the office worker fantasy painted the connection between consumption and success, the post-80s generation was the first in line to realize the dream. Today, even love comes with a price tag in China: to be on top, one needs a car, a house, and to be (made) beautiful. Youth have been in perpetual overdrive to earn, spend, and then earn some more just to keep up. This cycle has been put up for review as young people begin to come down from the status ladder in search of a more sustainable foundation.

In addressing consumers about this sensitive issue, McDonald's "Zero Burden" campaign commercials feature actress Xu Jinglei (from the movie *Go Lala Go!*) as the sympathetic post-70s generation white-collar host. The commercials show the famous office lady icon interviewing youth in McDonald's restaurants to understand their shifting values. Christine Xu discusses the behind-the-scenes angle of the spots, "It's not just a commercial, we asked the actress to interview youth and see how they reacted to this kind of philosophy: enjoy a simple life.... Some of the interesting things that we picked up are not from our scripts."[41] Topics covered in the final campaign reflect life issues particularly relevant to the post-80s' consumption woes, including housing, cars, and beauty. In the spots, interviewees respond to conventional assumptions in a new way ("Why buy when I can rent?" "I'll ride a bike instead," or "I prefer to wear very little makeup"). The campaign presents McDonald's as an empathetic supporter ready to help a generation reconsider its choices. For Xu, the result is about building a long-term connection more than it is about boosting the immediate bottom line. Xu states, "When we do marketing, it's not just about how much we spend and how much we get; it's about forming a relationship and emotionally bonding."[42]

In a similar vein, Euro RSCG produced a report detailing some key shifts in young Chinese attitudes towards consuming. In this analysis, the authors refer to Chinese "prosumers" as trendsetting agents of change. The study asserts that 80 percent of prosumers are in active pursuit of uncovering what can give them personal happiness, not blindly following a prescribed shopping list.[43] Even if they are not yet confident in shifting behaviors, attitudes are being put up for review.

This distinct transition in consumption attitudes and behaviors was apparent in research I conducted that was published in *Women's Wear Daily* in 2008, ranking the top ten retail priorities among Chinese youth.[44] In this study, youth looked at consumption in a way that I termed "retail tourism." Young Chinese shoppers were keen to try leading-edge products and retail to uncover new information—and were willing to travel for the experience. They were on a shopping expedition, uncovering unexplored territories and sharing their discoveries with friends on and offline to help map out a fresh landscape.

When I repeated the exercise in 2010 for *Ad Age China,* consumer priorities had shifted significantly. Young shoppers in 2010 had already moved past the shiny appeal of retail tourism and were trading in exploration for a more grounded and predictably efficient shopping experience.[45]

Two years and a global economic crisis later, the tone was more conservative. In 2010, young shoppers moved location up four notches from #10 to #6 on their list of foremost priorities. These consumers were gaining expertise quickly and preferring relevant and reliable to new. Respondents in 2010 jumped reputation up four positions from #7 to #3. Youth's relationship with shopping and expectations for retail were shifting.

This is not to say that the new model Chinese consumer was looking to step away from the cash register—not by a long shot. Young shoppers were evolving what they wanted and how they went about getting it in order to bring the notion of success back down to earth. This reevaluation could not have happened without the support of youth's chosen social circles. As only children, set adrift from their parents by a steady import of unexplored experiences and values, youth increasingly felt disenfranchised from older generations. They came to terms with the idea that how things had been done in the past would not suit them, and they pushed forward their own microcosms to help refine new models of success.

Now, when young generations assess their next moves, they look for status symbols that will be recognizable in their chosen social circles. Experiences and personal development, two segments that had been largely ignored in China's rush to develop, have become increasingly important.

MAKING A U-TURN

For youth, the holy grail is to find ways to secure society's benchmarks for success on their own terms. Reversing the trend and moving away from top-tier cities in order to afford a higher quality of life (with a lower cost of living) is increasingly attractive. To rebalance, some youth are heading to lower-tier locations in search of a more attainable version of the Chinese dream.

When I presented the topic of reverse migration patterns on my company blog in early 2010, the assertion was met with surprise and disbelief. I told the story of a top-tier socialite who followed her husband to live a simpler life as an entrepreneur in Ningbo, and of a trainer who opted to leave his well-paid position in Shanghai to develop a career in Nanjing. Migration patterns follow opportunity or avoid risk and, despite popular convention, these polarities are still fluctuating.

Employers are taking note of the appeal of lower-tier cities and increasingly reconsidering their own migration. For companies, relocating businesses away from tier-one areas can decrease costs. For recruiting and managing employees, being closer to home has the potential to reduce migrant workers' feelings of isolation and stress that arise when they leave their support networks. Consumer-focused businesses also benefit from moving deeper into areas with less penetration.

THE POST-90s SHAKE FREE

Perhaps the most risk-friendly individuals are China's next generation work force: those born in the 1990s. This generation has experienced less of a generation gap with their parents than the post-80s and have grown accustomed to steady development. Less burdened by expectation to lead the country into a new era, the post-90s have shown greater confidence in living life in an unconventional way. Disillusioned with the pitfalls they have seen the post-80s suffer, they are eager to expand their sense of freedom—from consumption to creation. Unlike their status-trapped older cousins, the post-90s are more individualistic and apt to find value in the experience over the outcome. Priorities for this generation include exploring their talents, expressing themselves, and discovering what they can contribute to the world. They are not as quick to pursue work and consumption solely to meet society's expectations.

Because of their willingness to go against the grain, the post-90s generation is exploding the country's established work/life paths. Different from the post-80s, the post-90s feel less attached to established tradition and are eager to break out of the office worker dream. While becoming the "boss" has long been a goal for most Chinese youth and their expectant parents, the post-90s are less likely to equate success with responsibility. For them, success means freedom. They want to explore interests and pursue new possibilities. They want to be (literally and figuratively) their own boss, but not necessarily the boss of others.

In my work mining consumer insights and analyzing trends across mainland China, I have seen the intrepid post-90s breaking the mold—setting up their own businesses not only to make money but also to share their passions with others, to build communities, and to test their own abilities. Even when they do not opt to start up their own businesses, their attitude of entrepreneurialism differentiates them from older colleagues. Fueled by greater access to fresh ideas, more open to change, and committed to self-expression, workers of the post-post-90s present an unusual challenge for employers.

THE CULTURE GAP

With more options on the table and increased confidence to grab opportunities when they see them, young workers are becoming hard to attract—and even harder to maintain. Joint research conducted on the post-80s generation workers and managers by the China Youth and Children Research Center and the Beijing New Talent Academy revealed some key definitional differences that often perplex and exasperate Western employers. Their findings validated employer fears—but also opened up questions about why these differences exist and what can be done to overcome the culture gap.

One of the key asymmetries between Western employers and young Chinese employees came across in the study's analysis of job-hopping. Eighty two percent of young respondents reported that they "highly agree" or "fairly agree" that job-hopping is not a sign of being disloyal to a company.[46] From their point of view, changing jobs was part of a non-negotiable cycle. They simply could not afford to be left behind.

With the mind-set that change is imminent, youth are taking it upon themselves to steer the conversation to their benefit. Young Chinese are looking for work and success to be meaningful—on their own terms. They are asking tough questions about how work makes them feel about themselves and how it enables (or disables) other parts of their lives. In the past, they would easily slide from one job to another for a little more money, a slightly better title, or an easier commute. In the new paradigm, young workers have upped the ante to reflect higher expectations for long-term and increasingly personal development. In addition to a competitive salary, youth expect training, career progression, and the opportunity to pursue personal interests.

This is easier said than done. One hurdle is that Chinese often do not have the confidence and cultural training to do what they need to do in order to stand out in a multinational company. Having been educated in a linear system that prizes rote memorization and falling in line, youth often stumble over their background while striving to realize their ambitions in MNCs. Conventional definitions of security are often at odds with employer expectations for creativity and leadership. For both employer and employee, this is where it gets tricky.

For global companies, managing creativity and battling back old behaviors is a constant challenge. As Doctoroff observes, "They [global companies] have to create environments where self-expression is safe and non self-expression is dangerous. They have to turn the system and the hierarchy against regression to the mean. That's a difficult thing to put in a test tube."[47]

THE VALUE OF ADAPTABILITY

These differences in work-related values can be deeply concerning. And, without a willingness to learn and an open-mindedness to change from both sides, they can become insurmountable. In my work with Western senior executives, the question of how to attract, manage, and maintain young workers often comes up. Many of these managers have experience working with young professionals and assume that Chinese counterparts will act and respond much the same as other youth in other countries would. They are caught off guard when this proves not to be the case.

Employers are puzzled by workers' constant engagement with real-time virtual connectors, like sending instant messages, cruising social networking sites, texting, and playing online games. Management is often distraught by the lack of input from employees in company meetings and aghast at how quickly young employees will abandon their posts. They begrudge the amount of one-on-one management young employees require and snicker at the influence parents exert in their children's careers. They do not understand the cultural motivations for these behaviors and are often looking for a quick fix; they want to see less but get more. The gist of their challenge is: how do we get our teams in China to act like us?

But this is the wrong question. Young Chinese see the situation differently, so they will be apt to draw different conclusions that will, in turn, spur different actions. Modernizing, not Westernizing, the new Chinese worker is challenging employers to adapt to their way of seeing the world.

ATTRACTING THE NEXT WORKER

A survey conducted in 2011 by ChinaHR, under the global employment site Monster Worldwide, helped create an index to illustrate new graduates' changing vision. In the index, recent graduates prioritized four key factors: compensation, brand, culture, and development. Of the respondents, the majority 0.99 voted that brand was their highest priority. Development followed at 0.98, culture came in third place at 0.96, and compensation was fourth at 0.91.[48] These results show a relatively balanced (albeit highly demanding) ranking and relay a confidence on the part of respondents in choosing an individual path over merely following a single group-determined priority.

These multiple values are particularly impressive compared to the report's historical findings. In the past, graduates exhibited a much less balanced approach to assessing employers' values. In the 2008 index, compensation was the most attractive to new grads at 0.87, brand ranked second at 0.67, development was an afterthought at 0.20, and culture ranked in last place at 0.12. What these workers wanted was not a long-term career; it was short-term status and consumption power.

Among these four categories, the 2011 survey specifies directives that youth would recognize as signs of an employer brand's value in a category. For example, a clear career path is listed first under development, one that provides opportunities for mobility while providing a stable foundation. Reinforcing new attitudes about consumption, youth also align diverse employee benefits before salary. In this model, compensation is measured by more than just a paycheck. It is a comfortable working environment, stable employment, and

competitive income level—in that order.[49] This new map highlights
the next iteration in young worker priorities. The dream is evolving away from short-term thrills toward longer-term thinking about
how to integrate life and work.

CORPORATE PATRONS

This new wave of worker is creating a following. Innovative government incentive programs are opening up, designed to help young
entrepreneurs get their projects off the ground. Start-up capital, risk
assessments, and reduced taxes are among the support options available from the state.[50] However, this new direction not only offers an
opportunity for youth, but it also presents a means for companies to
build a stronger connection with young constituents. By helping to
build the tenets of entrepreneurialism, companies can develop their
own employer brand reputation and tap into a hungry and inventive
type of idea maker.

In 2009, the L'Oréal Fund for Students Employment and
Entrepreneurship awarded 1 million RMB in financing to 27 teams
from two hundred candidate groups hailing from more than 70
universities across China. Each winning group, across high tech,
e-business, environmental, and even philanthropic fields, was
granted 10,000–100,000 RMB in corporate financing. The L'Oréal
group also organized mentoring for the winners from their own corporate pool; management from all functions including marketing,
human resources, legal, sales, research, and development chipped in
to advise budding start-ups.[51]

MOBILIZING ENTREPRENEURSHIP ONLINE

Taobao has been a powerful channel for youth to try out entrepreneurship with very little start-up capital or long-term commitment.
The most bare-bones examples include freelancers who auction their
time. The Taobao model is popularly recognized, and most youth
can recount their favorite success story. The moral of these stories
often involves how personal passion can lead to profit, how per-
sistence can overcome obstacles, and how working as a team can
deliver triumph.

Unencumbered by heavy setup, youth are able to manage online shops in their spare time, selling items that will be profitable or supporting categories or brands that they care about. This kind of personal curation is a key means of educating consumers and has become a driving force behind niche markets like vintage clothing and toy collection. On Taobao, youth are laying the foundation, helping to refine subgroups and allowing for trends to translate between large and small cities across China.

The youth-focused Chinese fashion brand Vancl has taken advantage of young people's ability to market and sell online with an online campaign named "Vancl Star." In this program, the brand converts consumers into a part-time sales force. By registering on the campaign's social networking site, users can create their own mini-Vancl shop, selecting and styling their own collections using Vancl products.

Shop owners who attract the most comments and fans are elevated to Vancl Star status. Given a featured position on the site, top users are also rewarded with coupons to be applied to Vancl purchases and have the chance to appear in the brand's advertising. Beyond accolades, there is an opportunity for financial compensation; the brand shares 10 percent commission with Vancl Stars whose visitors purchase items by clicking through photos in their personalized shop. The brand stated that they anticipated sharing roughly one billion RMB of its profits with Vancl fans.[52]

MAPPING NEW ROADS

Youth are no longer seeking to be merely employed—they want to be engaged. Illustrating this point, Steelcase office furniture produced a composite of post-80s workers' characteristics and a list of six critical shifts in the study *New-Gen Workers in India & China: Reshaping Their Workplaces & the World*. The report profiles China's post-80s generation workers as being unique from past generations in that they are self-centered, energetic, active, optimistic, confident, trend-conscious, and communicative.

These traits help classify post-80s' behavior in the workplace. Although they often require special mentoring and revised expectations, the post-80s are keen to contribute, express opinions, and feel a sense of ownership for their efforts. For their social sense of well-being, access to a variety of communication tools (primarily real time) is critical for a happy work environment. In comparison to older generations, they are self-centered, but their attitudes and actions are still largely informed by connection to their chosen communities.

Steelcase credited the post-80s for driving six key changes in what Chinese employees are seeking from their employers. The company outlined these changes as:

1. From Harmony to Identity: shifting from societal expectations to personal fulfillment
2. From Teamwork to Collaboration: sharing ideas across groups
3. From Job Security to Growth: establishing development as more important than security
4. From Supporting the Work to Supporting the Worker: enabling social networking
5. From Worker to Explorer: developing career paths with room to experiment
6. From Work & Life to Working & Living: seeking a work/life balance[53]

The post-90s generation will surely set the bar higher in terms of independence and individualized expectations. Their tolerance for change and rebellion against the norm is more formidable than that of their cousins, the post-80s. Nonetheless, the post-90s still seek ways to modernize and customize their own Chineseness, to seek a solution to a problem that is yet to be fully understood.

Neither generation of Chinese youth subscribes to one single definition of success. New paths are cobbled together by individuals who balance group expectations, personal passions, and lifestyle considerations. To manage this quest for balance successfully, Lynton suggests employers develop a serious and credible strategy to attract and maintain young employees. She recommends that employers "talk about using technology, developing careers, contributing to growth and society. Talk about employees as people with families and other interests that make them well rounded. Talk about these, and then demonstrate with action. Remember, the young talent wants to be idealistic, but they are also skeptics."[54]

For young workers who have become leery of values that have been handed over to them by a rapidly developing society, the time has come to reassess success. In their own analysis, youth are calling to task previous expectations of working to consume. They are evaluating how they can explore a more personal measure of success without stepping out of the bounds of their cultural identity. These highly adaptable youth are taking on a new challenge: when failure is eminent, redefine success.

LOOKING BACK

Although working in a foreign office was seen as a ticket to new professional and consumer freedoms after China opened up, this dream has since fallen flat for youth. Extended competition with little release has left many ragged and discouraged. The quantity of contenders with similar qualifications and dreams has left many feeling discouraged. No longer able to afford the Chinese dream because of skyrocketing housing prices, the concept of the working poor has taken root. To scale back from an imminent sense of failure, youth are now looking for a more balanced work and consumption lifestyle. Increasingly, they consider entrepreneurship as a means of achieving this goal. Youth are less and less satisfied with foreign companies as employers; companies need to look more critically at their people strategies to recruit, develop, and retain future talent. As the two generations (the post-80s and the post-90s) approach work differently, a thoughtful strategy is necessary to ensure cohesion.

LOOKING FORWARD

This chapter is meant to help you think more deeply about connecting to youth. How could the information be leveraged in these scenarios?

1. How can companies develop an employer brand that appeals to young workers—and their families?
2. How can managers help different generation employees work together successfully?
3. How can companies provide safe channels for employees to express new ideas—and discontent?

CHAPTER 3

TIPPING GENDER SCALES: FROM BOYS RULE TO GIRL POWER

I'd rather cry in a BMW car than laugh on the backseat of a bicycle.
—Ma Nuo, fashion model, born in 1988[1]

IN 2009, A SHANGHAI CARREFOUR CASHIER MADE HEADLINES for literally taking to the streets to advertise her demands for a mate.[2] It was not just that Sister Feng was a woman grabbing the reins of the mating ritual or her untraditionally flashy methods that attracted attention. She drew a media blitz for what was perceived as her overly lofty ambitions. At a pint-sized 4'8", with dark skin and an exceptionally wide mouth with buckteeth, Sister Feng was fatally unattractive by Chinese standards. The fact that she was not a traditional beauty was only one strike against her. Sister Feng also did not possess important family connections or an exceptional academic pedigree.

These shortcomings, while irredeemable by Chinese society's strict standards, seemed of little consequence to the ambitious 24-year-old. She penned her requirements for suitors as: an internationally minded 25- to 28-year-old graduate of Peking or Tsinghua University holding a Master's degree in Economics and residing in an eastern coastal city. Not only was she asking for China's crème de la crème with high income and access, she aspired to claim a looker with no strings attached. Sister Feng required that suitors be handsome, stand at 5'7"–5'10", and not have had prior marriages or girlfriends who had undergone an abortion.

A far cry from the old practice of relying on matchmakers and parental intervention to find a mate, China's mix of new feminine confidence and an oversupply of bachelors has created a climate of lady's choice. One blatant example of this is a dating website, 51Taonan.com (translated literally as "I want to find a man"), built like an online bazaar where women are the buyers and men are the commodities. When they see a profile they like, female users click to add bachelors to their shopping cart. If they are not satisfied, women can put the men's profiles back up for sale or even suggest them to a friend. Despite its appearance, the site tries to make the commercial angle of its business more subtle with the slogan, "We sell romance, not men." But the reality is that for Chinese women empowered by choice, bachelors are increasingly seen as commodities.

YOU'VE COME A LONG WAY, BABY

Well-positioned women in China today are emboldened by their roles as brides and income generators—and empowered by their ability to make personal decisions. Their influence is both social and economic, allowing them to call the shots like never before.

China Market Research Group estimates that in 1950, women contributed 20 percent to household incomes. The group posits that this number rose to 35 percent in the 1990s, and it expects that by 2014, women's contribution will rise to 52 percent.[3] Even among blue-collar migrant workers, men are often relegated to construction jobs, while women may be earning significantly more as maids or masseuses.[4] It is possible for wives to outpace their husbands' earning potential.

Eager to test new personal power and income potential, women in China are twice as ambitious as women in the United States, according to New York's Center For Life Policy. The organization conducted a comparative study of college-educated women and found that two-thirds of Chinese respondents thought of themselves as very ambitious, compared to one-third of American respondents. Career-minded Chinese women aspire to climb the corporate ladder, with over 75 percent hoping to hold a high-level position, compared with just over half of those sampled in the United States.[5]

PLAYING A PART

Of course, this headline does not apply to all Chinese women—education, location, and income gaps are severe in China. But the finding is a firm departure from women's historical standing. Traditionally, women in China have been placed squarely at the bottom of the totem pole, always below a man. The notion of the "three obediences" refers to women who were first required to obey their fathers, then their husbands, and then, as widows, their sons.[6]

A popular 2001 television commercial illustrates women's traditional role. The scene opens with a mother washing the feet of her young son, perhaps three years old, in a bowl placed on his bed. She finishes the job, gives him a loving tickle, and goes to get a larger bucket to wash her mother-in-law's feet. The boy, watching his mom at work, fills a bucket on his own and surprises his mother by offering to wash her feet. The tag line at the end reads, "Parents are children's best teachers." This spot for a domestic pharmaceutical company sums up the filial cycle—reinforcing the natural order of three generations living under one roof, with the daughter-in-law as the linchpin caregiver.

Perhaps this calm scene could have kept looping in China if not for the one-child policy. Lacking a comprehensive social security system and enforcing a birth control plan, the government essentially pushed most parents to roll the dice with a single offspring. If they had a boy, they had a better chance of their son moving his adult family in with his aging parents, working to support and care for them in their old age. Having a daughter, on the other hand, meant that parents would exert energy and resources, raising her with little hope of not being abandoned when she married into her husband's family. A daughter's parents would be left to fend for themselves when she moved, as dictated by tradition, into her husband's family house. Under the one-child policy, having a son was regarded as a means of ensuring future survival, while raising a daughter became a short-term investment.

ONE AND "ONLIES"

When the New Zealand city of Christchurch suffered a 6.3 magnitude earthquake in 2011, Chinese parents who lost children who were living there asked for additional compensation above and beyond what victims' families from other countries would normally receive. The appeal was based on their unique emotional and financial reliance on their children. Chinese parents claimed that the loss of their one and only child in the tragedy would be more significant than other parents' losses, as Chinese parents' financial and emotional investment could not be recouped.

But the one-child policy is hardly just a numbers story. This bargain has irrevocably changed the dynamics of both the group and the individual in China and has shaken up the politics of gender.

TIPPING THE UPPER HAND

Today, the combination of the one-child policy and the nation's historical preference for boys has led to a tipping point in China's gender relations. Fifty years ago, boys outnumbered girls 106 to 100.[7] In 2011, by demographer Nicholas Eberstadt's estimation, 123 male children existed for every 100 females under the age of four years old.[8] In some areas of China, including Jiangxi, Guangdong, Hainan, and Anhui provinces, baby boys have outpaced girls by 30 percent—or more. As these boys come of age and look for a spouse, the odds will be stacked against them.[9]

The Chinese Academy of Social Sciences predicts that one in five young men will not be able to find a wife.[10] In an American context, this would equate to ten cities roughly the size of Houston populated by frustrated bachelors.[11] With an estimated surplus of forty million single men of marriage age by 2020, China's gender expectations are being renegotiated.[12]

This imbalance, felt across China, has revolutionized gender roles and the traditional power balance between men and women. Urban middle- and upper-class young women already sense their increased value in society, their girl power if you will. In Jiangsu province, parents of daughters in upper economic classes have realized that girls hold the "upper hand" in marriage. Some of these families

Figure 3.1   Couple photo books show new girl power

have initiated advantageous contracts for their daughters, including inheritance rights for the wife, allowing the second child to take the wife's last name, and encouraging the husband to move into the wife's family's house or the house that the wife's family buys for the couple.

These concessions would have been inconceivable just one generation ago. In Chinese culture, it has long been a foregone conclusion that the husband's family holds all of the power and makes decisions for the present, past, and future generations. But as parents have come face-to-face with an oversupply of bachelors to potential brides, traditional rights and responsibilities have become more malleable.

THE NEW UNDERDOG

At the beginning of the twenty-first century, a widely accepted assumption showed signs of being reversed. For decades, women in rural areas were the last to reap the rewards of China's Great Leap Forward into modernity. Removed from the hustle and opportunity of the economic miracle taking place in China's cities, rural women suffered doubly—disadvantaged by their gender and their location. Often burdened by economic hardships and looming isolation in their small communities, women in the countryside became the largest group of suicide victims in the country.[13]

In 2011, when the temperature was taken again on the population's suicidal tendencies, a starkly different and surprising picture emerged. No longer were rural women the most likely to succumb to taking their own lives. Rather, their desperation had transferred to a group that was thought to be sitting securely in the most powerful seat in the country. China's Ministry of Health reported that rural suicides had decreased by 30 percent while urban suicides had increased.[14] This shift in the prevalence of suicide from the country to the city was not the only surprise. Suicide was no longer a woman's issue: men outnumbered women in taking their own lives. This dramatic turn of events is just the beginning of the tale of how gender has transformed itself in China.

A QUALIFIED PACKAGE

As women assert more power, bachelors and their families are the ones paying the price. It is not hard to connect China's high rate of personal savings with its gender ratio problems. Attracting a wife has become serious business. According to the National Bureau of Economic Research, the need for a man to provide a suitable "package" to attract a bride accounted for about half of the nation's increased household savings in 1990–2007.[15] In areas where the gender gap is more pronounced, savings rates were higher as parents were forced to chip in to help their sons woo a bride.

As a result of a young suitor's need to provide a sufficient package to attract a wife, financial pressures, suitability, and real estate have become the hottest topics in China today. One blogger estimated that attracting a bride in Shanghai (including courtship, wedding party, honeymoon, housing, remodeling, and of course, a car) requires a bachelor—also known as a "bare branch"—and his family to spend a whopping 1.4 million RMB. Saving this sum would take the average white-collar worker 15 years to earn, not taking inflation and steadily rising housing prices into account. With this hefty price tag, securing a wife becomes an all-consuming, highly stressful project that requires contributions from the whole family. Currently, it is necessary for two, sometimes three generations to pool resources to construct a qualified bachelor profile. For the majority of families, providing a house is the key concern.

A HOME OF ONE'S OWN

James Farrer, the director of the Institute of Comparative Culture at Sophia University and author of *Opening Up: Youth Sex Culture and Market Reform in Shanghai*, explains the housing crisis as a backlash from living through a period of not having sufficient resources: "The materialism of modern China has a lot to do with the culture of scarcity under socialism. In some ways, the current obsession of having your own place reflects the obsession of a previous generation."[16]

While previous generations most often married and moved in with the husband's family without question, today's individualistic youth are more and more finding it unacceptable to do so.[17] Encouraged by parents and peers to strive towards home ownership, the post-80s in particular dream of a home of their own to escape the constant eye of parents and in-laws—where they can be free to decorate, eat, sleep, and live as they please. These young people's desire for their own home is not surprising in a culture that prizes modern symbols of success and expects youth to be at the forefront of new consumption experiences. What is unique is that parents have so readily enabled and elevated home ownership as a criterion for finding a wife into a national obsession.

A survey by *China Youth Daily*'s Center for Social Research showed that 35.6 percent of more than 2,400 people polled would not commit to marriage if they did not own an apartment or a house.[18] Signaling the emotional benefit of property ownership, *China Youth Daily* revealed that over 80 percent of respondents linked happiness directly with home ownership.[19] This response demonstrated why, despite soaring real estate prices, most mortgages (60 percent to 70 percent) are being taken out by people under 40 years old.[20]

Owning a home has become so synonymous with finding a wife that few pause to reflect on how this national mania came about. There is a joke that ambitious mothers-in-law are the real instigators behind the property boom and, in some ways, it is. Property development advertising reflects parents' influence in pushing youth towards real estate. One ad in Shanghai reads, "Those who get married and don't buy a house are regarded as hooligans!" and another in Wuhan warns, "Mother-in-law says, 'the apartment has to have three rooms!'"

To satisfy this ambition, family members must pool resources. Reminiscent of Japan's housing bubble, when having three generations sign for a collective mortgage was not uncommon, China now offers intergenerational mortgages. In recognition of the group effort required to afford real estate, banks have adopted programs that put not only young couples but also their parents on the hook to pay back the Chinese dream. The term "Nibbling Off of Elders Group" refers to youth who rely on their parents' support to buy their way into society's increasingly demanding inner circle.

CULTURE REFLECTS CRISIS

The unfortunate combination of skyrocketing prices and unforgiving requirements for a qualified bachelor has led to a phenomenon dubbed "house slaves." This term refers to those who postpone plans and dreams in order to work single-mindedly to afford a roof of their own. A 2009 survey conducted among netizens in Chongqing asserted that 74.7 percent considered themselves house slaves, and 18.1 percent thought of themselves as "house slaves-to-be."[21]

Concern has mounted that young Chinese are trading their idealism for property, essentially being held hostage as single-minded workers in order to afford the roof over their heads. The conversation has not been limited to official channels, however; pop culture has lifted its own inspiration from society's crisis of conscience. Singer Huang Zheng's song "Sell" is an example of how the subject is provoking creative responses that resonate. The song's video follows different people as they react to a single real estate advertisement, revealing desperation as onlookers calculate how many years they would have to work to afford the dream of owning a home.

Dwelling Narrowness, meaning "living like a snail," is a television drama with a social message. The writer Xiao Fuxing describes the series as a mirror of the "cruel and hateful destruction buying a house is for the emotional value system of a generation of people."[22] Connecting characters with the crisis gave viewers an opportunity to watch—and discuss the problem from a close (but not dangerously personal) point of view.[23]

More than a commentary on housing prices and the national obsession with home ownership, the narrative also set up a debate among viewers on the value of love versus money. The popular web portal Sina surveyed viewers to determine if they would choose the poor boyfriend or the rich official if they were in the main character Haizao's position. Of the 6,447 respondents, 46.2 percent chose the official, while 22.2 percent chose the boyfriend. The popular reasoning among respondents was that, "Love with material benefits is better."[24]

PAYING THE PRICE OF GIRL POWER

By saving tirelessly to afford steep marriage prerequisites, bachelors and their families have arguably suffered from the gender imbalance. Bachelorettes, on the other hand, have enjoyed more earning and spending power than ever before. Without the burden of having to save for a home or pay rent since they are often living with their parents until marriage, these women can afford to buy what they want, when they want it.

Not limited to everyday purchases of household goods, women are flexing their consumer muscle in categories that have typically been reserved for wealthy men. Because of extremely high import and engine size taxes, ultra-luxury cars carry a price tag in China more than double that of what they would be sold for in other countries. Despite this, women of means are increasingly opting to step into the driver's seat. For example, the number of women buying Ferraris in China is double the worldwide average, and three times the number of Maseratis sold to European women are now being sold to Chinese women. In China, females account for 30 percent of Maserati sales, and women are now inspiring the brand to add color options such as red and bordeaux to appeal to their increasingly feminine consumer base.

ON MY OWN

There are many successful role models for women to emulate in China. *Hurun Magazine* (the publisher of China's annual Rich List) named Zhang Yin, the head of Nine Dragons paper recycling company, the richest woman in the world with a stately personal account of 5.6 billion USD. Zhang is part of a growing class of powerful women with significant disposable incomes and influence.

Ambitious women are starting businesses on their own; the magazine *China Entrepreneur* estimated that in 2010, there were more than 29 million female entrepreneurs. Although still unequal in wealth and number to their male counterparts, Chinese women are gaining global recognition for their commercial prowess. Globally, 11 of the top 20 wealthiest self-made billionaire-ettes are Chinese. The first three spots on the global ranking of the wealthiest entrepreneurial women are occupied by Chinese, while American super-entrepreneur Oprah Winfrey is ranked in ninth place.[25]

All of this earning and spending by women seems like a marvelous pinnacle in China's gender evolution, but it also poses a substantial threat to the way society operates. Women in urban areas are putting off (some even rejecting entirely) the idea of settling down. In 2005, the average age for women to get married was 23.5, while for men it was 25.9.[26] Three short years later, in 2008, when the numbers were tabulated again, the average marrying age for women had risen to 29.6 years old, and men to 32 years old.[27]

Anxiety about women putting off marriage is mounting. The crux for preserving the traditional family structure is now getting these empowered bachelorettes to transition into more conventional roles, to resign their independence in favor of marriage and motherhood. In this equation, single women in their late twenties and thirties have been dubbed *sheng nv*, China's so-called "leftover women."

LEFTOVER WOMEN

The phenomenon of women choosing the single life over marriage is causing a great deal of raised eyebrows. Although the unflattering term "leftover" has been levied on them, Farrer sees these singles more as reluctant pioneers: "China is a society in which marriage is expected. It's hard to be the first generation of women who are not going to get married, but that may be what we are seeing. This is the first generation of women who actually have a lot of resources, and a fairly sizable sliver won't get married at all, many perhaps regretting they never found the right guy, though some undoubtedly happy they escaped the shackles of marriage."[28] Although the term "leftover" seeks to simplify and perhaps even vilify single women's status, the causes behind the phenomenon and ramifications for the future are more complex.

The very existence of leftover women is a threat to the presumed order of Chinese families. Women now perceive their value as a professional as being at times equal or even superior to their roles as wives and mothers. To measure perceptions, Sina conducted an online survey about what netizens considered to be their personal achievement index. In response to the question about which accomplishment women should have made by the age of 30, 94 percent of female respondents selected "having their own career," while a puny 6 percent opted for "a good marriage." Women are enjoying careers, and not just for the money—they are lapping up the feelings of accomplishment, independence, and personal satisfaction that they receive from their work.[29]

While the option of marrying later in life may seem like a very cosmopolitan choice limited to trendsetting tier-one bachelorettes, it is also drawing attention in China's more traditional lower-tier cities. In the coal mining town of Taiyuan, Shanxi province, for example, one matchmaker estimates that her client base of 30-year-old singles consists of approximately three thousand women but only two hundred men. This means that for every one leftover man looking for love, there are 18 ladies his age skirting social assumptions that a woman should hurry up and marry and have kids.

Although society is not sure what to do with women making a decided turn away from traditional expectations, many brands are targeting them as a dynamic new segment. Leftover women were subtly targeted in a campaign for Benz (as Mercedes-Benz is known in China). In one treatment, a professional-looking woman wearing a stylish trench coat smiles into her mobile phone. She is leaning one high-heeled foot against her Benz that is parked on an empty rooftop, with skyscrapers in the background. The message is clear: she has made it. Another version in the series shows a woman jogging in a fashionable running suit beside her Benz in a groomed urban park. This woman is confidently taking time to enjoy life. Noticeably absent in these images is the entourage that normally accompanies women in making a car purchase (a husband, child, and often in-laws). Benz is speaking to a new successful, independent woman who does not need to consider requirements other than her own. The copy describes her as an individual: good natured, confident, elite, and healthy.

PARENTAL INTERVENTION

To find a match is not as simple as boy meets girl. Today, there are more than twenty thousand matchmaking agencies in China.[30] The agency Century Love claims to have found matches for three million members, leaving only 170 million more in the company's love queue.[31]

Young people's choice to marry later, if at all, is stressing out parents eager to see their children move into the next stage of expected development. From the parents' point of view, most never anticipated such independent, mobile children; their dreams were rooted firmly in their children settling down with a spouse, house, and child. Looking to protect this dream, parents are anxious for sons and daughters to find a mate before they are aged out of the prime marriage window. These concerns are causing parents to take initiative to push the process along.

Until 2005, it was illegal for people to marry while still in college, but dating on campus has begun to enjoy a new parent-approved reputation for helping youth along the road to commitment.

Anxious parents are now hoping to get the jump on their children's laggard marriage views by helping them find "the one" before graduation. Outside the realm of typical expenses, so-called "love funds" are a new line item in college students' allowances earmarked specifically for dating before graduation.[32] Even if their children are unsuccessful in the first round of college dating, parents hope that footing the bill will encourage their little treasures to learn critical social skills to find and compete for Mrs. Right in the near future.

Some parents provide financial support, while others take it upon themselves to look for a mate. Anxious parents lining up at weekly marriage markets is common in China's big cities. Mothers and fathers armed with pictures and CVs of their only child congregate in public parks, advertising their child's qualifications, including height, education, income, and information on the size and location of the apartment (for sons). The actual brides- and grooms-to-be are not in attendance—many youth would be embarrassed by their parents' matchmaking efforts, and often do not live in the same city anyway. No matter, as this is a market for parents.

Parents' role in finding a spouse for their child draws public interest and empathy. Pandering to the notion that mom and dad can influence and participate in the matchmaking process, the popular Saturday night dating show *Date on Saturday* has recently spun off a new series called *Mom and Dad Match-Making Group*. Other entertaining televised series pose filial singles and their opinionated parents side-by-side in the search for love. Although they want to help, parents cannot keep up with current notions of love and courtship. For their part, youth–while eager to please their parents–are not convinced that there is value in responding to the past and ignoring the freedom of modern love.

MADE-OVER MISTRESSES

Even the notion of concubines has taken a new twist in a modern context. For men, having a girlfriend on the side is still almost expected when they achieve a certain level of status, but for women, the game has changed. China's newly confident, independent, and income-oriented women have turned the tables on what society can expect from modern mistresses. Empowered by a sense of choice about when and if to get married and an understanding of the value of their feminine wiles in a gender imbalanced society, mistresses have become increasingly forward about their choices.

In a 2008 survey conducted by *Hurun Magazine*, mistresses were estimated to account for one-third of luxury product consumption. Although companies do not market to this segment overtly, it carries weight and association. Online, netizens refer to Mini Coopers and BMW 3 series cars as "mistress cars." Certain real estate developments are also known as "mistress villages," that is, enclaves known for their convenient, yet separate, proximity to wealthy businessmen.

There are two terms used to describe modern mistresses in China. The first, called *er nai*, or second wives, are assumed to be emotionally more akin to a real second wife, and they often have long-term relationships and harbor deep feelings for their partner. They function as a second family, with some women even raising children born out of wedlock. But unlike a first wife, second wives operate behind the scenes, without the social benefits allotted to a legally recognized partner.

The second type of modern mistress (or mister in some cases), on the other hand, is not interested in playing house. This type, known as *xiao san*, or "little three," often takes a utilitarian approach to the intersection of love and money. While material gifts have certainly been a hallmark of men's relationships with mistresses in the past, one kind of *xiao san* is taking the relationship from behind the curtain to demand a more public recognition. This wave of women views their choice less emotionally: for them it is a distinct career opportunity. Looking for a sugar daddy to supply a luxurious lifestyle, this relationship is often marked by luxury apartments, cars, and experiences that the wealthy patron provides in exchange for the little three's company.

Disobedient to the assumed code of mistress discretion, these independent-minded *xiao sans* have been particularly vocal in asserting their rights. Looking to be recognized as a professional group, little threes have organized into an association that has moved quickly out of the shadows and into the spotlight. One group, China's Association for the Care of Xiao San refers to its members as "professional mistresses of the new era."

DEBATING A NEW PLACE

Society's treatment of modern mistresses mirrors its grappling with the role of money in relationships and young women's willingness to break with tradition to pursue a new paradigm. In a 2009 survey, 16.5 percent of respondents thought it was acceptable to become a mistress of a rich man, and 14.8 percent thought an extra-marital affair was acceptable as long as the love was true.[33] While these feelings would have been kept behind closed doors in the past, the role of money and love in—and outside of—marriage is now a matter of public debate.

Mistresses, although not approved of by the general public, are certainly no longer operating underground. The proliferation of mistress matchmaking services advertised on college campuses across China speaks to the perceived viability of the relationship as a job with specific duties and compensation. Although some universities have cracked down on the practice, these women, often from lower-income families in smaller cities, are lured by the luxury lifestyle being a mistress affords. Without older, wealthier boyfriends to foot the bill, the dream would be nearly impossible to realize.

As marketing to eligible young undergraduates has kicked up in recent years, groups including the Guangdong Women's Federation and the All-China Women's Federation have organized in an attempt to keep young ladies from entering into these transactional relationships.[34] To discourage young women from choosing the life of a mistress, Guangdong province has initiated a pilot program aimed at dissuading primary and middle school girls from being seduced by glitzy promises when they get older.

A Beijing lawyer named Zheng Baichun has also taken up the cause of defending young women. But unlike activists in the south, Zheng takes action after women have become mistresses. His website is designed to educate women about their legal rights and help those who are often hesitant to ask for help. Unlike his comrades in the south, Zheng's point of view is not moral; it is acutely legal. For example, one of his cases deals with how to pursue child support for children born outside of marriage.

Both sides—those against women becoming mistresses and those advocating for mistress rights—are pushing society to deal openly with the phenomenon of mistresses. In doing so, they are sparking a deeper dialogue about women and gender in China. Their convictions speak to new gender roles, the wealth gap, and the struggle to incorporate traditional group dynamics with modern individualistic values.

EXPANDED CIRCLES

In China, youth date and participate in sex for the first time at a later age than their cohorts in the West. Farrer explains that China has age-appropriate assumptions about sex that preclude youth from engaging in sex at an age on par with their international counterparts. "This sort of pressure on kids to be academically focused at the expense of every aspect of their private lives means that adult behaviors of all types are completely delayed until university, if not to some extent beyond. What you see is a real delay of what it means to be an adult and most Chinese believe sex is an adult behavior," states Farrer.[35]

Although they may reach sexual maturity later than their international peers, young Chinese are still a far cry from previous generations in their country. Shaking loose traditional, somewhat transactional ideas about courtship, they are experiencing relationships, not just dating. Open-minded and more confident than their parents, youth today are flexible about how they meet, how they date, and even how (or if) they marry.

The combination of increased migration and the proliferation of the Internet has taken people further apart while bringing them closer together. In the preurban migration era, Chinese were confined to the communities they lived in for most, if not all, of their lives. These boundaries defined with whom they would be able to interact and also ensured family and social repercussions for behaving outside of expectations. Now, with migration, a girl from the north can travel to an eastern city, meet friends from all over China, and marry a boy from the south. In this way, her identity in her hometown becomes less critical and her understanding of herself becomes more complicated. The ability to go online has taken this network to yet another level. No longer bound by face-to-face interactions, youth are able to encounter and develop friendships with people in other cities and even other countries. This virtual playground has given young people an opportunity to see and experiment with different rules of behavior. They can play with their identities and even safely arrange hook-ups for anonymous sex without worry of ramifications in their own real-life communities.

A wider circle for socializing has led to an increased level of acceptance for strangers and new ways of meeting people. In a recent survey, 67.9 percent of respondents reported that "blind dating is not embarrassing," while 23 percent were open to personally posting a dating advertisement to find love.[36] Youth are more open and less critical about how they will form relationships; they all recognize it is critical for them to create connections.

BEHIND CLOSED DOORS

Sexuality among youth is a critical area that has largely been ignored by the general public until recently. This does not mean that youth have not been curious or even sexually active; rather, it means that they have been engaging in sexual activity without having much formal knowledge. In 2010, according to the first national survey of adolescent reproductive health, 22.4 percent of single (male and female) youth between 15 and 24 years old were sexually active. Most likely, the majority had never engaged in a formal conversation about sex with an adult. Having only minimal sex education, 51.2 percent reported not using contraception the first time they had sex. Respondents' awareness of pregnancy and disease prevention was also skimpy—only 14.4 percent were aware of how HIV could be transmitted or prevented.[37]

Young people are not equipped with proper information before they engage in sex and they face more ominous social ramifications from being pregnant than from aborting a pregnancy; therefore, abortions in China are an accepted after-the-fact form of birth control. Among sexually active females, 21.3 percent reported accidentally becoming pregnant and 91 percent of those reported choosing to abort the pregnancy.[38] As many clinics in China offer "set-menu"-style abortions, including exams, surgery, and necessary drugs for 880 RMB,[39] getting an abortion can be a relatively uncomplicated experience. Unlike the United States, China also has minimal moral and religious objections to abortion to contend with and almost no examples of single teenage mothers.

Despite young people's interest in sex, adults have by and large chosen to turn a blind eye to youth's sexual activity. In 2002, the Beijing Municipal Women's Federation studied parents' role in informing youth about sex and found the link to be weak: 74 percent of parents avoided discussing sex with their children.[40] Of the parents surveyed, only 3 percent said they would engage in an open conversation about sex with their children.[41] To tackle the issue, schools have gotten involved, at least to a token extent. Beginning in the fall of 2010, a pilot sex education program was launched in high schools and universities in 21 provinces across China.[42] But the mandatory course, "The Truth about Life, Love and Sex," is less about how to have sex responsibly than it is to promote premarital chastity.

Sexually active but not formally educated in sexual matters, Chinese youth are looking to find their own way. The Internet acts as an illustrative how-to guide, allowing youth to take notes on others' first-hand experiences and access pornography. *China Youth Daily* conducted a survey of over three thousand teenagers in 2010 that showed that 79.2 percent of respondents relied on the Internet as their primary source of information about sex.[43] Schools and parents ranked dead last in importance as a resource for sex education, which supports the Beijing Municipal Women's Federation's findings. Without a formal curriculum or guidance, young Chinese often learn what is sexy but not how to be safe.

SEXUALIZING CELEBRITY

Until recently, sexuality in China was kept sealed politely behind closed doors. While other countries have experienced a long string of celebrity sex tape scandals, China did not get a peek inside the private sex-capades of its pop culture icons until "Edison-gate." Before 2008, Canadian-born Chinese Chen Guanxi (aka Edison Chen, commonly referred to as Edison) was on top of the world. One of China's top entertainment figures, Edison influenced popular culture in his music, clothing line, acting, and modeling. Because of his strong youth appeal, he was a sought-after figure for brand endorsements, pulling in big bucks from deals with the likes of Levi's, Pepsi, and Adidas to be the face of their Chinese marketing.

All of that combusted in January of 2008, when Edison found himself in the middle of the country's first sex scandal involving a pop icon. After he took his personal computer in for repairs, his intimate files were exposed and leaked across the Internet. "Edison-gate" was born.

At the time of the scandal, sex in the mainland was a personal and innately private act. Mainstream Chinese youth had never seen such sexually explicit images of their favorite stars. The combination was irresistible, but the photos went quickly from trivial entertainment to potentially explosive. Government authorities and national media focused on controlling the situation, while fans incorporated this new open sexuality into their vocabulary. Despite threats from the police that any person showing or posting the photos in any way could be detained for up to 15 days, interest did not wane. The chat room Tianya Club slyly posted a collection of the images, which were viewed close to twenty million times per day.

The scandal posed a host of new questions, including how to resolve dueling images of women's sexuality. How should young fans feel about Zhang Baizhi (Cecilia Cheung), a superstar who, while engaging in some pretty playful sex scenarios with Edison, was not only married but had a young son? How could they reconcile their anger at Zhong Xintong aka Gillian Chung (one half of the squeaky-clean pop music duo Twins), who had promoted herself as a virgin, despite photos proving otherwise? Edison-gate posed risky questions and forced an uncomfortable debate.

Serious consequences were quickly levied for creating this kind of controversy. Public humiliation and even death threats chased

Edison. Transformed from icon to villain, the star fled his home in Hong Kong and retreated from the Hong Kong entertainment industry. The scandal was too hot for brands, and they raced to distance themselves. Edison was abruptly released from movie roles and lucrative contracts with brands, and the women involved faced similar commercial punishment.

But shortly after the ruckus erupted, a change in youth's attitudes became palpable. A few months after Edison-gate broke, a young woman who worked at a Kappa sportswear store in Shanghai claimed that a video of her having sex had been stolen and leaked online. A police investigation uncovered that she had released the footage herself and was subsequently charging set rates for appearances at bars, clubs, and other events. If Edison pushed the country to reconsider the private lives of public figures, this girl (dubbed "Kappa Girl") forced the question of whether sex itself was worthy of celebrity.

These two incidents, both of which delved into sex and privacy issues, have educated and inspired a new wave of youth to redefine the line between private and public sexuality. Today, far removed from the shock and awe that Edison-gate initially brought to the fore, Edison Chen and his lady friends have made a triumphant return to pop icon status. In December 2009, Edison opened up new retail brands in the mainland, including expanding his JUICE boutique brand in Shanghai. His fashion brand CLOT even collaborated to create a pop-up shop in Shanghai called "Man Is In The Forest" in 2010 to showcase Disney's creative collaborations with smaller niche brands and artists. Waves of post-Edison-gate, youth-created sex photos and movies underline the fact that public sexuality has staked its place in young China's modern vernacular.

THE VALUE OF SEXINESS

This opening up of society has given sexiness a glamorous makeover. Even a 2009 military parade in Tiananmen Square celebrating the sixtieth anniversary of the founding of the People's Republic of China got in the mood; the women's militia donned pink uniforms that were pretty hot by any military standard. This new sexiness does not necessarily have anything to do with sex acts per se; rather, it is about promoting an individual's worth in society. As Farrer puts it, "Now, there is a real commercialization of sex, and the old adage is once again renewed: sex sells.... To be sexy is good and to not be sexy is bad. To be marketable, to have sexual capital is a good thing."[44]

As youth have emphasized the value of sexiness, companies have followed to feed consumers' new tastes. In the past, sex shops in China's larger cities were advertised as "health centers." Overwhelmingly patronized by middle-aged male customers and staffed by apathetic older women in hygienic white coats, the centers were anything but sexy. In 2010, we did research on sexiness for a client and found that these sterile environments were upstaged by privately branded shops lining the coolest streets in trendy neighborhoods. Young entrepreneurs were engaging with customers as guides, repackaging a taboo subject into a hot trend. What was once considered serious, adult behavior was being remade into a fun pastime for a new wave of confident young consumers.

NEW PATHS DOWN THE AISLE

Although sexiness is being rebranded to address new consumer attitudes, the change does not signal a total transformation of sexuality and relationships. In general, Chinese tend to do less comparison shopping of potential partners before marriage than people in other countries and usually have only a few romantic relationships before tying the knot. Despite this "slow and steady wins the race" approach to commitment, young men and women are also increasingly open-minded about courting and not rushing to the altar. A recent study found that 17 percent of respondents recorded an emerging flexibility about so called "flash" marriages, those that occur when the couple has known each other for less than one year.[45] When youth do find love, they are taking a broader perspective on the steps required to reach a marriage proposal.

The pace of courtship is just one example of youth's openness to experimenting with relationships. Taking a decidedly individualistic approach to marriage has opened up young people to adopting new marriage trends that would have once been unthinkable. These "try before you buy" ideas were not popular among their parents' generation, but for young people eager to take a chance and guard their personal happiness, these concepts are growing in appeal. A recent poll showed that 48.6 percent of respondents accepted the idea of cohabitation before marriage.[46] Akin to cohabitating is the notion of a "trial marriage," essentially living together with the intention of getting married. This trend allows a couple to experience life under the same roof and also provides more time to save for a notoriously costly and extravagant wedding. (Bills for middle to high-end ceremonies in Shanghai on average are double those in the United States, but costs are often reimbursed with gifts of money from guests called *hong bao*).[47]

On the other end of the spectrum of an extravagant and expensive ceremony, the idea of a "naked wedding" has taken root, particularly among the stressed-out post-80s generation. A naked wedding does not require a big budget for the event, rings, and honeymoon. Just nine RMB for a marriage license cover the cost of a naked wedding. Although simple, the concept has inspired two television series to date. Symbolic of bachelors' exhaustion from the chase for a bride, a

Figure 3.2   Post-80s' divorce ceremony scene from the movie *If You Are The One*

2010 *Netease* survey found that 74 percent of men accepted the idea of a naked wedding. Women, on the other hand, in their relatively powerful position, were not so eager to negotiate; only 25 percent accepted the idea.[48]

BREAKING UP (ISN'T THAT) HARD TO DO

Just as youth have reenvisioned dating and marriage concepts, so too have they reexamined the notion of divorce. Unlike other countries that have many established channels for couples to work through their problems, couples in China are frequently left to fend for themselves. When they cannot mend a relationship, youth are often not intimidated by the idea of changing course to pursue personal happiness. Because of this, the post-80s generation has been at the forefront of rebranding divorce. For these unconventional leaders, divorces, like marriages themselves, merit celebration. Media attention has followed this phenomenon with interest as young people often part ways on friendly terms, some even going so far as to host banquets to toast their newly single status. The 2010 movie *If You Are The One II* opens with a divorce ceremony attended by fashionable black-clad guests, and later follows the main characters to Sanya for a trial marriage. In a recent poll of post-80s' attitudes about divorce, 61 percent of respondents in Guangzhou reported that a divorce ceremony was a good idea.[49] For these youth, a change in relationship status is not as socially detrimental as it was in previous generations; embracing change has been a common and critical skill.

Reflecting women's increasing power in relationships, wives tend to be the instigators of divorce. A court in Wenzhou, Zhejiang province, found that, among post-80s, wives requested 75.5 percent of divorces.[50] Another survey covering Wuhan, Tianjin, Changsha, Nanjing, and Beijing found that wives initiated 71.3 percent of divorces, while husbands initiated 26 percent. The remaining 2.7 percent was attributed to parents.[51] This research points to women's willingness to instigate a change in status and their powerful position in transforming gender assumptions in society.

THE NEW GENERATION OF MOMS

As post-80s and post-90s youth have come of age, their ideas about personal relationships have shifted markedly away from those of previous generations. Their decidedly individualistic perspective often clashes with traditional relationship responsibilities (with mates, families, and communities). This clash is leading young people to experiment to find a more natural balance that allows them to express independence while staying connected to their core peer group.

Parenthood is the next battleground for this test of wills between individuals and the group. For China's first generation of only children, the fear of becoming a "child slave" (parents who lose their freedom to take care of a baby) is grave. Many are too addicted to the trappings of independence, such as rashly changing jobs and splurging on elaborate shopping sprees, to trade them in for parental responsibilities.[52] Some young women are flatly deciding that the costs outweigh the benefits. A 2008 study reflects women's shifting attitudes toward motherhood: 12.5 percent of female respondents did not want to have children, a 10.5 percent increase from the study results three years prior.[53]

But not all young women are denouncing parenthood. Many are building on what they have already learned about themselves and are eager to apply these personal ideas to their roles as mothers. They look forward to becoming parents—as long as it does not mean they have to leave their freedom and personal passions behind. Campaigns for Pizza Hut and KFC, among others, are highlighting their commitment to help young moms find balance. Ads present women who are able to order dinners delivered to satisfy family obligations and allow them to finish work at the office or taking care of themselves. The message to young moms is simple: we help you be who you need to be, so you can be who you want to be.

Young mothers are not waiting for a product to help them manage. To secure their independence, post-80s generation women are adopting a concept called "child pooling," a means of sharing childcare duties so that moms can get a break. Play groups alternate between homes, with members taking turns hosting and organizing meals, entertainment, and educational activities for the children. To balance their own needs and motherhood, digital moms are

networking online, forming groups on QQ and other social networking sites to welcome new members whom they would not have
met in any other way. Motivated to protect their independence and
armed with a formidable digital network, these mothers have created
a cross between a modern "mommy and me" group and a Cultural
Revolution kindergarten. They rely on each other to provide time
away from parenting and also leverage the power of their social circle
to make group purchases of key products at reduced rates.[54]

These new moms are just the latest installment in the country's
evolving gender story. A power map is being redrawn to help both
men and women redefine what they expect from relationships –and
themselves.

LOOKING BACK

Boys have always been favored in China, but now as the one-child
policy has tipped the gender balance, women are taking their turn at
calling the shots. With more income, opportunity, and confidence,
China's first generation of single women is forcing society to reevaluate
the rules. For middle and upper class women who elect to continue
on the track of getting married and having a family, they are more
and more able to rewrite the rules in their favor. These new wives and
mothers are changing the terms of the gender contract in China and
making room for the idea that marriage is a more flexible choice—not
a foregone conclusion.

LOOKING FORWARD

This chapter is meant to help you think more deeply about connecting to youth. How could the information be leveraged in these
scenarios?

1. How can new marketing and product developments enable women to
   balance individual and family expectations?
2. How will marketing to the family be affected by youth's revised
   approach to the family unit (delaying marriage and children, accepting
   divorce, etc.)?
3. How can marketing create new aspirational profiles to ease the burden
   for life-long bachelors? And support the rise of "leftover" women?

CHAPTER 4

ABOUT FACE: SEEING NEW BEAUTY CODES

I think individuality is kind of sexy.
—Li Yuchun, pop star, born in 1984[1]

WHEN NETIZENS LIFTED PICTURES OF A HUNKY stranger from a photography community forum and reposted them across social networks including Tianya, a frenzy overtook China's fashion-focused digital communities. The handsome man's seemingly haphazard styling took the current mix-and-match trend to the next level. He had draped a long black down coat over a leather jacket and oversized jeans that he belted with multicolored fabric shreds. The look was topped off with mussed, longish hair and a dangling cigarette. "Too cool!" exclaimed young Chinese fashionistas. Other photographs of him wearing women's clothing circulated online and, instead of drawing ridicule as might be expected, his gender flexibility only added to his fashion-forward credentials.

News quickly spread and in less than a week, the images had lured millions of viewers. Young netizens got to work comparing his style to models swaggering down foreign runways and his looks to Asian actors, including Takeshi Kaneshiro and even the Oscar-nominated Ken Watanabe. They photoshopped his face onto the covers of international men's fashion magazines, ad campaigns, and movie posters to demonstrate how easily he could blend into an internationally cool vernacular. His image was altered to fit into a *Pirates of the Caribbean* poster (cast as handsome Captain Jack

Sparrow), and it also took Leonardo DiCaprio's famous spot behind Kate Winslet in a still from the movie *Titanic*.

But this awe-inspiring fashion maven was not another run-of-the-mill Internet celebrity in China. He was a homeless man in his mid-30s wandering the streets of Ningbo, an outsider by anyone's standards. Nevertheless, youth forgave these shortcomings, and new fans nicknamed him the Beggar Prince, the Handsome Vagabond, and Brother Sharp (the name that stuck) as an ode to his sharp dressing skills.[2] Less than two weeks after the images were first posted to Tianya, a search on Google using the Chinese term for "Brother Sharp" yielded more than fifteen million results.[3]

There was a rush to capitalize on the unlikely fashion hero: a book was penned by Brother Sharp's cousin, and a movie was optioned. *Xi li ge* (Mandarin for "Brother Sharp") was even launched in Jiangxi province as an online fashion brand. Designs in the collection took inspiration straight off of Brother Sharp's back (baggy and somewhat dirty-looking jeans, plaid button downs, shirts with holes). Images on the site showed models strutting these grungy looks, some sporting the same dangling smokes and mussed hair for which Brother Sharp was known. Unlike the accidental sensation that started it all, the message was a purposeful declaration against the norm. The brand's slogan shouted, "Refuse to be normal, we want to be trendy!"

Although the overt commercialization of this phenomenon was contrary to what made Brother Sharp an overnight celebrity in the first place, the fact that such a forsaken character could become a fashion icon at all is telling. Admiring the appearance of someone at the bottom of the social order was a revelation that spoke to youth's questioning of what success looks like. It revealed a movement rumbling to the surface. In new China's second act, youth are not questioning the value of traditional beauty or its place in society, but they are allowing for more variation in what is understood to be beautiful.

Brother Sharp was put on a pedestal for demonstrating the mainland's ability to fit into an international fashion scene; his look was just the kind of scruffy cool that other countries had pulled off successfully. Most still tiptoed around what "scruffy" meant because on the road to riches, rags were the last thing status-obsessed up-and-comers wanted to pack. The fact that youth embraced such a shabby-chic icon demonstrated that definitions of success were moving in more than one direction. Old definitions were clearly being compromised. Brother Sharp's dark skin, shaggy hair, and haphazard dress were a far cry from other coiffed and manufactured icons. His rebel appeal had nothing to do with an ability to earn and provide; Brother Sharp embodied a new kind of spontaneous sexiness, the kind young Chinese would not be bringing home to mom.

As youth seek to determine their own place in society and the world, they are repainting a picture of what is acceptable and even aspirational. This shift is partially in response to lines of societal acceptance that in the past were drawn too tightly to be inclusive, and partially a result of a new confidence in redrawing those boundaries to their own benefit. Youth are moving the beauty lens from one single angle of acceptance to refocus on a new crop of ideas, inspirations, and applications. As the world races to incorporate Chinese outer beauty, Chinese youth increasingly look inward to find a more diverse and inclusive appeal.

OUTER BEAUTY

In 2008, Sun Feifei took the stage to win third place in the annual Elite Model Look competition. Although models from all over the world had competed in the prestigious event since it was established in 1983, Sun was the first Asian to break into the top three. The competition's recognition of a Chinese beauty talent was perhaps inevitable. After all, the annual contest had been hosted in China for five of the past ten years. The Elite Model Look competition was not the first international contest to award its highest honor to a mainland beauty. Zhang Zilin had been crowned Miss World in Sanya the year before, and local pageants had popped up with men, women, and even children strutting down runways all over the Middle Kingdom.

This focus on China is not surprising given the high value the country places on physical appearance and therefore, its impressive

consumption of beauty products. For Chinese, economic development and beauty seem to go hand in hand. In 2010, China's beauty
industry expanded by 12 percent, and it is predicted to grow more
than 10 billion USD by 2015, the most significant growth of any
country in the world.[4]

Courting China's super beauty consumers used to require less
localization but now, as the market has become more competitive, Chinese models have graduated to become the new "it" girls
of upscale marketing. Givenchy underlined this point in 2011 by
choosing a primarily Chinese and all-Asian lineup to parade its cou-
ture collection down the runway. But Chinese models are not just
being touted as the new face of luxury. Brands are borrowing their
appeal to represent other modern attributes. For example, Victoria's
Secret adopted Liu Wen to represent a new sexiness in the brand's
first dip into the Asian model talent pool.

Beauty brands are also signing Chinese models to act as the face
of their marketing efforts. Liu Wen was transformed from sexy siren
to elegant sophisticate as the new face of Estée Lauder, and L'Oréal
signed actresses Yao Chen and Jiang Yiyan to represent Biotherm
and Shu Uemura, respectively. Even the Japanese brand Shiseido
shifted its strategy from a Japanese-born beauty to Chang Chunxiao,
a Chinese model / actress / singer / author.

China's rise as a superpower is toppling previous assumptions
about who rules the laws of attraction. Brands from the West,
Japan, and Korea are now bowing to court the very consumers who
once hung on their every move. From follower to leader, China and
Chinese beauty are being repositioned front and center. As designers
from the world's fashion and beauty epicenters clamber to localize
to varying degrees, there is a more fundamental question percolat-
ing in the mainland itself. What do the meanings and the expressions of beauty look like in China now?

THE BEAUTY CODE

Over time, even as ideals fluctuated, society has tended to decide by
consensus on one specific beauty archetype against which all others
are judged. From foot binding nearly a century ago to today's popular

double eyelid surgery that creates an upper eyelid with a crease, the pursuit of beauty has always been a serious venture. Contemporary standards of beauty, while they have shifted over time, have moved in unison. Elements of beauty that have held fast are delicate, and include a small nose, big eyes, cherry lips, a rounded and petite jaw, a lean body, and light skin. The picture-perfect specifics of this look are not meant to act independently; rather, they are meant to convey a sense of balance and harmony. As Tom Doctoroff, the chief executive officer of Greater China at J. Walter Thompson (JWT) and author of *Billions: Selling to the New Chinese Consumer* and *What Chinese Want*, confirms, "Beauty, like everything in life, should be 'harmonious.' Chinese want to stand out by fitting in. That means being 'perfectly normal.' Round faces, smooth skin. When women use skin whitening products, they want to smooth out blemishes, not shine."[5] For most Chinese, beauty is recognized as a recipe of attributes that work as a group, not as an isolated or outstanding feature.

The generally accepted ideal is not meant to convey what is average; however, it is a reflection of perfect "normalcy." When the process to find suitable Olympic medal presenters for the Beijing games began, recruiters searched for female candidates who were between the ages of 18 and 25 years old, with a height between 5'6" and 5'10." The hunt was on for candidates with "a regular appearance with standard proportion." Standard proportion in this case was judged as *san wei* (the proportion between chest, waist, and hip circumference). Even candidates' smiles were judged. An etiquette class for prospective award presenters asked candidates to hold chopsticks in their mouths to ensure a perfect smile (defined as the exposure of 6–8 upper teeth).[6]

FLOWER VASE

The race to embrace feminine ideals is a far cry from the so-called "Iron Girls" who were raised during the Cultural Revolution.[7] In the 30-plus years since reform and opening up, beauty standards have returned to social, not political, power. Today's young made-up fashionistas strutting the streets of Beijing and Guangzhou hardly resemble the uniform appearance of the Iron Girls who walked before them.

Under Mao, women were gender neutralized; the pursuit of beauty was a vilified and punishable offense. Displays of femininity, including long hair, makeup, jewelry, and using red paper to color lips (cosmetics were not readily available) were all strictly forbidden. In that era, women pushed the mirror away to buckle down to the serious work of the revolution. Under this system, beautification was a liability, not an asset. Mao once hailed in his poem that: "China's daughters have high-aspiring minds, they love their battle array, not silks and satins."[8]

When China opened up in the 1980s, a return to femininity became a sign, not of political backwardness but of progress. Iron Girls were ridiculed and pushed aside to make way for the new face of China. Young women with exposure to higher education and media messaging rushed to buy au courant cosmetics, hairstyles, and icons to explore a new direction and keep pace with society's development. But even as they purchased products, they were careful not to overdo it. To be seen as too good-looking was risky. Women were careful not to be seen as a "flower vase," someone who is beautiful on the outside yet vapid and of little use inside.[9]

Although the Iron Girls were seen as out-of-step, elements of their legacy remained. Students from Beijing University in 1993 denounced beauty contests as "meaningless Western culture" and scolded contestants for their lack of "self-respect and spiritual pursuits."[10] Gao Jing, a female student at Beijing University, was credited with writing a story called "Peking University Rejects Beauty Pageants," an article that was published on the front page of the *Beijing Youth Daily*.[11] In 1994, the All-China Women's Federation issued its stance on beauty pageants; it would not support, endorse, organize, or participate in the contests. That same year, 22-year-old Pan Tao traveled to South Africa to compete for the Miss World title, but after that, China took a hiatus from international pageantry. Recognition for being attractive was a compliment outside of China, but it carried confusing associations inside the mainland. China did not send another delegate to the Miss World or Miss Universe pageants until the early 2000s.[12]

Figure 4.1 Couples dressing among friends, lovers, and families signals belonging.

Research I have conducted in lower tiers reflects this complicated and delicate balance between inner and outer beauty. For women in smaller, more traditional communities, beauty is a double-edged sword. Coming off as too attractive can be off-putting, yet being seen as not attractive enough can be negative as well. As Doctoroff observes, "People's identities and definitions of success are always dependent on societal acknowledgement."[13] The key is to stay within a strict parameter—pacing oneself evenly with the group, not falling behind, racing ahead, or being left out.

THE CODE FOR BELONGING

Log onto any social networking site in China, and you will be greeted by a gallery of youth peeking out from behind their avatars, hoping their look will incite a response. They are looking for attention from their existing contacts and also prospecting to catch new people's interest. But if you look closely, you will see a common language strung between the images. Some of the most popular poses for girls include holding up two fingers in a "V" gesture, puckering up for a kiss, and making a heart with their hands. These youth are distinguishing

themselves, although not drastically. They are embracing subtle dif-
ferentiations, but rarely engaging in sweeping displays of singularity.

These standard poses online actually relay unity and belonging.
A "couple space" on Renren (a Chinese Facebook-like community)
has a similar but decidedly more close-knit social function. Profiles
are created and managed by couples, not individuals, who wish to
present themselves and communicate with others as a team. Pictures
and updates are posted to show off their togetherness and friends
respond in turn to them both.

Offline, couple dressing is a popular style among youth to show
that they are a unit that belongs together. Sometimes the association
is expressed by simply wearing the same T-shirt, while other times a
couple embarks on head-to-toe twinning. This matching can occur
between friends or boyfriend and girlfriend. As the post-80s grow
up and have children of their own, family-style dressing (husband,
wife, and child) has emerged as a natural transition. T-shirt designs
targeting young families use video-game iconography (Plants vs.
Zombies, Angry Birds, etc.) and characters including The Smurfs
and Astro Boy.

Figure 4.2   Beauty is a group decision that includes friends and family.

FROM ACCESSORY TO INVESTMENT

Make no mistake about it: beauty is a tool in the Middle Kingdom. But it is not a lofty declaration of self-actualization. It is not about personal satisfaction and individual aesthetics; instead, it is an investment in building social capital. This association is particularly acute in the case of luxury-branded fashion and cosmetics.

To help luxury brands better understand their customers in China, my team conducted a series of in-home interviews, digging into the closets, cabinets, and inner thoughts of young luxury consumers. One participant that sticks in my mind was Elsa, a 28 year-old from Ganzhou in Jiangxi province. She is what McKinsey's 2011 study *Understanding China's Growing Love for Luxury* would identify as a middle-class aspirant, a lower-tier city native who buys luxury goods, but not all the time and not across all categories. Even though this segment may seem like an insignificant shopper by other markets' definitions, it is estimated to make up 51 percent of the total luxury-consumer population in China.[14] With rising incomes, knowledge, and opportunities, middle-class aspirants are a force that cannot be ignored.

When Elsa worked for a global public relations company, she would regularly travel internationally, snatching up luxury goods along the way. But when she decided to drop out of the corporate world to try her hand at freelancing, her budget took a hit. She no longer felt that she needed to keep up with the office-lady lifestyle, so she scaled back spending on luxury bags and accessories. For her, it did not make sense to carry a Gucci or Louis Vuitton bag if she was not going to an office. Elsa had no illusions that she would be able to afford a 360-degree luxury lifestyle complete with a fancy car, clothes, and experiences—nor was she sure she wanted it. Continuing to spend on skin care, cosmetics, and fragrances from up-market labels was a different story; that was an investment in her future. Using lesser products might affect her appearance, impacting the quality of her professional and social life. Elsa's rule was that if it touched her skin, it needed to be the highest quality—and luxury was quality. Even when she was unemployed for a few months and money was tight, she still would not consider downsizing in these critical areas.

THE INVISIBLE CV

Being attractive has a certain social ritual in China, but overall, the pursuit of beauty is highly practical. Charles de Brabant is an ex-L'Oréal executive, a current partner and Asia director at the luxury human resources consulting firm Saint Pierre, Brabant, Li and Associates, and adjunct professor of Luxury Branding at the China Europe International Business School (CEIBS). Brabant explains, "Chinese are extremely pragmatic and packaging counts. So probably the better you look, the more likely you are to get a job. We may not like to say that, but that's a reality."[15]

The case of the 2005 Miss Asia contest winner, Wang Lei, is an obvious example of looks enabling access. After winning the Miss Asia crown, the 20-year-old, who hailed from Harbin, was offered permanent residency by the Shenzhen Bureau of Labor and Social Security. This special permission (which is notoriously hard to get) did not sit right with many Chinese who had lived in the city for decades with little hope of ever achieving this kind of privileged status. Based only on her looks, Wang had been given the gift of special consideration above and beyond what ordinary Chinese could hope to receive. The bureau defended its offer in a fairly transparent way, noting Wang's "special expertise in the cultural industry."[16]

Parameters have been established that reinforce the link between traditional beauty and traditional success. While the West has established antidiscrimination laws and litigious enforcement of employee rights, laws against hiring or firing based on appearance are not commonly enforced in China. When a Chinese individual first applies for work, physical appearance is front and center. On the top of most CVs, a mug shot of the applicant looking clean-cut and malleable to the company's requirements peers back at the recruiter. Explicit demands for eloquent speech, minimum height, and pleasant facial features are commonly advertised, especially for public and client-facing positions. But some descriptions can teeter on sounding like personals ads, describing desirable smiles, figures, and personalities as critical requirements for consideration.

Mixing appearance requirements with professional qualifications is not limited to the private sector, however. In 2010, Chengdu authorities openly sought female law enforcement officers based on looks and age, explaining their approach as a way to enhance the district's image. Requirements for these pretty police included being 18 to 23 years old, over 5'2", and attractive with a good temperament. This was not the first case of equating feminine wiles with representing the government. In 2004, Hunan province tried to recruit candidates with "symmetrical breasts" for civil servant positions.[17]

For job seekers, being attractive is a way of standing out—and fitting in. When they apply, they not only need to stand out from other applicants but also show that they can fit into the overall corporate image. For women who do not make the grade, there are consequences. In 2011, the Women's Federation of Foshan (Guangdong province) reported that 33.6 percent of female college students suffered discrimination based on their appearance when looking for a job.[18]

UNDER THE KNIFE

Women have been bold in seeking new ways to fight against genetics in order to squeeze their way into the narrow definition of traditional beauty. Modern science gave the gift of cosmetic surgery, and Chinese women opened the package with glee. The success of Hao Lulu, China's first surgically enhanced beauty, helped popularize the idea of cosmetic surgery. Before her trip under the knife, Hao was an unemployed fashion writer from Beijing, struggling to make it in a competitive field. Plucked from obscurity, she hit the big time when she agreed to undergo six months of procedures donated by the EverCare Medical Institute as a televised marketing ploy dubbed the *Beauty Dreamworks Project*. Media frenzy followed Hao's every operation, and when she unveiled her final transformation, she landed a starring role in a Taiwanese television series, *Meteor Garden*.[19] Turning cosmetic transformation from a private matter into a public spectacle, Hao's story declared cosmetic surgery as a shortcut to a better life.[20]

The fever for going under the knife has helped to catapult cosmetic surgery to the fourth-largest consumption category after housing, cars, and tourism.[21] Banks now offer cosmetic surgery loans to help eager customers speed up the process. Popular surgeries include creating double eyelids, making the nose narrower and higher, and performing liposuction and breast implants. Few cases of leg lengthening exist, but they do speak to the preference to be tall (but not too tall). Cosmetic procedures are available across China, at deluxe as well as back-alley clinics. Korea, a cultural and beauty Mecca for young Chinese, has become a popular destination for cosmetic-surgery tourism; packages are sold that include both the procedures and travel. Yestar, a clinic in Shanghai advertises its competitive advantage plainly: "Korea is very far, Yestar is very close."

Young women often receive procedures as gifts after graduation to help give them a leg up on the job market. For older women, using science to reverse aging allows them to stay current in an increasingly youth-obsessed culture. And cosmetic surgery is not a tool uniquely available to women. Men are also electing to have surgeries that will help them bump up the value of their appearance. Men, too, are looking to leverage their looks (surgically enhanced or otherwise) to achieve a better job, more money, and enhanced status.[22] As Doctoroff points out, "Beauty is a means to an end. Plastic surgery, a no-no many years ago, is now hot. But it's not for self-actualization. Plastic surgery reinforces the notion that beauty is an 'asset' to be leveraged."[23]

The Chinese Association of Plastics and Aesthetics estimated that three million Chinese underwent cosmetic procedures in 2009. A *China Youth Daily* survey showed that 71.5 percent of respondents believed the plastic surgery boom was a result of modern values linking looks and competitive advantage. Of those polled, 49.4 percent asserted that cosmetic surgery's popularity was a reflection of the opinion that "changing your appearance can change your life and make dreams come true."[24] The plastering of advertisements for cosmetic surgery clinics in factory cafeterias and across districts frequented by factory workers reflects this claim. Here, the message is clear: beauty can change destiny.

CITY JADE MEN

Changing one's destiny is a mission that has pushed the nation forward; however, as social landscapes have shifted, gender-based connotations have evolved. Metrosexuals are known as "city jade men," a segment that spends a great deal of time, money, and effort on personal beautification and on developing a reputation for sophistication and style. For city jade men, this is more than a hobby. Pragmatically speaking, being attractive provides the same competitive advantage in work and marriage for men as it does for women. Maybe more. James Farrer, the director of the Institute of Comparative Culture at Sophia University and author of *Opening Up: Youth Sex Culture and Market Reform in Shanghai,* suggests that men may be more socially obligated to stay attractive because of the gender imbalance. As he notes, "The gender imbalance leads to late marriage for men. It puts people in a holding pattern so even well-off men marry later. It means that there's more of a market for male sexiness."[25]

This need to be seen as attractive is pushing the market for male beautification into new territory quickly. Basic skin cleansing and moisturizing products are being moved aside to make room on the shelves for lines that offer more sophisticated benefits like anti-aging and anti-oxidation. Procter & Gamble (P&G) estimates that approximately 65 percent of Chinese men now use skin-cleansing products.[26] By P&G's approximation, growth in the men's cosmetics sector has shot up at twice the rate of the total beauty market in China.[27] L'Oréal is positioning itself by putting brands in front of men at every price point: Biotherm for the luxury market, L'Oreal Paris for the premium mass market, and Vichy for the pharmacy market.[28] These companies are racing to help men look good and keep pace with enhanced social expectations. And with so much competition to get the job and the girl, the market is expected to explode. Market research firm Euromonitor International calculated that the category's growth in China will be five times faster than it will be in North America in the period leading up to 2014.[29]

Figure 4.3   For city jade men, beauty rituals are becoming a normal part of their routine.

THE MASCULINE MYSTIQUE

Some key concepts are crossing gender lines. In one television spot, a successful metropolitan professional uses Nivea's whitening products to help defend against sunlight, pollution, and natural darkening of the skin. The commercial touts an equation between outstanding whitening and outstanding success. But the target of the ad is not a woman—it is a man. Just as women have pursued whitened skin for social status, now so do men. The ad's hero is not only picking up points from his colleagues at work, but members of the opposite sex are fawning over him. An attractive bystander sighs to his girlfriend how lucky she is to have him.

As companies plan for this influential consumer segment to grow, they are pausing to take a look at who the new beauty consumer is and how he differs from his counterparts in other markets. While macho sensibility has kept movement in men's skin-care and cosmetics categories comparatively sluggish in the West, a lack of machismo among Chinese men is an opportunity. Chinese men are driven by competition and are less judgmental about what is required to achieve their goals.[30] Not bound by the West's highly masculinized stereotypes, Chinese men have created a footprint in fashion as well.

Cutting their teeth on luxury accessories, men now account for a full 45 percent of the 1.2 billion USD market for luxury handbags in China. In the United States, where packing a Gucci or Prada bag may be received as effeminate, men account for a measly 7 percent of handbag sales overall.[31]

The need to be attractive has inspired a new rush of men's fashion and lifestyle media. Magazine offerings include versions of international publications (including *Harper's Bazaar Men's Style, GQ,* and *FHM*) as well as homegrown Chinese print and online resources with names like *The Outlook Magazine, Manse,* and *Trends Men*. It is the job of such publications to educate city jade men about the latest and greatest developments in fashion, cars, gadgets, and girls.[32] Sprinkled amid other content is advice about cosmetics and skin care. Although *GQ China* runs a feature on men's cosmetics in every issue, an editor told *Bloomberg News* that readers want to see two or three times that amount.[33] Men understand that to compete in today's market, they need to cultivate an image that demonstrates their savvy and appeal.

OPENING UP AND BRANCHING OUT

Because of the prescribed social and economic benefits of being attractive in China, it is no surprise that men as well as women are pursuing assistance to help boost their status. Unlike previous generations, youth are becoming much more flexible about what constitutes beauty. While it is still critical to be perceived as attractive in order to get ahead in a larger social sense, young vanguards have cracked open a door to let more than one beauty standard guide their behavior. For them, the divergence is about incorporating individuality into the equation. As Brabant observes, "One way of augmenting your status is eventually to have your own individuality, which is a big change. Second generation wealth needs other ways to differentiate themselves."[34]

Youth today are increasingly flexible in their definitions of beauty. Lenovo ThinkPad's *xiao ben* (meaning small notebook) campaign allowed users to try on ten different style genres on a branded mini-site. The audience could watch a man and a woman undergo the transformations, or swap in their own photos to imagine themselves in a new way.[35] This makeover madness was fun, but the reality for most youth is that they engage in fashion experiments all the time. Most will make short-term commitments to fashion, rotating closets, interests, and identities to suit a mood or occasion. Fashion can be a situational tool to help the wearer fit into different surroundings. For example, a worker in an American company may choose a relaxed American-style ensemble for work, trade that in for a romantic British sophisticate number for a date, and then pull off whatever style friends have elected for a night out on the town. For youth, this chameleon-like behavior is both about fitting in—and branching out.

Unlike cohorts in countries with more developed subcultures, fashion is a fun and flexible tool that Chinese youth play with freely. It does not carry the same serious social connotations for stepping in or out of line. Buying into a new look does not necessarily mean adopting a new point of view complete with new friends, new taste in music, and new hangouts. Fashion is simply expected temporary experimentation. While there is a serious following for "cosplay" (short for "costume play"), most youth engage in their own form of this pursuit without recognizing it.

And why shouldn't they swing from one image smack into another? Style mash-ups are evident across modern culture. In music for example, the country's top pop stars are chameleons in their own right, moving freely from sappy ballads to hard rock to hip-hop. Zhou Jielun (Jay Chou), the Taiwanese king of pop in the mainland, even delved into a fast-paced country-and-western jam with his song "Cowboy On the Run"—and fans followed. The video for the song shows the singer sauntering around a 1950s-style American diner outfitted in full Western regalia (vest, chaps, cowboy hat, and boots). This image came from the same album that showcased Chinese style rhythm and blues (R & B) in the song "Blue and White Porcelain," and Chinese-style rock in "Sunshine Homeboy."

In this playful context, Western symbols of rebellion lose some of their potency. Style-wise, some of the monikers of Western dissent are simply a matter of personal preference, not territorial posturing.

Tattoos, piercings, and wild, spiky hairstyles in bright colors are more of a stylistic choice than a statement of defiance or of belonging to a counterculture.

RECLAIMING STYLE

In 2011, when Joan Rivers and the crew of E! Entertainment Television's *Fashion Police* proclaimed Fan Bingbing as the winner in the show's "Bitch Stole My Look!" segment, fans watching on Chinese video-sharing sites went wild. They were watching one of their own get marked by American fashion critics as an up-and-coming trendsetter. Fan, one of China's biggest stars and #9 on Forbes China Celebrity 100 of 2011, did not just win the fashion showdown. She bested one of America's biggest stars, Jennifer Lopez. While Lopez took a no-frills approach to the pink wrap-around Elie Saab dress, Fan paired it with a sequined cardigan and a matching turban that she had styled out of a top. Lopez's take was elegant but expected; Fan won for being creative and theatrical.

Youth are catching up quickly with global trends and movements that were lost when China closed its doors to the rest of the world. Today, fashion and lifestyle magazines dedicate pages in each issue to helping readers understand historically important designers and movements that will enable consumers to make sense of the fashion world as it moves forward. As fashionistas rediscover the past, vintage stores on- and offline are developing a reputation for curating history.

Old and new, Eastern and Western influences are colliding in this exciting experimentation phase. *Xiao qing xin*, literally meaning "little freshness," is a hybrid composed of derivative styles mixed with home-grown elements. The result manifests in a simple, thoughtful, and clean aesthetic across fashion, interior design, visual art, and music. Think shabby chic meets Indie Pop. The style's appreciation of creativity and the environment can make it look like the fashionable Chinese face of the LOHAS (Lifestyle of Health and Sustainability) movement. Followers generally exhibit creative expressions that clearly represent tribal membership and subscribe to a unique set of consumption priorities. Their reputation is both tied to environmentalism and fashion.

When domestic brand Haier chose to pinpoint *xiao qing xin* style with its "Everyday Xiao Qing Xin" campaign on the popular social networking sites, Douban, it was taking a calculated risk. Not many home-appliance brands had tried to tap into Douban's young and trend-conscious user base, but Haier was looking to make a connection. The brand was launching a relationship between its air conditioning products and a group of influential, fashion-conscious youth with an interest in environmentalism.

The campaign allowed users to upload their *xiao qing xin*-style photographs to compete to win Fujifilm Instax cameras, a cool prize for young shutterbugs. The audience shared images produced in classic *xiao qing xin* style, including overexposed shots of girls taking pictures in nature, close-ups of simple flowers, and cropped angles of blue sky. The images were a visual complement to the message behind the product. To educate youth about air-quality issues and promote its product, Haier initiated a poll on Douban, asking users, "What do you do to fight against air pollution inside?" Several videos featuring young painters and interior designers were posted to educate on the benefits and inject cool capital. By connecting values, the brand was able to foster a meaningful connection with an influential group. The campaign was well constructed and offered members a means of expression and recognition within their group.

NEW SKIN-COLOR SPECTRUM

While trend hunting in Beijing in 2006, I ran into a pair of Chinese friends on a shopping spree. One had clearly embraced the traditional preference for whitened skin, while the other was conspicuously tan. Surrounded by shoppers who had adopted couples' dressing style, these two stood out for their dissimilarity. One was on a more traditional beauty track, while the other was stepping into new territory.

The preference for white skin predates Western influence in China, and its contemporary popularity is associated with an urban, white-collar ideal. Researchers note that the media's constant presentation of lightened skin is partially to blame for society's single-mindedness, but at the root of the issue is a message. Associated with manual laborers who have to work outside to earn a living, tan skin has had unappealing social implications in China. Today, when everyone is seeking to urbanize and move up the social ladder, looking like one has been exposed to the elements working outside has dubious value.

A pale visage remains a compelling, subconscious way to communicate higher social and economic status. White skin signals that a person is urbane, elite, and protected; he or she is situated safely inside the ideal. A study conducted by Nielsen found that 30 percent of Chinese respondents used whitening products either daily or weekly. Compared to consumers in other countries, Chinese were most likely to use whitening products on a daily basis and least likely not to engage in whitening at all.[36]

When I did research in Shanghai on tanning, I found that the trend had taken a turn in direct opposition to the original assumptions. Respondents felt that tan skin (while not a fit for everyone) was a symbol of wealth, not of poverty. Tanning salons were popping up, travel was popular, and bronzing potions were widely available. Youth understood that those with a tan were willing to foot the bill for these options and had the ability to do so. In this environment, a tan was not a symbol of poverty; it was a pronouncement of wealth. Even if they were not willing to try on a bronze tone themselves, young women were attracted to the idea of a man with a tan. Their association had evolved from a laborer to a cosmopolitan assertion of wealth and a new kind of sexiness.

This is not to say that tanning has replaced the alabaster skin fetish in China, not by a long shot. The notion of pale skin is being joined by the idea of tanning, but not overthrown; light skin is just as much of a competitive advantage as ever before. In one ad for Olay White Radiance Ultra UV Protective Fluid, two popular celebrity rivals are dressed in white and pitted against each other to determine who is the real whitening queen. On one side is Lin Zhiling (Chi-ling Lin), a Taiwanese model and actress who has been referred to as "the first face of Taiwan" by Taiwanese media. On the other side is Xu Xidi (aka Xiao S or Little S), also a famous actress, singer, and top television hostess in Taiwan. The two women are often compared and have developed a reputation for rivalry. "PK" (meaning "player killing") is common slang meaning "versus" that is derived from gamers, and is used in the copy to catch young people's attention. The use of celebrities is almost expected, but the beauty brand's use of youthful language and playful competition between the stars made the ad memorable.

The power of pale skin is reflected in the saying, "A white complexion is powerful enough to hide seven faults." But while the concept is still dominant, it has been adapted. As consumers pursue a traditionally mainstream aesthetic, they increasingly want their beautification process to be suited to their own unique needs. As the beauty landscape evolves in China, new terms are created to reflect consumers' demands for personalization and to help differentiate products in an increasingly crowded market. ZA's True White, Olay's White Radiance, Neutrogena's White Vitality, and Chanel's Precision White all propose slightly different messaging set against a traditional value.

MAPPING IDEALS OF BEAUTY

I worked with a client to investigate how beauty is perceived and how concepts move across the Middle Kingdom. I found that tier-one trendsetters, with the greatest exposure to international media, held fundamental beliefs about beauty that were very similar to what the client's brand had experienced in other territories. When I asked respondents to explain their beauty icons, these young people cited a smattering of international celebrities and models, including American socialite Paris Hilton and British supermodel Agyness Deyn.

When I researched lower-tier cities, people's enthusiasm for international beauties waned. In the lower tiers, aspirant respondents favored Hong Kong celebrities such as Shu Qi and Zhang Manyu (Maggie Cheung), while mainstream interviewees were more comfortable with popular mainland figures such as Fan Bingbing, Gong Li, and Yang Lan. They did not make their choices based on looks alone, but rather, selected icons because of a combined package of physique and character. Less exposed to international figures and more inclined to stay within the norm, lower-tier women did not look for a far-away version of beauty, instead aspiring to icons with looks and reputations closer to home.

Their judgments were most certainly tied to how they themselves were judged within their communities. More traditional lower-tier respondents were assessed on their ability to fit in, not branch out. Tighter standards within their communities forced women to look good, but not too good. They considered it important to keep up with what was available (they were well informed about brands, cosmetic surgery, and celebrity gossip), but hesitated to go beyond their social circles' expectations. On the other hand, peer pressure for top-tier respondents with more exposure to different media and marketing demanded a curated ideal with international influences. They were judged on their ability to create a personal image that was both globally relevant and unique.

UNTRADITIONAL FACES

As China has opened up economically and culturally, traditional beauty ideals have not been tested so much as they have been joined by a new tolerance for variance. Access to diverse beauty codes and avenues for acceptance outside China have helped youth to develop an appreciation for a broader aesthetic. While most youth still adhere to normative values, outliers have found increased tolerance and even success because of their difference.

One example of how a new look can find an audience in the mainland is Fei Xiang (born as Kris Phillips in 1960 in Taipei). When the Taiwanese singer took the stage to perform at the annual televised China Central Television (CCTV) New Year's Gala in 1987, he caused a ruckus. At least part of the 27-year-old's stellar reception could be attributed to his uncommon appearance. Not only was he the first Taiwanese to perform in the mainland, his heritage (his father was American, and his mother Chinese) gave him a look with which mainlanders were not overly familiar. The pop star, at six feet tall, towered above most other performers, and his muscular physique, blue eyes and wavy hair all added to his exoticism. Women swooned at his mix of Chinese refinement and Western proportions. Wearing a red tuxedo jacket and leopard-print cummerbund and flashing dance moves straight off of MTV, Fei advertised his difference instead of trying to mask it.

The performance helped propel the singer to become an overnight sensation, and he sold 20 million copies of his album, *A Voice on The Ocean*. When Fei went on tour in 1989, he was met with 63 consecutive sold-out stadium crowds in 12 major cities, setting a record that has been hard to beat to this day. His unusual look surely helped him differentiate and develop a dedicated audience.

A dozen years later, when model Lv Yan (aka Lu Yan) made it into high fashion's inner circle, Chinese were confused. Like Fei, Lv too did not resemble the conventional beauties that mainlanders were used to seeing on television or in magazines. She was too tall, her eyes too small, her nose flat, and her skin freckled. By strict standards, she was considered an ugly duckling. Coming from a mining town, Lv seemed doubly burdened by her unusual looks and unlikely background—hardly a candidate to be plucked from the mainland to grace foreign ad campaigns. But still, there she was, one of the first successful Chinese to break barriers and rise as an international high-fashion model. She graced international runways, fashion magazines, and was named runner-up in 2000's Metropolitan Top Model Competition, the most impressive showing for a Chinese contestant to date. Since then, the icon has made her film debut in the made-in-China Hollywood production *The Painted Veil*.[37] Her success caused young people take a second look to see if they could determine what the foreign fashion industry saw: market value in being different.

BOYISH / GIRLISH CHARM

In Kate Fox's book *Watching the English: The Hidden Rules of English Behavior*, the author breaks down universal elements of dress into three core categories: sex differentiation, status symbols, and affiliation signals. Throughout history, China has had a few gender-bending heroes who have veered away from this code. Legendary war heroine Hua Mulan disguised herself as a man to serve in the army on her father's behalf, and Jia Baoyu, the main character in the classic novel *Dream of the Red Chamber*, is known for his sensitive and effeminate demeanor. Gender-flexible figures today have had to fend off their share of haters, but they also have inspired a devoted group of followers. What these heroes represent is more than a willingness to dress up; they parade their outsider status to a cheering crowd of young people who feel like outsiders too. The applause is encouraging. Although raised to follow the mainstream, most youth see themselves as not fitting in—and hope that one day they too will be given the opportunity to receive praise for what makes them unique.

When Li Yuchun took to the stage to compete in one of China's many televised singing competitions, she easily stood out from the crowd of high-pitched and girly female competitors. But it was not the 21-year-old's singing talent or her dancing that drew attention. Almost four hundred million Chinese tuned in to catch a glimpse of the overnight sensation's boyish physical and vocal stylings.

In loose jeans and a black button-down shirt, without makeup or long lustrous hair, and even singing songs written for male vocalists, Li seemed an almost laughable underdog. Still, there she was, helping the show attract one of the largest viewing audiences ever in the mainland and bringing in over 3.5 million short message service (SMS) votes from viewers to win the title. After Li won, an editorial in the *China Daily* wondered how a democratic system could elect the singer least able to carry a tune.[38] But it was not her singing that caused the crowd to respond; rather, it was the fact that she was there at all—presenting an alternative—that made fans openly cry during her performances.

Four years later, another androgynous-styled contestant, Zeng Yike, took the stage to compete in *Happy Girl* (another *American Idol*-like program). Like Li before her, Zeng drew attention for her looks and criticism for what many perceived as a lack of singing talent. When she advanced to the top 20, one judge, Bao Xiaobo, took a bold step, proclaiming that if Zeng moved ahead, he would leave. And just like that, he resigned and unceremoniously walked off stage. Bao's stand stirred up debate among fans over the value of the show: was it to promote good singers, or was it to showcase people who were different?

These two figures, unflatteringly nicknamed Brother Chun and Brother Zeng, have been met with applause and ridicule for their boyish styles. Netizens brought the nicknames to life with photo-shopped pictures of the stars' heads plopped on top of Rambo's body and also the bodies of video-game characters, bodybuilders, and even that of Jesus Christ. Clearly, the question of girls presenting their masculine side has made some people uncomfortable. While youth are becoming more liberal in loving, hating, and debating the phenomenon, conservative media and social experts are making gender ambiguity a dangerous issue. An online survey of over two thousand adults by China Youth Daily's Social Research Center showed that 65 percent feared the unisex craze would lead to more abnormal or errant behavior.[39]

For youth looking for a mainstream outsider icon, Li and Zeng have great allure. Fans are drawn to them not for what they do but because of how they do it. Their message is about more than a style. It is about daring to go against the current—a relatable, modern, and aspirational message for youth overwhelmed by society's rigid demands. These vanguards are leading the way for youth to imagine themselves coming out into the open with their differences. The appeal is about social transformation.

Brands are picking up on this trend as well and adapting their marketing to appeal to changing consumer attitudes. When Maybelline selected Zeng Yike as the face of its new Clear Smooth Minerals BB Cream, an all-in-one moisturizer, sun block, and foundation, the pairing may have seemed like an odd match. But Zeng was not selling beauty; she was selling the promise of being oneself. "My voice may not be the most popular, but I dare to be myself," declared the 20-year-old in a television commercial. Similarly, when Clairol put the short-haired Li Yuchun in front of the camera to hype Herbal Essences, the brand was not looking to demote idyllic long hair, it was reaching past its category to the consumer. Herbal Essences was tapping into youth's desire to feel the liberation they associate with Li's uniquely open difference. And that is what many stressed-out youth want to hear: that there is a place for them, that there is a possibility to be imperfect and still be accepted.

While girls' adoption of a more masculine or androgynous appearance is becoming more permissible, boys' exploration of their feminine sides is still uncomfortable. Gender-detecting software in the Middle Kingdom is a means of ascertaining a player's gender so that there can be no misrepresentation among gamers. The effort is meant to keep online players on their own side of the gender fence, primarily obstructing males from taking on a female persona.

In the mainland, few men (old or young) would dare go public about advocating an open and flexible gender identity. A handful of young men are moving in this direction. When Liu Zhu stepped up to compete in *Happy Boy* (yet another singing competition), he was asked if he was trying out for the wrong show. Clad in a brightly colored pop-art dress and blue tights, his hair loose in feminine curls, the 19-year-old from Nanchong was taking a brave leap of faith. When one of the female judges questioned him about his Manhood, Liu remained confident. He said, this was how he always dressed, and he argued that it would be a farce to present himself differently just to take part in the program. Liu wanted to be judged on his singing (he was talented), not on his appearance.

Most Chinese were not even familiar with the Mandarin term for cross-dresser (*weiniang*) before Liu made his appearance on television. The fallout included the inevitable debate about moral decline, but most youth came out on Liu's side, as they did for Li and Zeng before him, for his courage to be himself.

MOVING ON

Tired of chasing elusive standards of success, many youth have started to come down to earth in terms of their own expectations. They are acknowledging that living up to perfection across all areas (meeting demands set forth by family, friends, teachers, and employers) is impossible and they are creating an alternate playing field. In this model, youth do not have to single-mindedly chase external ideals at the expense of internal interests and happiness. They are rebalancing themselves to find a place where being different, even being average, is acceptable. This fresh confidence allows them to branch out and explore new territory within themselves and creates diversified standards going forward.

The China Youth and Children Research Center conducted a study in 1999, 2005, and 2010 to determine changes in youth's attitudes across a decade. The findings showed that satisfaction with bodies and appearance increased from almost 77 percent in 1999 to more than 82 percent in 2005, and finally ticked up to more than 84 percent in 2010.[40] Similarly, the percentage of those content with their own characters increased from more than 71 percent to close to 77 percent, and finally topped 81 percent.[41] These statistics reflect a growing level of comfort and increasing confidence that what they have to offer (both inside and out) is worthwhile.

While being beautiful is an undeniable vehicle to gaining advantage in a tight race for jobs and spouses, youth are increasingly confident in expressing their individuality and determining their own parameters for beauty. More tolerant of difference in other people and themselves, young Chinese are opening up doors to let new beauty codes find a footing.

This shift in mind-set is an opportunity for brands to empower youth to establish their own laws of attraction. A 2011 commercial for P&G's Rejoice shampoo shows a young woman meeting a young man for a date. As one would expect from a hair care ad, the man is impressed by the woman's gorgeous, silky mane. However, as is rarely the case in a Chinese beauty spot, the location is not glamorous; rather, it is realistic. The young man apologizes for the simple street-side restaurant, promising next time to take his date somewhere better. She coyly plays with her chopsticks and tells him, "No problem, I like simple." The message is directed at something young people are increasingly feeling: fatigue from the pressure to constantly aspire to just-out-of-reach ideals. The young woman is not grasping at a glamorous lifestyle; instead, she is content with a more quotidian approach to dating—and beauty too.

Overwhelmed by mainstream ideals, youth are beginning to usher in a more tolerant approach to notions of both difference and average. Online, shoppers are increasingly exposed to models with normal faces and body types. *Ma dou* (meaning "cyber-models" in Mandarin) are not judged on their ability to fit into a perfect size, and *ma dou* agencies do not recruit for long legs and thin physiques like professional agencies do. These average types do not require catwalk training; they are booked primarily by online retailers looking for a relatable girl next door. Models are purposely chosen to appear as friendly faces for off-the-rack fashion, a more realistic and trustworthy example of how the clothes may actually fit on real customers.

When Maybelline selected models to appear in national campaigns to help promote the launch of BB Cream, audiences saw a global brand pick up on this trend. The selection of a professional model and a talent-show celebrity was expected; these two vocations were standard "go-to" figures for beauty brands to grab youth's attention. What was new was leveraging unknown and trendy young women, including a LOHASian (a follower of the LOHAS environmental movement), a freelance writer, and a blogger. While the public at large would not recognize these faces, Maybelline was making a statement by targeting segments that were slightly outside of the mainstream but not overexposed. These women were outside of average but not empty; they had personal points of view and passions. They were not perfect, and Maybelline's suggestion was that their position outside the ideal might be a good thing.

LOOKING BACK

Chinese beauty is assumed to be first and foremost about pragmatism, not aesthetics. Women (and now men) pursue a physical ideal to enhance their opportunities for success within the larger social framework. This quest for advancement in a highly competitive market has led to the popularization of cosmetic surgery and to China's own metrosexual clan known as city jade men. But as youth are exposed to outliers who have gained an audience for their difference, they increasingly accept new looks that veer from the traditional norm. While they do not question that being attractive is necessary to get ahead, youth are seeing more than one code for success. These divergent models suggest that being average (not the idealized perfectly "normal") is also OK and that a fresh balanced beauty includes looks, interests, and talents.

LOOKING FORWARD

This chapter is meant to help you think more deeply about connecting to youth. How could the information be leveraged in these scenarios?

1. How can brands communicate a balanced beauty that goes more than skin-deep?
2. How can companies embrace and encourage safe differentiation?
3. How can companies drive new routines and rituals for city jade men?

CHAPTER 5

SPEAKING UP: THE SEEDS OF ACTIVISM

> In my opinion, there are three kinds of business men: speculators, who only care about making money; businessmen, who have principles; and entrepreneurs, who not only create fortune but also value for society.
>
> —Ma Yun (aka Jack Ma), founder and chairman of Alibaba Group, born in1964[1]

IN A CONTROLLED POLITICAL CLIMATE WITH FEW WAYS TO express dissent, Chinese seek an acceptable channel through which to vent pent-up frustration. Although communicating political opinions can be risky, practicing consumer activism has become a safe and social outlet. One example of this kind of activism is KFC Super Tuesday promotion—a simple idea that went very, very wrong.

Using Taobao, KFC ran a marketing promotion in 2010 that encouraged fans to come into its stores at three different times of day (10 a.m., 2 p.m., and 4 p.m.) to receive 50 percent off on some of the most popular menu items. To qualify for the savings, customers had to present a coupon. This seemed easy enough. Electronic versions needed to be printed, but the promotion claimed that copies were also acceptable. Consumers were galvanized by the triple-threat attraction of limited time, reduced prices, and one of their favorite brands.

Crowds carrying coupons entered stores in cities such as Beijing, Nanchang, Guangzhou, and Nanjing expecting to get a great price on some of their favorite fast food. But the mood quickly turned when stores stopped honoring coupons, unable to tell which coupons were valid and which were not. Some consumers simply walked away mildly disgruntled at the inconvenience, while others used their mobile phones to activate a spur-of-the-moment protest. Going online, they spread news of the debacle directly to friends and posted pleas to a broader audience via Weibo. The tone of the appeals did not just connote a soured business transaction; consumers felt personally affronted. Why were some coupons honored but others were not? How could KFC do this? How could it break its promise?

Drawn in by digital appeals, angry supporters traveled to KFC stores to join waiting petitioners. In some cases, when customers turned into vandals, the police had to be called, and store operations were suspended. In what could be interpreted as real life *e gao* (online satire that expresses dissent in a humorous way), customers called McDonald's delivery service for meals to be sent to them—to be eaten inside KFC restaurants.

McDonald's wasted no time responding with its own campaign. It launched an almost exact replica of the KFC promotion with coupons that proudly welcomed copying and reposting. Nor did McDonald's

Figure 5.1   Crowds protest a promotion gone wrong at KFC stores. Photo by Liu Liu

bother with subtle nuances. A press release stated, "While other companies still stumble over fake coupons, McDonald's generously encourages customers to use photocopies of coupons."

A series of humorous viral videos supported McDonald's counter-campaign. One showed a young woman mistrustful of promotions. "If you lie to me, I will be heartbroken," she sobs into her mobile phone. At the end of the ad, she is convinced that the caller is sincere and proclaims confidently, "This time I met a reliable one." Another version takes a jab at the harm KFC did to consumers by showing a young man doing tai chi—preparing emotionally and physically to defend himself. Yet another execution depicts an office worker frustrated that she has wasted time copying useless coupons. Each ad closes with a promise from McDonald's not to abuse the trust of vulnerable young consumers. Christine Xu, vice president of national marketing for McDonald's, explains how the company decided which course of action to pursue, saying, "We had a debate internally to decide the fine line....We just want to make it fun, but we are not pointing a finger at KFC....It's about being socially responsible to the consumer; if you are too aggressive, people won't like you."[2] Her advice speaks to the fine line that brands tread with consumers. For a brand, the goal is to align with a cause without becoming the target of the next investigation.

LEARNING THE ROPES

Despite being the first foreign fast-food chain to open its doors in China in 1987, KFC, like everyone else, is still learning the rules of engagement in the Middle Kingdom. Brands are still learning largely because the rules are constantly shifting. New standards, values, and means are evolving and, over time, new organizations will develop to support them. But we are not there yet. For now, there is constant fluctuation. Even for KFC, an early entrant that has been applauded for its localized menu, managing risk and maintaining control is slippery.

Something as seemingly benign as a limited time promotion presents opportunities for problems to arise from every angle. KFC was not prepared for the number of customers who came through the door—and it was blindsided by factors they had not imagined. The company had not thought through all of the creative incarnations and potential players the promotion might attract. It was ambushed by third-party websites that had reposted the coupons to reach a much wider audience than KFC could accommodate. The incident was not only a stain on the fast-food giant's brand image, but it also had the potential to make a legal example of KFC's error. When the activity was initially investigated, KFC seemed in danger of a lawsuit, as the coupons clearly stated that copies would be accepted. Although the promotion was initially poised for success, KFC lost out by not preparing for glitches in the program. Xu advises, "Crisis management needs to be sincere and you need to be transparent. You have to treat a reputation loss more seriously than a loss in revenue."[3]

The first lesson in this example is that consumers—and both known as well as unknown third parties—have great potential to throw even the best-laid plans off the rails. The company had not fully realized the possible threat and scale of counterfeiting, and had not applied a system of checks and balances to differentiate authentic coupons from fakes. Stores were not able to protect the integrity of the promotion, and their failure to do so provided an opportunity for the competition to pounce.

The most valuable lesson in this scenario lies in how young consumers perceive their own power. When they feel disrespected, they are willing and have the ability to levy punishment—even on one of their most beloved brands. Partly despite (and partly because) KFC is such an iconic, Chinese-friendly brand, consumers were merciless in calling for retribution. Whereas this kind of bumbling might be expected from a lesser or local brand, consumers felt personally insulted by KFC's failure to deliver on its promise. For better and for worse, foreign brands (especially in food and beverage) are held to higher standards of quality and connection.

RISING SELF-PROTECTION

The job of policing companies is largely left to consumers themselves. Official channels (government agencies and government-recognized organizations) are often stunted by bureaucracy and corruption. While agencies are busy precariously balancing government and private interests, the job of protecting individual concerns is often left to individuals. To Protect themselves, regular citizens are banding together to share information and leverage collected influence. These citizen groups are demanding that companies and the government pay attention to their point of view and are turning monologues into dialogues.

This turn of events is nothing short of monumental. It signals the growing clout of individuals and groups outside of official channels, and leads to a demand for accountability from authorities. While little citizen-led activism existed before the economy opened up, greater income levels and private ownership have given people a vested interest in speaking up to protect their interests. Duncan Hewitt is *Newsweek*'s Shanghai correspondent and the author of the book *China: Getting Rich First: A Modern Social History*, which explores how China's social and economic transformation has affected the country's people. Hewitt asserts, "[Through the 1990s] people began to have a certain kind of voice and their own interests to defend. And that is something they didn't have before in a traditional socialist system."[4] Defending private interests is the first step on a ladder leading to greater participation in social causes.

BY THE PEOPLE, FOR THE PEOPLE

Since reform and opening up took hold in 1978, the government has had to constantly juggle power dynamics to maintain control. Achieving the delicate balance between protecting state sovereignty and allowing a modicum of nongovernmental participation has been a challenge. As China has opened its doors to economic development, new ideas, influences, and channels to voice dissent have crept into the system. Most vocal have been citizens themselves, and netizens in particular, who have taken aim at the powers that be, confidently criticizing nongovernmental organizations (NGOs), consumer brands, and even the government.

While the government has been sluggish in implementing regulations and providing oversight to protect consumers and to deal with human rights issues, this new breed of citizen is setting out on its own to police authority and set a distinct agenda for China. New groups often form online and take their interests offline to socialize, support causes they care about, and exercise their increasing power as consumers. They are using their collective influence to push forward causes they care about—whether the goal is to strike a better deal, advance group affiliations, or support issues that may not even directly affect them. These budding special interest groups are forcing a negotiation and are leveraging all of the tools at their disposal to make their voices heard. With less ability to participate politically and a social imperative to buy status, some youth feel most powerful in their role as consumers. As Hewitt states, "People have become much more conscious of their rights as consumers because China has probably become one the most consumer-obsessed societies in the past 20 years."[5] This obsession with consumer culture makes the act of consumption powerful and imbues it with social expectations both for consumers and brands.

TURNING UP THE VOLUME

Nowhere is word of mouth more convincing than in China. While some government-supported consumer protection agencies have been formed, the most influential policing has been done by consumers for consumers. Without well-established and transparent channels to defend consumer rights, citizens and the media have played active roles in communicating and resolving issues. Consumer hotlines, radio programs, and television exposés have all done their part to inform consumers (and companies) to be on guard against faulty goods and services. Even so, as the media is controlled by the state, the most trusted information still comes from average citizens.

The explosion of real-time information and extended social networks have given word of mouth a megaphone. As netizens have gone online to get advice, share opinions, and organize into groups, the information landscape has expanded and turned the tables of influence to favor expression by regular citizens. The Internet is not just the latest channel for word of mouth, but it is also the new consumer watchdog. With information more available and more immediate than ever before, Chinese are able to share, receive, and act on it in real time. Although formal, aggregated consumer review sites are still in their infancy, consumers are conversing about and comparing product quality and styling on their own. Their research often yields impressive results. Young shoppers arm themselves with the brand story, product specifications, price, and style comparisons before they make a purchase. Depending on the category, young consumers may also consider a product's manufacturing origins. This sharp shopper expects that making a choice is a social investigation. To get it right, they seek out knowledgeable resources to help them analyze brand claims.

JUSTICE STARTS ONLINE

More voices are speaking up, demanding to be let into the conversation, and creating challenges to controlling communication. Netizens are aiming for more than just patrolling brands, they are on the look-out to right wrongs. Enabling netizens to connect to each other in real time, share content, and add to each other's narratives with pictures, audio, and video, Weibo (the generic term for "microblogging services") in particular has the potential to be a game changer. Communicating at this velocity has exposed a number of frauds (including those perpetrated by the government and the extremely rich and well connected) to the light of day and popularized the idea that citizen reporting is important—and possible. Over time, the question will be how Weibo will adapt to preserve the integrity of information shared and manage the threat of that information.

Without proper regulation and transparency, citizens have little faith in the government's abilities to police and audit misdeeds. Wrongdoers can seem untouchable either because of wealth or government connections. Multiple scandals erupted in 2011 that proved that monitoring corruption was within the scope of netizens' ability. Fueled by a constant flow of real-time information and a social circle that values contributing to the dialogue and exposing false claims, netizens have stepped into an important and exciting role.

When a pretty 20-year-old woman, Guo Meimei, began flaunt-
ing her glamorous lifestyle on Sina Weibo in June 2010, netizens'
attention was roused. Their interest was piqued by pictures she had
posted of herself lounging in the first-class cabin of an airplane,
displaying her collection of Hermès bags, standing in front of her
own "little horse" (a white Maserati), or driving her "little bull"
(an orange Lamborghini). Although she listed her previous career
as an actress, she also claimed to be the general manager of a company called Red Cross Commerce. The name, sounding similar
to the Red Cross Society of China, the country's largest and most
well-known charity, provided netizens with cause for concern. The
profile of Guo Meimei Baby, the siren's Weibo handle, was marked
with a "V", meaning that the identity had been verified by Sina.
This prompted netizens to research further, to dig into how her
lifestyle had been paid for. Most pointedly, they were looking to
see if the Red Cross Society of China had played a part in funding
her excess.

An investigation was launched, and netizen detectives shared
the results in a visual diagram that charted Guo's connections to
high-profile organizations and individuals. Enthusiastic, collabora-
tive searching uncovered the link: Guo was being bankrolled by a
higher-up in an organization connected to the Red Cross.

Speculation about corruption in charitable organizations, and
the Red Cross in particular, was not new. Chinese had long har-
bored concerns about the Red Cross's work in China, and the organization had failed on several occasions to provide the necessary
transparency and accountability to boost confidence. The origins
of such skepticism likely stemmed from the organization's special
status in the mainland. Despite being one of the few bodies autho-
rized to solicit financial support from the public, its staff is paid
by and answers to the government.[6] With this sticky standing (one
foot in the private sector and the other in the government) and
multiple, similarly named groups with murky links to the parent
organization, the Red Cross in China seems to present more questions than answers.

When the Guo Meimei incident inspired netizens to investigate
and shine a new spotlight on the Red Cross, accounting errors and

questionable finances came to light.[7] Citizens' feverish digging and the exposure they brought about provided a warning: with new technology and enthusiastic citizen detectives, under-the-table deals would be increasingly challenging to pull off. A new breed of equipped and expert young patroller was ready to sniff out the truth and demand accountability.

In the same month as the Guo Meimei scandal, another incident played out online. Youth demonstrated a typical approach to political criticism: planning an assault with humor and Photoshop. This time, it was not a pretty rich girl that inspired a double-take, it was an awkward-looking photo of three government officials inspecting a road. When the photo was posted to a government website, netizens guffawed at the obvious doctoring of the image. Inspired by the figures seemingly floating above the road, netizens blasted their own renditions of the image, using Photoshop to place the officials on top of Rio de Janeiro's Christ the Redeemer statue, to surround them with dinosaurs in prehistoric times, and even to show them walking on the moon. This creative protest was picked up by the international media, which spread news of the embarrassment abroad.[8] The government had no choice but to respond—and explain. The incident (smartly dubbed "cropoganda," in reference to the evident Photoshop cropping) provided another example of a new power dynamic that allows citizens to set rules, lobby complaints, and force authorities to answer for their actions.

A CRITICAL EYE ON BRANDS

While brands were once exciting status symbols, relationships have been compromised and complicated over time. When asked why they would prefer to buy goods outside of China, respondents to a McKinsey survey demonstrated a clear lack of faith in mainland retail. Of the luxury buyers surveyed, 62 percent thought making purchases outside the mainland was a quality guarantee, 58 percent believed they could access a wider selection, and 53 percent believed they could only get the latest products outside of China. Although Chinese consumers are notoriously price sensitive, cost was not the primary motivation for choosing to buy abroad (40 percent were motivated by price difference).[9]

While the McKinsey study focused on higher-income consumers and their relationship to shopping outside China, a lack of trust in mainland retail is not reserved for the wealthy. A similar distrust can be seen in average and even lower-income shoppers, especially in reference to domestic goods. As Chinese learn to express power and to influence transactions, they develop important skills to protect themselves in the battle against faulty products and suspect brands.

THE PRICE OF SAFETY

Just as the world outside has become suspicious of the made-in-China label, so have Chinese. And with good reason. Generally, there is not a clear chain of ownership mapping a product's movement from conception to shop floor, making accountability almost impossible. In the best of these scenarios, consumers are duped into buying a poor-quality product at a high price. At worst, health-and-safety epidemics have been unleashed that have cost consumers their lives. Food and beverage safety has earned a position front and center. Tim Minges, the chairman of PepsiCo in China underlines this concern, "[Food safety] is the number one concern of Chinese consumers today, it's not so much about price, it's not inflation; it's food safety."[10]

Domestic food-safety issues have changed people's perception of foreign brands, which are now regarded as the safer choice. As consumers look for additional measures to protect themselves, foreign brands have been repositioned from status symbols to safeguards. "It used to be cool to be Western because of the badge value... then it became about affordability, then it became about trust.... Now, one of the strongest calling cards is 'foreign and therefore safe,'" states Minges.[11]

For consumers, foreign food and beverage brands offer an enhanced perception of safety—one that they are willing to pay for. This has opened the door for brands to go premium. Minges explains, "[Safety concerns have] really changed the perception of brands....Now, consumer surveys suggest that Chinese consumers believe well-known brands are better quality and, more importantly, expensive products are better quality. You see that now in the market, you see a lot of premiumization for that very reason."[12] For consumers who can afford it, purchasing premium products is seen as an insurance policy.

Exposed

The preference for foreign goods and the willingness to pay a premium price came about virtually overnight when the poisonous chemical melamine was uncovered in baby milk formula in 2008. Unfortunately, the occurrence was hardly a one-off mistake; 22 domestic manufacturers were found to use the dangerous thickening agent to reduce costs and boost protein content. Almost forty thousand children reportedly visited hospitals, and approximately thirteen thousand of those under three-years-old received treatment for ailments caused by the tainted formula.[13] To further shake consumer confidence, a foreign partner in one of the primary offending manufacturers announced that it knew of the contamination but that the government had chosen to hold off on a public recall.[14] Three years later, the bitter memory was refreshed when 178 primary school students were hospitalized after drinking contaminated milk at school.[15]

From infancy to adulthood, consumers face dangerous choices. The milk scandals were shocking but hardly isolated; similar stories are easy to find. When the government investigated the selling of fake alcohol in clubs, they turned up 140,000 bottles of evidence and rounded up 483 suspected culprits. The initial bust was likely just the tip of the iceberg. In two days, police raided 272 production and sales outlets and confiscated three hundred devices for making fake spirits. A total of 13.5 million articles of counterfeit packaging were also seized, including caps, boxes, and labels to dress up imposter products to look like better-known brands.[16] One investigation in Beijing alone divulged ten thousand sham bottles, including whisky labeled Chivas, Johnnie Walker, and Jack Daniel's. These bottles, which cost about ten RMB to produce, were being prepped to cheat consumers out of as much as 580 RMB in stores and clubs.[17]

In my research, I have encountered many youth who hesitate to drink in clubs because they fear they will get sick from drinking fake alcohol. Coverage of a 2011 Beijing raid validated their hesitancy. Cheap nonbranded alcohol was found in bottles as a filler— but so was methanol. From childhood through adulthood, from studying hard to letting loose, consumers manage the risk of being turned into victims at every turn. Confronted with fake products, unclear production chains, and limited accountability, consumers know that they have to stay on guard. There are no true guarantees. Only degrees of security are for sale.

Outside of food and beverages, fake products can pose a different kind of threat—to their reputations. In my research, I have found that trendsetting youth understand the business of copycat goods (they often know the sellers or understand the business), but refuse to buy fakes. Among more image-conscious circles, sporting copies is the equivalent to admitting that one is not a real fashionista, athlete, or digital maven. The choice of real or fake is a reflection of personal authenticity and credentials. For Chinese youth, purchasing a trusted brand or upgrading to a premium product means protecting themselves from potential health hazards or reputational damage.

POLITICAL PURCHASING

In a consumer-centric culture, what a person buys is a deeply telling statement of who he or she is. Brands can signal that a person is smart, stylish, rich, or in-the-know. But if the brand originates in a country that is perceived to be less than pro-China, the message is more than personal; it is political.

Intensely nationalistic, mainlanders often swing their support towards or away from nations based on their dealings with China. While making a comment against China is risky, protecting the nation is encouraged. As brands are seen largely as extensions of their country of origin and Chinese are accustomed to casting votes with their wallets, consumption and politics easily join forces. If a country takes an unfavorable political or commercial position towards China, Chinese will often levy retribution by boycotting that nation's brands. For example, in 2010, when China and Japan butted heads over maritime rights in the Diaoyu Islands (disputed but uninhabited land in the East China Sea), consumers in the mainland boycotted Japanese hallmark brands including Toshiba and Sony. As a result, *Economic Daily News* predicted a bump in sales for competitive brands from Taiwan such as Acer and Asutek.[18] The assumption was that consumers would punish brands associated with Japan and turn their support to non-Japanese makers.

When the Olympic torch was passed around the world in 2008, Chinese watched in shock and dismay as the torch received a less than stellar welcome in the West. Prior to the Olympics, most mainlanders had had very little exposure to Westerners' feelings about Tibetan liberation, and they were unprepared for what was to come. While torchbearers met resistance in London and San Francisco, the Paris leg was seen as particularly egregious. Chinese officials had to change plans and put the torch out at least three times due to security concerns. Images of the pretty young torchbearer Jin Jing fending off pro-Tibetan activists from her wheelchair incited an uproar of anti-French sentiment in the mainland.

Chinese saw the French defense of Tibet as innately anti-China and quickly transferred their ire to French brands. L'Oreal, Vivendi, Renault, and LVMH joined 43 other French brands on a consumer-generated boycott list. Adding fuel to the fire, rumors started circulating that some brands may have lent support to the Dalai Lama.[19]

The French hypermarket Carrefour bore the brunt of consumers' nationalistic ire. Although the brand released a statement that it had not and would not do anything to "harm Chinese people's feelings," netizens nonetheless called for consumers to boycott Carrefour stores across China. On the designated day of the boycott, some protesters vowed to avoid the store altogether, while others waged small-scale physical demonstrations on location. One banner attempted to efficiently educate on the link between nationalism and consumption: "Support the Olympics; no independence for Tibet; boycott French goods; boycott Carrefour."[20]

Although the scale of the protest was less significant than efforts from other nations with more developed activist communities, the events marked an important jumping-off point. They served as an example of what ordinary Chinese could accomplish outside of recognized channels and emphasized the potential for organizing dissent online. But the protests also revealed new divisions in how the nation's best interests could be interpreted. The origin of the problem was simple enough: the boycott was organized in response to France's position on Tibetan independence. Activists took their outrage online to align and defend the group. But after that, a split occurred. Taking a cue from the new emphasis on individuality and personal power, a split in opinions occurred about what should come next. In one camp, activists launched a boycott intended to teach Carrefour that consumers were willing to prioritize the country's interests ahead of getting a convenient bargain. A second group disagreed and lodged a complaint that the boycotts were counter-productive. From this point of view, boycotting a popular brand that employs so many Chinese was not nationalistic, it was disruptive. While both sides were motivated by a love of country, the debate marked an evolving story about managing difference and opposing interpretations of what constitutes the country's best interests.

SAY WHEN

After the citizen-led boycotts against French brands, netizens took it upon themselves to police contributions to Sichuan earthquake relief efforts. A simple text message was sent in May 2008, listing foreign brands that were profitable but that also reportedly had not donated "enough" to the Sichuan earthquake relief efforts. The message attacked big names, including Coca-Cola, KFC, McDonald's, Nokia, Procter & Gamble (P&G), and Motorola, urged consumers to stand united against the companies listed. "If you have a conscience, please boycott these companies and spread this message around!" read one version of the message.

Donations from important figures and companies were a matter of public record and were broadcast openly across television, print, and online channels. A less official list was also circulated, an account from so-called "iron roosters" (connoting someone who is stingy; as in, it would be impossible to pull a feather from an iron rooster). Although anonymous and without clear methodology, the tabulation excited an audience. Consumers were asked to do more than passively observe the news—they were called on to help facilitate action. The message requested that viewers both boycott the brands listed and continue to update the index as new information was revealed.

Whether the allegations were true or not, these denunciations were more than just idle fodder passed online and via mobile phones. They resulted in organized physical action. A McDonald's store in Nanchong, Sichuan province, met with a hundred or so protesters who pasted a banner on the store's door reading "super international iron rooster." KFC restaurants in Sichuan, Shanxi, and Shaanxi suffered similar reproach. Windows were pasted with a list of iron roosters and the message, "We will boycott in accordance with our conscience! We pay silent tribute to the compatriot victims in the disaster zone."[21]

SELLING ♥ FOR CHINA

While many missteps demonstrate what not to do, solid examples of foreign brands demonstrating their support for China have been hard to find. Other than donating money, most companies have not made significant strides in getting involved or educating consumers on larger social issues. By and large, companies opt for small-scale brand-building activities rather than pioneering true leadership and empowering consumers to advocate for positive social change.

The events of 2008 were the greatest opportunity in recent history for brands to prove their China-friendliness. In the wake of the nation's conflict with foreigners over Tibet, MSN Messenger allowed users to add an icon (I ♥ China) to their MSN signatures. Roughly seven million digital youth eager to show their support and signal their membership in the group adopted the signature.[22] But when Tencent's QQ copied the activity, allowing users to post "Love China" to their signatures, the brand drew criticism for charging for the privilege. Consumers were disappointed that a brand would extract a fee for users to express their alignment with a cause, particularly one that had such obvious patriotic merit.

An offline example of consumer-facing corporate social responsibility was executed by P&G in partnership with the China Youth Development Foundation. Using in-store promotions to drive awareness and solicit consumer support, The Live, Learn, and Thrive initiative has exposed over 325 million consumers to the cause. But consumers are not the only ones that recognize the company's commitment to education, over 5,000 P&G employees have participated in the efforts. To date, the program has helped educate 100,000 children across China. This example of brands reaching out not only to make a quick sale but also to improve the community are just the tip of what is possible for consumer-facing corporate responsibility in China.

ONE IN A BILLION

The fact that so few companies and citizens themselves have experience participating in social causes is a reminder that this is still an early phase of development. For most in China, it is easy to get lost in the crowd. I did research in 2008 asking youth if they felt they could have an effect on social causes, and overwhelmingly, they did not feel powerful enough to drive change. At the time, youth believed that influencing social issues was clearly beyond an ordinary person's ability, it was an activity better left to celebrities, corporations, and the government. In the years since the study was conducted, the temperature has changed, and youth have exhibited more confidence in getting involved in causes they care about. Personal politics has become fashionable.

SMALL INTERESTS, BIG MOVEMENT

While citizens' establishment of formal, government-recognized organizations has been slow going (marked by stops and starts and then inevitably more stops), more casual assemblies of independent activists are gaining momentum. As many of these groups get their start online, they have the ability to attract people who never could have met otherwise and develop influence across offline borders. These groups gather based on interest or affiliation—young mothers members of alma maters, residents of a hometown, and hobby enthusiasts, including nature photographers and drivers of specific brands of cars. While seemingly innocuous, these groups that are organized around common interests represent a new phenomenon for China. As they attract members and start directing efforts and spending towards their own causes, they are paving the path for a civil society and forming China's first citizen-led self-interest groups. They are pushing their influence to protect themselves and issues they care about. When this approach is borrowed to further more controversial causes, it can push a confrontation between the marginalized and the mainstream.

OUT OF THE CHINA CLOSET

Unlike other countries that demonstrate higher levels of acceptance or resistance to homosexuality, China is relatively middle-of-the-road on this issue. Most gays in the country exist in a social Never Land with little fear of physical violence but also slim hope of living outside the closet. As they grow older, most gays expect that they will be required to balance a publicly straight identity with a privately gay one. By the time youth reach their late 20s, their families predictably become antsy for their only sons and daughters to find a spouse and have a child. Under heavy pressure, many gay and lesbian youth will step obediently into a straight life, albeit a life dotted with weekends and business trips to gay-friendly locales.[23] New dating sites propose a compromise, matching gay singles with straight marriage partners who are willing to engage in a platonic arrangement.

Homosexuality was classified as a mental illness until 2001 and although official recognition still seems far off, gay culture is becoming increasingly open, organized, and influential. In 2009, Chinese Lesbian Gay Bisexual Transsexual (LGBT) communities took an important step forward by openly promoting and celebrating Gay Pride week.[24] On and offline communities joined global celebrations, organizing activities that had both entertainment and educational value.

Regardless of its political purpose and awkward execution, the opening of the first government-backed gay bar in Dali, Yunnan province, in November 2009 seemed to underscore the public's focus on gay issues. The momentum did not last, however. Gay Pride festivals in 2010 and 2011 were comparatively less public, and the 2010 sold-out Mr. Gay China pageant was shut down moments before its opening ceremony.[25] The government was blamed for this effort to return gays to the closet. Rumors spread that officials did not want to attract international media attention on gay issues, regardless of whether they were positively or negatively reported. In China, official support for gays is often a case of two steps forward and one big step back.

BARKING UP A NEW TREE

The first stage of activism was about self-preservation but now, empowered by a sense of security, young idealists are moving beyond their own well-being. Efforts to address animal welfare are an example of this expanded sphere of influence.

In 2011, An Lidong had come to the end of another day working at his foreign-owned office when he decided to do something unusual. An was a young and enthusiastic dog lover who had experience volunteering and was keen to do more for a cause he cared about. He had heard that the Jingha Expressway was part of a route that carried dogs to be slaughtered and served in restaurants in the north. Hoping to save animals that he valued as pets (not food), An determined that it was the time and place to make a stand. As luck would have it, he saw a passing shipment of live dogs and managed to get the driver to stop. To rally support to free the dogs, An posted to his microblog and attracted 200 to 300 interested netizens and animal-rights supporters to help him stage a 15-hour standoff to redirect the dogs away from the dinner table. These rescuers, armed with water, dog food, and medicine, effectively blocked traffic to force a confrontation. One hundred police arrived on the scene to help control the mob and determine what to do next. But when the impromptu rescuers raised 115,000 RMB to buy the truckload of dogs, the crowd was able to disperse on its own and reroute the load to a shelter.

As animal rights activists applauded their victory, an uneasy realization set in. Even the capitol of Beijing was flatly not equipped to feed, shelter, and care for some five hundred homeless, trauma-tized dogs. With few fledgling animal rescue organizations and miniscule avenues for government support, resources were quickly stretched thin. Official media sources and independent citizens pro-moted the rescue and appealed for help across television, print, and online channels. Initially, the efforts attracted some one hundred volunteers a day to help care for the animals. Food and veterinary services were donated, and QQ announced that it would help under-write the expenses for the dogs.

But the story was not only about dogs. The rescue shed an uncom-fortable light on fissures that have erupted from high-speed develop-ment. It exposed a lack of infrastructure, a bitter wealth gap, and friction between modern and traditional values.

Rescuers' willingness to take a stand for animals drew criticism from those who felt their efforts could be better directed to other causes—namely those that would benefit humans. Critics argued that animal rights should be addressed only after basic necessities and human rights were secured. Many of the animals rescued were primarily mixed breeds from small villages and, the critics con-tended, having had limited human contact, the dogs were less than ideal candidates for adoption anyway. Like the Carrefour protests, the event raised questions about dealing with difference. With more confidence to speak up and distinct interests to protect, how would debate be managed and who would determine the course?

The incident exposed a gap in both wealth and ideology; the two main characters in the rescue were well cast to represent the divi-sion. Activist An was a young white-collar worker employed by a for-eign enterprise who was reportedly driving a black Mercedes-Benz when the rescue occurred. He had tools at his disposal—income, a social network, and confidence—to act on behalf of his passion. His youthful exuberance ran into a middle-aged man bound by responsibilities. The truck driver was a lower-income worker from the north who depended on delivering his shipment from point A to point B in order to feed his family.

MODERN CONSUMERS VERSUS TRADITIONAL CONSUMPTION

For older-generation northerners, eating dog meat is a tradition that is inexpensive and is believed to help guard against cold weather. But for cosmopolitan youth, eating dog meat is seen as an embarrassing and outdated conception that they are eager to replace. Young pet lovers see dogs as delightful, not delicious. They accessorize their furry companions with jumpsuits, play dates at doggie bars, and sporty shoes (four at a go). For many outside this circle of pet enthusiasts, this kind of spending is just shy of ridiculous.

Few animal rights laws exist, and only a handful of small, private organizations support animal welfare. Although there have been attempts to pass laws, advocates have not been able to overturn tradition and economic interests. In order to eradicate the practice of eating dogs (or cats), change will have to be initiated at the consumer level.

Although the topic of dog companion versus dog dinner may still be too volatile to attract a spokesperson, animal welfare has definite celebrity appeal. National basketball treasure Yao Ming was featured in a television commercial asking consumers to avoid eating shark fin soup, a traditional delicacy. His message was to support animal rights with conscious consumption.

GOING GREEN

At the beginning of 2008, an American journalist approached me about green marketing. Did youth care if products were environmentally friendly? Would they be more likely to buy if a product was organic or if the company's production processes were sustainable? These questions turned into running jokes in the office. At the time, there was a slim set of examples of green marketing experiments. These considerations were simply too far-fetched for most youth to bother with. From a young consumer perspective, there was very little motivation to make purchase decisions based on their environmental impact. For these pragmatists, the environment and its protection were far-away concepts; their personal well-being and the well-being of the environment did not seem connected. Although youth at the time were aware of the power of their wrath against certain brands, they had not made a positive link between their consumption and supporting larger causes.

With less popular expectation for youth to have a point of view on social issues and to act on their convictions, environmentalism was little more than an exotic elective. But when the government mandated that retailers charge shoppers for plastic bags to hold their purchases, people's understanding of the relevance of the green movement changed. While the fee was nominal, the price was still enough to grab consumers' attention and make the cause personal.

But the success of the initiative cannot be attributed solely to notoriously price-sensitive Chinese shoppers being asked to reach into their wallets. Magazines and influential pop-culture figures made the idea of reusable bags more than affordable—they made them fashionable. Global brands such as Diesel, Marc Jacobs, and DKNY, as well as independent local designers jumped on board, providing a mountain of stylish alternatives for young consumers to kick off a craze.

Fashion First

In 2008, a feature in one of the country's leading youth fashion magazines attempted to envision the next stage of environmentally friendly consumption. The spread included photos of trend-conscious youth trying on different ways they could make a small difference in a big problem. One of the ideas was to wear a handkerchief in their pockets instead of carrying tissues, and another was to use personal chopsticks in lieu of single-use utensils. Although many ideas were not mature executions, they did show an enthusiasm among young people to find new ways to consume and to voice their affiliation with a cause. While no clear second steps were taken en masse, the media coverage solidified the notion that looking out for the environment was modern, fresh, and fashion-forward. Youth who chose to pursue (at least verbally) a green lifestyle were perceived as trendsetters.

The initial success of reusable bags can be linked to price, but the long-term value of the initiative was in branding a Chinese green consumer. This marketing of the effort as a symbol of the modern, in-the-know fashionista helped turn the activity into a social and aspirational exercise. Brands were quick to pick up on the opportunity, but did little to push the cause forward. It was ultimately consumers who changed their behavior, not governments or companies. But without additional guidance and support, next steps have been slow going.

TRANSLATING ENVIRO-CABULARY

Many shoppers outside China are old pros when it comes to making environmentally friendly choices. They are well versed in the concept and understand the vocabulary of "bio," "green," and "organic." They are also confident that the products that carry these labels are regulated and therefore somewhat credible.

In China, however, green lifestyles are uncharted territory. A study conducted in 2009 at grocery stores in three cities showed that Chinese shoppers had less awareness than their Western peers about organic products. Compared to 80 percent of people in some developed countries, an average of 53.5 percent of Chinese consumers were aware of organic food. Thirty-six percent of consumers were familiar with one or two labels of organic food, while a puny 15.7 percent were aware of organics' product and safety benefits.[26] This not only shows a lack of awareness but also demonstrates that marketing has come before education. This curriculum will have to be reversed to create a long-term positive perception for consumers and real value for brands. For consumers, the benefits need to be clarified to have real meaning, especially since most green products are both less easy to find and more costly. OgilvyEarth's 2011 survey of consumer attitudes towards environmentally friendly consumption found that 53 percent of respondents think green products are too expensive.

Figure 5.2 LOHAS magazine's fashion-first appeal. Photo by Toni Young

Besides price resistance, hyperbolic claims are quick to turn off consumers looking for explicit and reasonable benefits.[27] Terms that generally guide choices abroad are thrown about in China without clear or standardized definitions. Translations of enviro-cabulary are largely feel-good adjectives used to convey a somewhat spiritual sense of balance with nature. The Mandarin translation for "organic," for example, can be understood as simple, healthy, and proximate to nature. With this fuzzy description, seeing the word "organic" on a package is pretty, but not concrete or impactful.

What most shoppers do know is that there are not adequate controls to regulate mainstream products. And there are certainly not measures in place to oversee niche goods. While consumers in more developed markets rely on clear-cut and regulated authority to monitor claims, Chinese have no such confidence. This leaves the real value of environmental messaging at a bit of a standstill. What is the advantage of green, which is at a higher price point than other options? Does it represent a social benefit to others (helping to save the earth), or does it offer a personal value (making the user look and feel better)? Without education or controls, how can the green revolution really be either? Without a clear impact, the differentiation becomes superficially tied to consumers' desire to be fashionable and trend-conscious.

CHINA-STYLE LOHASIANS

The global movement Lifestyle of Health and Sustainability (LOHAS) was kicked off in 1998 by sociologist Paul Ray and psychologist Sherry Ruth Anderson in their book *The Cultural Creatives: How 50 Million People Are Changing the World*. The philosophy behind the movement emphasizes a more sustainable cycle of production and consumption for companies and consumers. Members of the LOHAS movement, sometimes referred to as LOHASians, support brands and products that provide earth-friendly alternatives.

While the movement was introduced to the mainland in 2006, years after its adoption in the United States and other parts of Asia, trendy Chinese were eager to adapt the message.[28] Not only foreign, it held appeal for have's and have-nots alike. Youth who had grown up in a status-panic were happy to join a group that offered a life vest, a new way of living that emphasized simplicity over glitz and glam. For those who had already achieved society's status markers and were looking for more, LOHAS's message of personal balance and introspection provided a welcome dose of friendly and nonconfrontational spirituality—and another way to set themselves apart.

Although imported, LOHAS was not entirely foreign. It reflected traditional Chinese perspectives on balance and man's relationship with nature. Stirring modern looks and traditional values, LOHAS has been translated as "happy living." The mission is summarized as embracing three goods: do good, feel good, and look good.[29] At this stage, consumers are putting effort into the latter principles—feeling and looking good. The movement's reputation as a social and fashionable cause célèbre is reinforced in the magazine of the same name and LOHAS-themed social clubs in major cities. LOHAS is a niche culture with mass-market potential. Lacking well-articulated boundaries, the term has been adopted to fit some interesting scenarios in the mainland. Brands like Dairy Queen have capitalized on the term by launching low-fat and low-sugar organic mooncakes. The real question is, can LOHAS define itself clearly before its meaning is stripped of conviction? Like most concepts with loose guardianship, the idea is in danger of becoming so trendy that it becomes generic.

PLAYING FARM

The quest for the simple life has taken on cyber permutations as well with virtual farming games that allow users to grow crops and protect their harvests from thieving friends. At the peak of its popularity, Happy Garden, a game from Kaixin001, boasted that fifteen million users were logging on every day just to make sure that other players did not steal their crops.[30] The game offered buzz and an obvious vehicle to disseminate a deeper message.

The domestic, state-run company branded as Lohas even used Happy Garden to promote its juice product. In the game, users could plant seeds and then squeeze mature plants to make Lohas juice. The game did more than put a logo in front of Kaixin001's primarily white-collar user base to build awareness. It also engaged and edu-cated consumers about the product's five-step production process. This example was one of the few peeks behind the scenes to see how goods made it onto store shelves. Good for consumers and good for the brand, it also provided a golden opportunity for a company to articulate its value while helping audiences understand the category.

Interest in the game was used by small-scale farms to create a new direct-to-consumer offering. Farms allow individuals to rent small plots of land, decide what to plant, communicate with farmers about management, and order the results of their virtual labor to be deliv-ered straight to their door. It is virtual farming with tasty results: consumers at home pay in advance and plan crops with farmers. They can visit the farms or wait comfortably on the couch for the crops to be delivered. This instant, easy, and first-hand experience is helping to define concepts of "organic" and "natural" for city dwell-ers who otherwise would not have direct exposure to what these terms actually mean.

NEXT-STAGE ACTIVISM

The big question now is how the next stage of organized activism will evolve in China. Government agencies, interest groups, brands, and young change agents are all considering their next move.

One example of how a cooperative effort can play out is 1KG MORE. Independently launched by An Zhu in 2004 as an online network to combine travel and social activism, the NGO's mission is to turn tourists into foot soldiers. By adding one kilogram of school supplies to be delivered during their travels to rural areas, young backpackers turn a vacation into an act of volunteerism. Since its founding, 1KG MORE has expanded its reach to help more than one thousand schools and has supported thousands of youth tap into their personal power to contribute to the greater good. Participation is appealing because the activity is social and the effort is relatively small. It is an easy and fun way to feel con-nected to a large cause.

A clear mission and solid organization have helped attract brands to contribute. For example, Portland, Oregon-based footwear brand Keen partnered with 1KG MORE as part of its global Hybrid. Care corporate social responsibility efforts. P&G's Safeguard brand also worked with 1KG MORE volunteers to help educate students in rural schools about the importance of hand washing. This example shows how the cast of next stage activism can work together; there is an important supporting role for brands and a social, fun, and fulfilling part for young activists to play.

THE CONSUMER-SET AGENDA

Young consumers are increasingly bold in standing up for their rights as individuals and are getting closer to connecting choices to being able to make a difference. While the motivation for this new phase of conscious consumerism seems to be more about reputation than results, it is actually the first stage in integrating the political with the personal. Youth are assigning meaning to aligning with a cause and feeling out how membership will impact how their communities will see them—and how they will see themselves.

In their willingness to levy retribution against certain brands, consumers in China can seem to be some of the most sensitive in the world, willing to emotionalize issues and take them to an extreme. But, in the context of what they have had to contend with, these same consumers can be regarded as pragmatists who have learned the hard way to prepare for anything and everything. In their daily lives, they have to navigate to avoid fakes and inflated prices and also to consider carefully how their choices have an impact on their reputations. They teeter between functioning as confident independents and conscientious group stewards, operating in a way that can represent both their individuality and the subgroups to which they belong.

This balancing act provides a peek into a culture that is learning to deal with new divergences from the prescribed norm. As author and journalist Duncan Hewitt points out, "If you look at the level of debate in the Chinese media or just among ordinary people in their daily lives, there's discussion of many subjects that there wouldn't have been 20 years ago—despite the obvious restrictions in some areas."[31] This robust dialogue is helping to establish a new, multifaceted value system.

Youth are leading the way to encourage opinions and actions based on conviction. Digitally equipped and looking for recognition within their chosen communities, post-90s in particular are using activism to build social capital. These cluster communities encourage members to expand their influence and sway others to their way of thinking. Hewitt argues, "Some people would say that the post-90s are more 'on message' politically than some of the previous generations—particularly when it comes to issues of patriotism and national interest. Nevertheless, in terms of many domestic issues, they [the post-90s] seem to have a greater sense of their own self-worth, their own rights, their own individuality, and their own need for space."[32] For the post-90s and likely for generations to come, the personal and the political are one interconnected sphere.

LOOKING BACK

Without government or NGOs to establish order reliably, young netizens are leading the charge to hold officials and brands responsible for their actions. Eager to exert influence, youth are discovering a new form of power—not through organized politics or religion—but by leveraging their wallets. Shaped by years of dangerously loose systems of transparency and accountability, Chinese youth are demanding better products and more protections. Real-time online communication tools like microblogging have become key vehicles for netizens to accumulate and exert influence. These strategies are putting companies on the defensive and creating a new culture of consumer influence. As interest in social activism gains momentum among youth, brands have a unique opportunity to empower as well as assert and demonstrate their value.

LOOKING FORWARD

This chapter is meant to help you think more deeply about connecting to youth. How could the information be leveraged in these scenarios?

1. How can companies be proactive to redeem trust from disillusioned consumers?
2. How can companies promote easy and social roles for youth to participate in corporate social responsibility efforts?
3. How can brands participate in social media channels (like Weibo) to promote positive and monitor negative impressions?

CHAPTER 6

DRIVING SUBCULTURES: BUILDING A CENTER ON THE EDGE

When he says we are the history
We'll show you we are the future
It's not as good as we thought
But it's a story about you, you and me.
——Lyrics to "Back 2 The Future" by Queen Sea Big Shark,
a Beijing-based indie rock band, created in 2004

AS PART OF AN INVESTIGATION INTO NON-MAINSTREAM expression in different cities, I had the opportunity to interview the lead singer of a rock band called Groupie about local trends and subcultures. Living in Shenzhen, a coastal city fed by its status as a special economic zone, Denya (aka Xi Teng), the lead singer, had a bird's-eye view into how young people were styling rebellion.

She reminded me of an early Chinese Gwen Stefani. With heavy black eyeliner and messy hair, a girlie red plaid skirt contrasted with garters and stomp boots, Denya knew how to rock the image of the sexy starlet. But unlike the cold front adopted by many of her peer rockers in other countries, Denya was accommodating and even sweet. She brought us imported chocolates to munch on and offered to spend the weekend as our tour guide.

As a high profile member of the local non-mainstream scene, Denya played with her appearance as part of her job as a tastemaker. She watched fashion from all over the world and curated her own

Figure 6.1   Denya, the lead singer of Groupie, demonstrates her rocker style.
Photo by Feng Lei (Ayu)

style. She had favorite brands from China and abroad for most categories; she loved MAC cosmetics but preferred the local sports shoe
brand Li Ning. From a foreign perspective, she was all over the map.
She broke the rules that defined subcultures have led followers to
rely on. Her diverse choices made easy classification and prediction
impossible. But, from a post-90s perspective, she was right on track.

I spoke with Denya at one of her frequent gig spots, an outlet
of the True Colors bars, a chain of clubs that reminded me of a
Chinese Hard Rock Café. Complete with a branded lifestyle shop
downstairs, True Colors offered a total package experience. But
unlike the Hard Rock brand, True Colors (like Denya) did not
bank on one consistent image. Its value was in the diversity of
rooms, bars, and flavors on offer—literally something for everyone
under one roof.

With a fan base of young rebels, Denya forecasted that the post-
90s' outward rebellion would evolve from being shocking to becoming expected. "In Shenzhen, post-90s kids are crazy. Some of them
cut their wrists because they think it's cool to leave a scar there.
Post-90s are not mainstream, but I think the non-mainstream will

be mainstream in the future."[1] As we stepped onto the street from our interview, we saw a poster for a well-known domestic jeans brand: the model was winking and showing off his tongue piercing. Her prediction seemed to be coming true right before our eyes.

EMERGING DIFFERENCE

Embracing difference is not a practice typically associated with modern Chinese society. Much before and especially after the Tiananmen Square protests of 1989, the government took a stern approach to managing divergence from the norm. Foreign influences that emphasized individual expression were particularly troublesome for the state. Rock music was problematic, and the situation became especially grave when youth started forming their own rock bands and chanting locally relevant messages into the microphone. The 1986 song "Nothing To My Name" by Beijing rocker Cui Jian was used as an anthem to unite protesters at Tiananmen Square and give them courage to fight for their rights. Rock music and musicians were thus vilified for helping to incite rebellion, and the government took a firm hand to limiting their influence on state-run TV and radio.

The term *liu mang* (meaning "hooligan") was applied to anyone who operated outside the mainstream. This incorporated artists and other noisemakers whose independence was deemed a threat to conducting official business-as-usual in the Middle Kingdom. With little ability to access and cross-contaminate, subculture development was stunted.

Gradually, rock and other defiant Western-born music has worked its way back into popular culture. But now, style largely leads the way, not the substance of the message. Mainstream artists that make it big are often bubble-gum sweet in both looks and lyrics. Rock musicians, with less access to larger distribution channels, often find it hard to make a living from their music alone. Without state-approved media channels to help them reach an audience of critical mass, they are marginalized. Most have jobs that pay the bills and rely on music as an expressive outlet rather than as career-oriented practice.

Today, the abrasive connotations of being different have largely been stripped away. The term *ling lei* (meaning "alternative") refers to those who elect lifestyles that depart from the norm. In general, these youth pose little social or political threat and thus present a less criminal image of difference. Never the menace to society they were once perceived as, and now more controlled by monetary demands than political parameters, *ling lei* has become shorthand for youth who aspire to be fashionably out-of-sync. While their expression is more pose than politics, lifting difference from dangerous to desirable is a game changer. The introduction of more than one path to acceptance and personal satisfaction is a disruptive phenomenon in itself.

INTRODUCING NEW IDEALS

Embracing difference has not been easy. Breaking the mold has often been an uncomfortable experience for those who have defied convention to champion atypical ideals. Standing alone has been a particularly potent challenge. Singular voices find it difficult to emerge from the masses and, when they do, quickly realize the threat of being silenced. This was the case for an average girl who dared to catapult herself to become China's first self-appointed Internet celebrity in 2003.

Born to a peasant family in 1977 in Shaanxi province, Shi Hengxia (later to become known as Sister Hibiscus, Sister Lotus, and most commonly Furong Jiejie) was eager to get out and see the world—or at least have the world see her. Judged against China's traditional value system, Shi hardly seemed destined for greatness. She was not rich, exceptionally talented, well connected, or academically successful enough to warrant a second look.

For college, Shi set her sights on China's most prestigious schools, but her scores were not stellar enough to provide her with a place. Instead, she settled for the less impressive Shaanxi Technical College where she enrolled in technical engineering courses. Even after she began her studies, Shi found it difficult to settle into her station and attempted the exams again in the hopes of moving up and out of mediocrity. Her first posts to the BBS (bulleting board systems) of Peking University and Tsinghua University were made while she was dreaming of admission. Although anonymous, she pleaded her case and documented her struggles to climb ahead.[2] Despite not being accepted to either institution, she posted musings and pictures of herself lounging romantically around campus to university online forums.[3] She gained notoriety among students for her bold self-promotion despite rather unremarkable talents. The fact that a normal girl who was not even a student gained celebrity among elite super students is an accomplishment in and of itself. This feat was remarkable, but Shi did not set out to become a campus sensation; she was aiming for a much larger audience.

Establishing her own blog took her away from the small-time reach of closed campus forums and opened her message to a wider public. Unlike her peers, Shi was confident in leveraging everything about herself regardless of mainstream values that pointed to her dismissal. She was sure her story was interesting and important— even if it was not in a traditional sense. Shi's original stated intent in creating the blog was to detail her struggle to get into the country's best schools. Her assumption was that others would be inspired by her efforts, if not her success.

It did not take long for the blog to derail from its original mission to become a personal megaphone for her to boast about her superior dancing, singing, looks, and academic abilities. In her late twenties, an age when her peers from Shaanxi would already be married with children, Shi set her sights on fame. She became an unstoppable public relations machine, transforming herself into Furong Jiejie, one of China's fastest rising BBS stars. According to the Chinese-language search engine Baidu, Furong Jiejie's name remains in the top ten searches for "figures." This ranking puts the self-appointed celebrity in impressive company, among important literary figures such as Ba Jin and Lu Xun, and politicians, including Jiang Zemin and Hu Jintao.[4] Also on the list are cultural icons Mao Zedong and Bruce Lee. The fact that Furong Jiejie, a girl from the countryside with no obvious talents other than publicly praising herself, has inspired enough interest to be considered in such culturally critical company is nothing short of mind-boggling.

THE THREAT OF THE INDIVIDUAL

Self-promotion like Furong Jiejie's was (and is) uncommon for average Chinese, and her celebration of self was a revelatory statement. She indulged in self-praise for her natural abilities and claimed that others were similarly overwhelmed with admiration. One well-known post from her blog states, "I am so beautiful, when men see my body they get a nosebleed." Her boldness was decidedly outside of the norm and incited a response.

Not unlike Andy Warhol's iconic soup-can images, Furong Jiejie made people look with new eyes at something they saw every day. The implications of a normal girl shining a spotlight on herself were uncomfortable—and intriguing. Proponents loved her confidence and dubbed her "a pioneer in anti-intellectualism."[5] The fact that Furong Jiejie had determined and driven her own rise to fame made a statement, but so did the fact that her followers appreciated her despite prescribed reasons not to.

(UN)SAFE CELEBRITY

As Furong Jiejie moved from online cult celebrity to the main stage offline, her image graced the covers of magazines and she received significant airtime on television. Her story was picked up by international media and spread to audiences around the world, furthering her reputation as the most talked-about woman in China.

Things were really lining up for Furong Jiejie; the celebrity destiny she had predicted for herself seemed accurate and unavoidable. And in another country, it would have been. She was poised to be iconic on the level of an early Chinese Lady Gaga. But the government had had enough. The Ministry of Culture called for a blackout on Furong Jiejie, halting coverage of her on television, in print, and online. Although the content of her message was neither political nor pornographic, the seemingly benign girl from Shaanxi was cast as a threat. The government was not about to let the antiheroine become a symbol of modern China.

Furong Jiejie's story is at once an inspirational saga and a cautionary tale for youth who dare to define themselves as outliers. The lesson

Figure 6.2   Cosplay fans gather at Fee Café in Shanghai. Photo by Ren Gang

is that youth can find their own standing, as long as they do not create too much noise or step too far outside of prescribed boundaries.
To risk pulling the mainstream in a new direction is going too far.
Being a solo act is dangerous; it is safer to move anonymously or as
part of a group.

REINTERPRETING DIFFERENCE

Although stepping outside the norm as an individual can be risky
business, staying safely tucked into the mainstream is losing its
appeal. As youth struggle to define themselves as modern and creative, they are increasingly grabbing onto and extending subculture
groups into the Middle Kingdom. In these scenarios, youth create
a smaller-scale society that holds greater potential for success and
personal satisfaction than the larger framework. In this way, the role
of subcultures is less about cultivating a personal aesthetic than it is
about creating a more manageable and satisfying paradigm. Inside
subcultures, members are quietly and safely unleasing new models.

Stepping away from the mainstream to create separate identities has not been easy. Even finding the time and independence to
investigate personal interests in-depth has been a hurdle not easy to
surmount. Youth have felt the pressure and known the opportunity
to help support family aspirations, a duty that is almost impossible
to ignore. As students, free time is largely a myth as extra hours are
quickly filled with tutoring and other activities designed to prepare
youth for the work world. As a result, the exploration of hobbies
not tied to employment comes later in life than it does for youth in
other countries. Time and money to try new experiences off of this
grid are reserved for more independent young adults after they enter
the workforce.

It is clear that youth would prefer to have more space to explore
their interests, but that is not to say that with more freedom, young
Chinese would maintain subcultures with the same level of serious-
ness that youth outside of China have. What has been presented to
date is enthusiasm. For young Chinese, subcultures are an increasingly relevant and highly social toolkit that can be played with, at
little cost or consequence.

For youth, historical boundaries and hierarchies of imported subcultures are largely meaningless. Exposed to a world of foreign-bred
music and style genres almost at the same time has given youth
the freedom to experiment and propose their own interpretations.
Compared to international cohorts who were beholden to history
and preconceived notions about what a punk or a goth or a skater
represented, Chinese youth were open-minded. They welcomed a
host of new ideas as influences more than as icons. This flexibility
allowed them to mix and match music, interests, and fashion to suit
their own temporary and transcendent tastes.

To whatever degree they are able to explore or create on their
own, Chinese youth have a wider berth for experimentation than
most youth in other countries. *Fei zhu liu*, a term meaning "non-
mainstream" and associated primarily with the post-90s, is an
example of this flexibility. *Fei zhu liu* (known as FZL in Internet
shorthand) was first associated with youth who opted to look more
"alternative" than their mainstream peers. If this term sounds non-
specific, it's because it purposely is. While the term initially stood
firmly outside the mainstream, *fei zhu liu* has evolved to incorporate multiple styles in a nonexclusive way. To fit in as a FZL, youth
can try on defiant or fantasy-led Western styles or attempt a sweet
look more closely tied to one of the myriad of Korean or Japanese
cute subcultures. The only criterion is that they present their image
online for others to see and respond to. The web site fzlgo.com is a
one-stop shop teaching youth how to dress in FZL style, create FZL-
inspired images in Photoshop, and develop avatars, online names,
and signatures that will be recognizably "in the know." The site's
content underlines the actual key element of *fei zhu liu* culture: it
is a group that can express affiliation and membership online without having a standard, parallel outlet in the physical world. The
fact that *fei zhu liu* is recognized as a subculture despite not having
the specific music, style, or attitude allegiance that would normally
constitute a subculture is unique. Youth are playing not only with
elements of outside cultures, they are reimagining the primordial
definition of a subculture.

As young people cycle from one experiment to another, original cultural significance matters less than how they can adapt

and move it forward. Unlike indigenous subculture incarnations outside China, youth in the Middle Kingdom have no personal obligation to stay true to original meanings or roots. Their peers with the same conceptions will not act as social centrifuges either hinder movement. There is no value in being discreet; to separate from the masses, youth move in and out of derivative groups, combining symbols to create new meaning. In this laboratory, social value is in the experimentation, not in adhering to history or lineage.

THE BALANCING ACT

There is no doubt that the modern Chinese identity is sprinting into new territory. In 1981, while teaching organizational psychology in a management program in Shanghai, then MIT professor Edwin C. Nevis had a hard time applying Maslow's hierarchy into a Chinese context. Abraham Maslow's famous contribution to human developmental psychology (Maslow's Hierarchy of Needs) seeks to explain the different levels of human needs, from basic survival to advanced self-actualization. The predictive theory is often illustrated as a five-stage pyramid with physiological needs at the base, safety at the next level, followed by love/belonging, and then esteem. Self-actualization is at the top of the pyramid, the final stage in development.

Nevis's premise was that Maslow's theory had a certain cultural relativity, and required tweaking to work in cultures with different individual-collective and ego-social dimensions. Nevis dubbed his theory Nevis's Hierarchy of Needs (also known as the Chinese Hierarchy of Needs). To adapt the model to fit into what he saw as the Chinese frame, Nevis reshaped the pyramid to four levels, with belonging at the base, physiology and safety following, and finally, self-actualization at the top. For Nevis, belonging was the foundation from which Chinese could develop. Without it, the rest was not possible. Adopting subgroup identities is one way for youth to succeed in a highly competitive environment. In a smaller circle, belonging and moving towards more personal self-actualization becomes attainable.

COMPARING RELATIONSHIPS ONLINE

For communities outside of the mainstream to flourish, they would need to establish circles of belonging and find channels to recruit similar thinkers. The first step was to enable safe self-expression outside the mainstream. In China, individual expression was a revelation in itself, largely enabled by intimate online spaces. In 2008, a study called *Young Digital Mavens* was released by JWT and IAC comparing online attitudes and behaviors of Chinese and American youth between 16 and 25 years old.[6] This study targeted youth born between 1982 and 1991, providing a snapshot of the post-80s and their relationships with themselves, each other, and the Internet. Although the study was conducted several years ago, it still provides a valuable comparison point between Chinese and American cohorts and helps illustrate the intimate nature of Chinese youth's relationship with the Internet. To help understand how the Internet changed youth's ideas about expressing themselves, we can compare the study's findings of Chinese to American behaviors and values.

Anonymity online allowed the post-80s to feel safe expressing themselves in new and often deeper ways than they could in real life. This confident expression led to greater self-awareness and a deeper emotionalism, and enabled new ways of building relationships.

- 73 percent of Chinese agree that online they are free to do and say things they would not do or say offline versus 32 percent of Americans
- 69 percent of Chinese agree that "I have experimented with how I present myself online" versus 28 percent of Americans
- 66 percent of Chinese agree that "online interactions have broadened my sense of identity" versus 26 percent of Americans

The study explained some key relational differences between Chinese and their American counterparts—namely that Chinese are more willing and open to exposing themselves and developing meaningful relationships online.

For Chinese, the mask of anonymity online makes deeper connections safer than face-to-face interactions. Tom Doctoroff, the CEO of Greater China at J. Walter Thompson (JWT) and author of *Billions: Selling to the New Chinese Consumer* and *What Chinese*

Want, explains, "There is an evolution from sheer release to belonging to acknowledgment to platform-shining and then you even get transcendence but it's taking place in a parallel universe."[7] For Americans eager to build their personal brand in a culture obsessed by celebrity, the value of anonymous communication is decidedly lower.

- 48 percent of Chinese state things online often feel more intense than things offline versus 12 percent of Americans
- 63 percent of Chinese think that "it's perfectly possible to have real relationships purely online with no face-to-face contact," versus 21 percent of Americans
- 32 percent of Chinese admit that the Internet has broadened their sex life versus 11 percent of Americans

Enabling new ways of exploring and relating to themselves and others, the post-80s formed an intimate relationship with the Internet itself. As a testament to youth's appreciation for the medium, blog to book self-publishing services helped youth turn their blogs into printed memorials. A trusted advisor and sympathetic listener, the Internet became a true and important friend. The ability to express themselves and refabricate new identities was addictive.

- 61 percent of Chinese report having a parallel life online versus 13 percent of Americans
- 25 percent of Chinese report they would "feel uncomfortable if they were offline for more than one day" versus 12 percent of Americans
- 42 percent of Chinese consider that they sometimes are addicted to living online versus 18 percent of Americans

TESTING BOUNDARIES THROUGH BLOGGING

Established in late 2002, BlogCN became the first free blog hosting service provider in China.[8] By equipping youth with a cost- and risk-free mouthpiece, blogging became a welcome tool to further youth's quest for independent identities. The vehicle allowed unique self-expressions and supported dialogue—opening a door to fresh questions and divergence. Isaac Mao is a key figure in Chinese Internet culture—his credentials include but are not

limited to being the cofounder of BlogCN, director of the Social
Brain Foundation, and fellow to Harvard University's Berkman
Center for Internet and Society. Mao states, "Now, we find people
more easily and we can come together to find new missions and
even new ways to solve problems. Even if we can't solve them now,
we can imagine how we can in the future. It's a form of very disruptive change in China."[9]

But blogging was not only a vehicle for youth to define themselves and gather like-minded individuals; it allowed young Chinese
to move away from the masses to test the barriers of socially acceptable behavior. For instance, female bloggers like Mu Zimei and Ye
Haiyan (aka Liu Mang Yan or Hooligan Sparrow) challenged notions
about sex and gender by broadcasting their sexual encounters.[10]

Self-expression has become an unstoppable force online. Despite
government attempts to force bloggers to register with their true
identities, virtual-identity experimentation has been impossible to
curtail. The lure of the Internet as a safe, accessible and collabora-
tive space to reinvent oneself has proven irresistible. Dressed up in

Figure 6.3 Avatars online show personality but also membership

a self-designated avatar with a self-appointed name, address, and information, anything is possible for youth looking to explore how they feel and how others will respond. In this space, reimagining others is an easy next step.

CREATORS WANTED

Creation is a key element of engaging online. Adding to the conversation and providing new information enables netizens to maintain a place in the group; it is important not to be left out. In 2009, Forrester's Consumer Profile Tool suggested that there were almost twice as many Creators in metro China (defined as those who created or uploaded content such as videos, music, or text to be consumed by others) as there were in the United States (44 percent to 24 percent, respectively).[11] China also boasted more Critics (those who responded to content) than the United States (46 percent to 37 percent, respectively), and more Collectors (those who organized content for themselves or others using tags, RSS feeds, and the like) (37 percent to 21 percent, respectively). The United States had more Joiners (those who connected but did not necessarily contribute using SNS), 51 percent to China's 32 percent.[12]

In China, anonymity has led to safe and therefore highly creative, collaboration. Masked behind their computers or mobile phones, youth have bred memes that travel from one person to the next, encouraging new incarnations, new voices, and new meanings to be added to the conversation. Rarely is the originator known; after all, the purpose of the first spark is to ignite a conversation. For young Chinese, the expression of an original idea online is less important than how it can be mixed, matched, and made anew.

REDEFINING THE OUTSIDE

"Xiao Pang," or "Little Chubby," is an example of an identity that was borrowed and then reincarnated. The example shows how netizens are keen to call out and exploit difference. Their activity took one picture of a normal boy and catapulted a sensation. At first, it was just a picture; thirteen year-old Qian Zhijun was unwittingly photographed during a school traffic-safety activity. In the image, a cherubic Qian stood apart from his classmates. Next to their thin profiles, his face was very, *very* round. His sidelong gaze met the camera with suspicion, and netizens got to work imagining the rest. Described as "the face that launched 1,000 clicks,"[13] Qian's head was superimposed onto heroic figures such as Russell Crowe in *Gladiator* and onto the movie poster for *Lord of the Rings*. But it was also emasculated by netizens who suited him up as Doraemon and cast him as Kate Winslet in *Titanic*. Qian was also given larger cultural proportions by netizens who imposed his image on the Mona Lisa and Buddha.[14]

Qian's embarrassment turned into a success story. His recognizable face helped him land a place on television and parts in two films *Three Kingdoms: Resurrection of the Dragon* and *The University Days of a Dog*. Rather than shying away from the caricature of himself cobbled together by others, Little Chubby embraced his physique and fame to help promote the image of other heavy-set youth.

WEB SPACE IS MY SPACE

One young person I interviewed in 2006 was such a true digital maven that I hired her as soon as the project came to a close. On the outside, Becky seemed like any other college student—she lived in the dorms with five other roommates during the week, and then came home to doting parents on the weekend. She shopped with her mom, and they shared opinions to help guide each other's adoption of new fashion trends, and even explored do-it-yourself (DIY) together. Although Becky had not had a boyfriend yet, she was surrounded by close friends, many of whom she had known since childhood.

What made her memorable was that she was active on almost ten social networking sites and had made sophisticated judgments about each one. She had created profiles on different sites based on pursuing specific interests and expressing different parts of her personality. Some foreign sites were for making international friends and practicing English; local sites were used to keep up on local events; fashion sites were used to get feedback on style choices;

and music sites helped her connect with new sounds. She added and dropped virtual social circles ruthlessly as she came to better understand her interests and power within these communities. But that did not mean she was not engaged with each one; it just meant that she was flexible in her engagement. From one angle, Becky was acting as a digital chameleon, partitioning pieces of herself to make up a whole. From another point of view, she was not partitioning at all, but rather looking for a comprehensive solution. Becky never considered that one social networking site or profile could suit all of her needs; she believed that she would need to cobble together her own combination of sites to enable a complete expression of her personality.

FOUNDING VIRTUAL COMMUNITIES

The establishment of a meeting ground offline in Shanghai in November 2005, Chinese Blogger Conference, helped to cement bloggers as their own independent community. In this forum, bloggers determined status symbols and codes of conduct that were unique to the group. Despite blogger conferences being closed by the government in recent years, the power of online communities has remained.[15]

Like CNBloggerCon, Tudou Video Festival provides offline recognition for a largely online community. Unlike blogger conferences that focus on blogging as a medium of expression, Tudou Video Festival's focal point is on emerging talent in film and video. Recognizing young creative talent formally since 2007, the event helps boost voices that would not otherwise be heard. A case in point is the 2011 Golden Potato Award (for best overall film), which went to 23-year-old director Wang Zizhao for *Fearless*, the story of a young male virgin who takes a trip to a rural doctor. Inspired by the country's gender imbalance and young men's new and uncertain identities, the short film is poignant and edgy. Director Wang reportedly looks across to other online video creators for inspiration, scoffing that mainstream big budget cinema has lost touch with real life. As filmmaking is a less than conventional path, the Tudou forum provides important recognition for like-minded creatives to develop their own center of gravity. Even for Wang, his parents did not take his career path seriously and had not yet seen his film before it won the award.[16]

A LANGUAGE OF EXCLUSION

Online, groups can play with new values and expressions without the larger society meddling in their experiments. Born from the desire to build protective fences around these communities, new ways of communicating have come to life to divide intended audiences from the outside. Eager to separate into protected groups and gain status for their contributions, the post-90s have morphed their own breed of digital lifestyle. To do this, they developed a language that would self-select who is "in" and who is "out." The writing system, known as Martian language, is a post-90s invention and is entangled with both the reputation and identity of the generation. Insiders demonstrate their skills in creating new expressions and in understanding or placing the origins of Martian terms.

Unlike phrases common in the United States, such as LOL (laugh out loud), OMG (oh my God), and TMI (too much information), Martian language was initially used less for inclusion than as a means of exclusion. A creative combination of letters, numbers, and symbols, Martian language draws inspiration from various dialects, foreign languages, and pop culture phenomena. Dubbed by outsiders as "brain-damaged writing," Martian language uses extremely obscure symbols to express everyday activities and emotion.[17] Users play with rare characters, mix languages, and split words into parts to reconstruct surprising twists in expression, a veritable beat box of influences. To the uninitiated, these coded conversations can look like spy-speak gibberish. To the post-90s, they are small, exclusive salons operating in plain view.

Out of use and forgotten, *jiong* 囧 (originally meaning "brightness" or "window") is an Internet slang term that came out of obscurity in the mid-2000s to become perhaps the most recognized of any Martian term. Resembling a human face—two eyes with an open mouth—囧—the character connotes emotions such as embarrassment, scorn, or failure. The character is often combined with

"OTZ," "orz," or even merged to form 囧rz. Characters strung together symbolize a person who is prostrate on his or her hands and knees.[18] For gamers, "gg" means "good game," so combining orz+ gg = orzgg means, "You lost a game."

The term has become a product in itself. I knew this beyond a doubt when I saw cakes shaped as 囧 being sold at a local bakery. Li Ning also recognized the character's bankability and produced 100,000 pairs of Jiong sneakers, selling out in two months.[19] Kleenex used the icon for two editions of its mini tissue packs. Kimberly Clark's feminine product brand Kotex featured the character in a television spot, and Intel leveraged it in a forum for users to communicate their own 囧 experiences.

Martian language has come a long way from its original intent to create a coded, unique expression that only those "in the know" could understand. Taking Internet slang from the realm of the exclusive to the mainstream, new terms are being co-opted into everyday offline language. Popularized in 2010, the term *gei li* (meaning "awesome") has been used by less-than-hip officials, in news stories, and has even found its way to star in marketing campaigns in both China and Japan. The niche term was originally derived from a line used by the Monkey King in the Chinese-dubbed version of a Japanese anime.[20] Beyond its initial adoption as one word, *gei li* has been morphed by creative, experimental netizens into the English "gelivable" and the French "très guélile."

Using tools like Martian language, youth are finding ways to lock down their own communities as separate from the mainstream. While netizens push to individuate, brands are hoping to communicate that they too, belong in the club. Taking advantage of the need for youth to get deeper exposure and demonstrate their knowledge has become big business.

PUTTING SUBCULTURES ON STAGE

The excitement was palpable in May 2011 as fans prepared to enter Midi Festival, Shanghai's first multiday, multistage outdoor rock festival in over three years. They had a lot to look forward to besides a great day spent outside in the sun; 40 plus bands and disc jockeys

(DJs) from around the world were lined up to rock forty thousand anxious fans.

"Rock" may be an overstatement, as most music festivals have strayed from catering to hardcore music buffs to creating an experience with wider appeal. The Shanghai stop on Midi's ambitious 2011 tour was an experiment in just how far festivals could go. Shanghai was not necessarily known for its music scene, and interest in attending an outdoor festival had not been tested in a while. Shanghainese were more reputed as mall rats than live music fans. Still, crowds jumbled excitedly into Pudong's Century Park through gate 5, chattering and posturing in anticipation of what the day would bring.

Once inside, the congregation moved past young designers and artists displaying their products for sale. Some may have stooped to pick up handcrafted notebooks or homemade jewelry displayed on a blanket by a friendly looking artsy type. They may have conversed about the artist's process or encouraged each other in some small way before moving back into the stream to carve out a place on the lawn.

Unlike rowdier incarnations in more developed markets, music festivals in China are fun and friendly. Bands may be on the stage, but they are rarely the headliners. The real attraction is people-watching and witnessing something unusual in art, music, and fashion. Music festivals are a crash course in subcultures for curious youth.

From their perch in Shanghai's largest park, concertgoers could experience the carnival-like atmosphere. Sipping mojitos for the first time and munching on barbecue for the millionth, youth were inundated by new sights, sounds, and ideas. They got a peek inside groups that they would not normally interact with and even got a look at different incarnations of their own tribes.

On the lawn, youth dressed to resemble punks, goths, and bohemians all turned their heads to check each other out. Some were faithful to the subculture they were emulating, but many more were mashing elements to come up with their own styles—a little British punk here, a little Chinese retronationalist there. Young alchemists were experimenting across time and territorial boundaries to develop their own genres. They were leveraging symbols from adopted subcultures and mixing them with national and generation-specific markers to create their own hybrid looks. From the local retro pool, youth were grabbing onto the iconic Chinese rock uniform (blue-and white striped shirts paired with red scarves) as well as reclaimed striped armbands, Feiyue shoes, and Lei Feng caps. They were mingling in elements of their own generation such as post-80s and post-90s T-shirts, comic figures from their youth, local designers, and even DIY. All of these items were paired together in experiments meant to grab attention and convey that the wearer was a good mixologist, not just a straight copycat.

This chemistry experiment was also apparent on stage. While some bands were derivative, others dipped into multiple genres to cultivate a more unique look and sound. Shanghainese band Top Floor Circus rocked its own hybrid music, alternating crooning in Shanghainese dialect with experimental instrumentals.

For youth, social activism (like subcultures and music) is stylish so it was only natural that a cause would make an appearance. The cause célèbre of the festival was the plight of bears, specifically educating youth in how to help protect caged bears from having their bile robbed and turned into an ingredient in traditional Chinese medicine remedies. Black and white posters of an illustrated bear holding up its index finger and pinky in fraternity with festival rockers lined the stage and reminded youth of the festival's ties to something larger than a good time.

Whether or not youth in Shanghai could have an impact on the issue was of little consequence. Promoting a social cause was symbolic, an essential part of creating a fashionable and modern experience. Youth concocted their own activist outlets at the concert as well. A more friendly incarnation was young people who held up signs offering hugs to strangers. On the rebellious side, stickers that read "I (broken heart) Z F," meaning "I hate the government," were sold and worn on site.

The stickers were defiant—and ironic—as the government has been a key partner in driving festival culture out of the shadows to flourish in the mainland. When China's first school of rock music, Midi, held its first festival in 2000, it may have more closely resembled a college house party. Held at the school and showcasing mainly student acts, Midi 1.0 was more about the music than the fanfare. But now, heading into its eleventh year, the show had evolved beyond scrappy posters, amateur bands, and cheap beer. Despite government-imposed setbacks in 2008 that brought the curtain down on Midi's mission to rock, it had evolved into a serious brand that was setting records.[21] The year 2011 was designed as a big expansion period; six months of events were scheduled, and the festival was moving into its fourth event in one year.[22]

Since the beer-soaked music bash that started it all in 2000, festivals have been popping up and taking hold across the Middle Kingdom. Midi is no longer the only game in town; in 2009, the number of events increased to 44, and in 2010, that number more than doubled to over one hundred.[23] While developed markets have a more robust festival scene (Germany, for example, hosts over three hundred music festivals a year), China is on a fast track.[24] The proliferation has been allowed (and even propelled) by city governments that have changed their tune from opposing festivals to welcoming them with open arms and budgets. The foray into youth culture is not philanthropic, however. It is part of a larger commercial strategy. The goal is to brand cities as creative centers and position them to profit as China redirects its reputation from factory to creative hub.

To capitalize on this increased appeal and outdo one another, city governments have been eager to host festivals and brand themselves as culture zones. The concept has moved beyond the bright lights of China's biggest cities to rock fans outside of tier-one locations. Zebra Music Festival has picked up the beat in Chengdu, Hangzhou, and now Shanghai.[25] Smaller festival brands include the Snow Mountain Music festival in Yunnan and the Roaring Hooves festival in Inner Mongolia's Gobi Desert. More sophisticated incarnations have localized to differentiate festival brands and cater to individual cities and the people who live there.

Modern rock festival culture in China is about many things—including music. Perhaps the most important part of the experience is providing young people with the confidence and inspiration to pursue their interests. Shifting from focusing on the music to elevating brands and fashionable lifestyles in general, festival culture has gone from outlier to experience mall. This is a much more attractive proposition for government agencies and brands that recognize the increased potential for profit.

ALL FOR ONE, ONE FOR ALL

Metersbonwe, one of the biggest youth-focused fashion brands in China, has offered up conventional styles at mass market prices. With mandopop sensation Zhou Jielun (Jay Chou) as the brand's spokesperson and stores sprinkled across most cities and towns, Metersbonwe is known for its mainstream appeal. When Metersbonwe launched marketing and products related to subcultures, youth's movement towards niche identities was formalized.

Like its young customers, the Chinese brand has no sense of legacy or debt to subcultures to uphold. Free to explore, Metersbonwe is pushing multiple messages at the same time, offering up different expressions like a Swiss Army knife. Some expressions have targeted nationalists, post-80s cohorts, and friendly feminists. Limited-run collaborations with indie designers have even been sold next to perennial basics. Speaking to niche groups helps keep Metersbonwe from falling into a newly dangerous place: too general to matter. But speaking multiple languages at the same time is tricky business, and down the line, as consumers' expectations mature, the brand will need to fine-tune its approach. As subcultures build their own vocabularies, structures, and meanings, brands will be forced to do the same.

COCREATING CHINA'S OWN SUBCULTURES

The evolution of subcultures is not a foregone conclusion in the Middle Kingdom. Youth are still determining which elements are useful, which need to be tweaked, and which will be tossed to the side to make room for something better. For brands that have firm roots in subcultures outside China, there is a process of localization and legacy building that needs to take place before they can assume any lasting influence in the mainland. This is a balancing act between representing core values and building room for new interpretations to lead the way. Converse is one brand that understands this challenge.

In 2008, most global sports brands elbowed each other to stake their claim on Olympics fever. Brands plastered images of athletes glammed up in China-friendly scenarios and slapped traditional Chinese symbols onto products to sell their nod to flattered consumers. The rush of attention was exciting but the similarity in approach made it difficult for youth to decipher a brand-specific point of view. Brands did not tightly carve out their own place; they went for "safe."

But in this heated battle to own the Olympic moment, Converse took a gamble. In Shanghai's bustling shopping district Xujiahui, Adidas and Nike billboards battled athlete to athlete. And then there was Converse. Images from Converse's "Love Noise" campaign did not showcase a Photoshopped fantasy of larger-than-life moments; rather, they gave viewers a glimpse of local bands on a grassroots tour. Unlike other brands that had leveraged musical acts in their marketing, Converse was not backing a mando or cantopop sensation with mass appeal. Converse was putting its name behind two Beijing-based indie groups.

Outside of indie music circles, audiences were not likely to recognize Queen Sea Big Shark or PK14—but spotlighting the mainstream was hardly the point. Converse was making a dramatic statement by planting these groups on a billboard in a high-traffic area. Images showed band members crashed out on the ground and wreaking havoc on stage. Set opposite major sports brands' highly produced marketing, Converse's gritty, behind-the-scenes peek inside a subculture stood out. The brand could have reached back into its own history to pull out previous associations with Western indie icons like the Ramones or Nirvana, but "Love Noise" was more than a recycling effort. Converse was helping to create recognizable indigenous figures to push local non-mainstream movements forward. It was helping to develop a movement—and rebuild its significance—from the ground up.

Conveying the brand's connection to music was not a one-and-done task. First, Converse gave some of the most important bands in China's indie music scene a platform. Sending Queen Sea Big

Shark and PK14 on the road in their own tour bus, the brand documented and broadcast the road trip to give fans a more in-depth idea of what it means to be indie in the mainland. The road trip itself did not focus on tier-one entry points, but rather it took on more epic dimensions by covering five thousand miles by bus, hitting five lower-tier cities, and rocking out with local bands along the way. The tour, although backed by a major brand, was meant to stir enthusiasm in lower tiers, and it shot straight for small venues in Nanjing, Hangzhou, Changsha, Wuhan, and Xi'an, playing to crowds for the low ticket price of 30 RMB.

The opportunity to go to shows, watch the documentary of the tour online, and look up at larger-than-life billboards all served to expose old fans and new recruits to the indie music scene and lifestyle. Broadcasting the movement gave the subculture heroic standing, and intimate details seeped into the mainstream, simultaneously developing a broader as well as a more dedicated base. Ian Stewart, Marketing Director, Asia Pacific at Converse explains the strategy, "While core fans want a core story, the wider audience wants to be entertained and inspired in general and I hope we are successfully doing this."[26]

After presenting the appeal, the brand encouraged participation. After educating youth on the subculture, Converse helped young Chinese get involved. After the music tour, the documentary, and multimedia marketing exposed them to tenets of the indie lifestyle, Converse turned the tables on audiences to encourage them to participate. The brand's crowdsourcing of extras to appear in a video and help compose lyrics for Queen Sea Big Shark allowed young Chinese to put their own spin on the scene and get recognized for their involvement. Prizes did not veer from the mission: winners received a paid trip to check out Midi Festival in Beijing and a shopping spree in Converse stores. Like the tour, auditions for the video went off the expected map. Often overlooked fans in Chongqing, Shenyang, and other unexpected cities lined up to see what would happen next. By crowdsourcing, the brand provided a back-stage pass into a creative process and gave winners a sense of status and recognition within the subculture.[27]

After educating and encouraging involvement, Converse continued to nurture local indie culture by publishing and distributing a zine. The first issue, called "Music Holiday," profiled local bands and wrapped content with graphics clearly aligned with an indie aesthetic. Converse did not stop at the Middle Kingdom's borders to appeal to mainland Chinese, however. The brand took acts on the road to Singapore and the United States, documenting the reception abroad for consumers at home to experience vicariously.

When I ask music creators, especially in indie spaces, about the fashion vocabulary they use to express their tribal membership, the conversation almost inevitably turns to Converse. Not afraid of differentiating and willing to take a long-term perspective to develop an audience, Converse has made itself a valuable asset among burgeoning subcultures.

Different lines within the brand lend to a multidirectional trajectory: Chuck Taylor targets music fans, Star Chevron targets sports fans, and Jack Purcell targets art and fashion fans. Stewart emphasizes, "I think when it comes to Converse and our approach to connecting with the wider demographic, we don't want to necessarily only have one face—we hope to bring cultures together so that kids can appreciate a range of inspiring lifestyle stories—skate, indie music, street basketball, art, and fashion."[28]

But even with multiple lines to spin stories and connect with consumers at different life and culture points, Converse has to be ready to adapt its offering to fit in a Chinese context. It knows that applying cues from youth culture abroad isn't a simple cut and paste exercise.

Few skateboarders in China for instance, resemble their international counterparts. With early pressure for kids to achieve, the sport is not a pastime for teenagers; it is an activity that youth may attempt later in life, when they are 20-something and already working. At this point (and often not before), youth have some extra time and money to divert to their own interests.

This dominant social structure requires brands to adapt to fit in with what is possible. Stewart advises, "Respect and appreciate that that's the paradigm...and then you work around it, you don't try to force it, you don't walk away from it, you just create a marketing story and paradigm that aims at different demographics with a different story and different objectives."[29] Converse is not waiting for the landscape to bend, it is adapting to fit in.

Converse has since applied the formula it developed for indie music to tap into skateboarding. Taking skaters on tour to different locations in China's outer limits and broadcasting their experiences back to youth online, Converse has drawn an audience of skaters and young people interested in seeing new places and having unique experiences. Like it did with bands, Converse has taken young Chinese skaters to foreign spots and promoted their positive reception abroad back to eager youth at home. The result is a double win; it taps into nationalism and demonstrates other, more relatable angles from which to see skaters and skateboarding. Stewart claims, "[Chinese] kids want to get information about journeys and adventures and discoveries. They love to see the context and dimension of these faces so rather than a skateboarder just doing tricks or a musician just singing songs, they want to know behind the scenes. And then there's the national pride of having someone from their country go to Los Angeles or Austin or Singapore and totally getting embraced."[30] Youth are able to participate, even if tucked behind their computer screens, and experience the thrill of acceptance from an outside audience. Witnessing behind-the-scenes adventures gives them the opportunity to see the world from the perspective of youth like themselves.

LEAVING THE PAST BEHIND

As youth sculpt foreign subcultures to fit into a local context, they inevitably change the meaning and representation of original culture codes. Current mash-ups from fast-moving chameleons are sure to yield results that veer into new territory. As Stewart hypothesizes, "Now, youth are taking bits and pieces but they're not panicking about getting it wrong. In five or ten years' time, it will be their homegrown interpretation of whatever that genre is.... I think of all the cultures in the world, China will move fastest away from [the current] retro mania."[31] Converse itself is taking this dive into the future, not relying on old credentials to win a new audience. Instead, the brand is taking the time to build the foundation for Chinese to decide what comes next. Converse isn't trying to relive its heyday; instead, it is providing youth with the support and encouragement to create their own.

As they build on existing models, youth look for ways to do more than just copy what has been done. With no responsibility to preserve imported subcultures and a unique cultural context that both impedes and mandates expression outside of the mainstream, youth are creating a new center on the edge.

LOOKING BACK

Youth are increasingly seeking ways to step outside of the mainstream. Although acting as a true individual can mean risking being ostracized or silenced, seeking refuge in a smaller community can provide more options for personal expression and comparative success. Despite being sheltered from developing their own interests until young adulthood, youth are increasingly experimenting with imported subcultures and making moves to create their own. As these renegades seek to define their own mini-societies, they find new freedoms to mash and tweak assumed absolutes to their benefit. Online communities have played a significant role by developing a safe movement away from the mainstream—evolving from a means of anonymous self-expression to creative collaboration zones to emerging subculture guides.

LOOKING FORWARD

This chapter is meant to help you think more deeply about connecting to youth. How could the information be leveraged in these scenarios?

1. How can youth-targeted brands support local subculture development—instead of recycling eras from other countries?
2. How can brands track, connect with, and encourage movements their audience cares about?
3. How can companies provide (online and offline) recognition for youth's contributions?

CHAPTER 7

REBRANDING CHINESENESS: NEW CHINA, NEW IDENTITY

Shang Xia belongs to Chinese culture and belongs, therefore, to the whole world.

—Jiang Qiong'er, Shang Xia's CEO and artistic director, born in 1976[1]

WHEN I ARRANGED TO MEET FRIENDS AT THE LAUNCH party for Shang Xia's first store, I, like most guests, imagined I would see a mini, Chinese-styled Hermès. After all, the legendary French house was financially backing the Chinese brand and was responsible for the media buzz that preceded Shang Xia's launch. When I entered Hong Kong Plaza, on one of Shanghai's primary retail rows, Huaihai Road, I found something smaller and smarter than I had anticipated. The event itself was surprisingly low-key for a luxury brand in China—there were few cameras, no overt celebrity presence, and no over-the-top glitzy floor show. Instead, artisans were demonstrating their crafts, showing how the products were made, and telling the stories behind the design of various clothing, furniture, and fashion and home accessories.

For now at least, Shang Xia is leveraging time and effort to differentiate the brand. Items in the product line are time-intensive commercial works of art. For example, it takes four months to create the jade chain used in one pendant. It takes two Mongolian craftswomen a week to produce a single cashmere garment employing a modified technique previously used to make yurts. Products and processes are imbued with meaning, and even the product mix speaks a new language. Not led by conventional category-driven apparel or home furnishings, its assortment follows a cultural activity. On offer are tea sets, chairs, porcelain dishes, apparel, and jewelry—all relevant to reenvisioning the Chinese tea ceremony.

Besides its vanguard approach to storytelling and product assortment, Shang Xia is an anomaly in many ways. In contrast to other luxury marks, the brand is not aligned with a specific family or personal lineage. The name Shang Xia itself speaks to the brand's unusual mission. Meaning literally "up down" or "topsy-turvy," the concept is a mirror meeting of opposites. Its existence poses a central question about the possibility of luxury coming from a country known for mass-production. Its challenge is to eschew the factory image and elevate traditional Chinese handicrafts to compete in a European-dominated luxury market.

Although its mission is unique, Shang Xia is not going it alone. Its cooperation with Hermès strikes a chord that is hard for many straight-laced nationalists to accept. It raises the question: is a brand backed by a French company too foreign—or not foreign enough? At the very least, Shang Xia is a well-publicized provocateur revealing how notions about China may be reframed in the future.

Shang Xia is part of a breed of innovative Chinese brands brought to life by a new generation of entrepreneurs. Jiang Qiong'er, the 30-something design mastermind behind the brand, has both the local lineage and training abroad to merge points of view from both China and the West.

China has earned a reputation for massive scale manufacturing, but is eager to become known as more than a factory. The next challenge is to reposition from executing someone else's ideas to producing its own. Shang Xia's bold intention is to create products and experiences that match the quality and design of any other luxury product made in the world.

INVENTING MEMORY

Shang Xia started not by introducing new products as most breaking brands do, but by building a contextual foundation. The idea of recent Chinese history fitting into a modern luxury framework had not been established, so Shang Xia took the necessary step back to create a platform for moving forward. Its inaugural exhibit, *Pass It On*, was displayed outside the store and featured a collection of old family photographs and personal souvenirs that were not previously associated with having luxury value. The brand offered a limited-edition of 3000 memory boxes including a 322-page book of vintage personal photos, a model airplane, a classic ring made of tin, crystal beads, a train ticket, red scarf, and a letter from a 21-year-old girl to her younger self. These pedestrian items are by themselves not luxurious; similar tokens can be unearthed in most people's closets. But the original presentation allowed Chinese to feel a sense of common history with the brand and encouraged audiences to reconsider their memories as meaningful and worthy of rediscovery. Each year, the brand aims to create a special cultural object to add to its collection of modern pieces with "found heritage" rooted in China's past. These efforts are helping Chinese to embrace their own indigenous traditions and craftsmanship, helping consumers build contemporary meaning for Chinese traditions. The goal is to give Chinese heritage a sense of prestige, place, and purpose among upwardly mobile consumers. It is no longer just a question of what history outside of China means; Shang Xia is reopening the doors to the past to craft a narrative on a grander scale.

THE CONFIDENCE OF LUXURY

Shang Xia's strategy is a decided step away from what luxury brands have typically presented in the Middle Kingdom. It lacks the flash and conspicuous status that most brands jangle in front of Chinese consumers to get their attention. Its appeal is quiet, and at price points ranging from 180 RMB to 500,000 RMB, it is both accessible and exclusive.

This modesty speaks to upwardly mobile Chinese looking to demonstrate their connoisseurship in a more refined manner. In China, true power is subtle. According to Tom Doctoroff, "As the Chinese consumer becomes wealthier, his relationship with society evolves....The benefit structure has evolved too—from more blatant status projection to more substance-driven. It's always about substance that shines."[2]

Shang Xia's tea ceremony concept is a symbol of traditional Chinese hospitality and ritual that will serve the brand as it moves outside of the Middle Kingdom. The next stop after China? The brand has its eyes on the luxury capital of Paris.[3] But even in planning this move, Shang Xia is not losing sight of the real power consumers. While efforts abroad will introduce Chinese luxury to Europe and may bring in new Western fans, the true value may be in boosting the brand's credibility among Chinese who will appreciate the prestigious outpost.

COMING OUT

Rising levels of consumption have inspired brands from every corner of the world to pack their bags to satiate consumer appetite for the new and different. While foreign brands calculate how to localize, Chinese brands are implementing sophisticated marketing to showcase their origins. More confident in the value of their own culture and inundated with options, consumers are driving the need for both camps to personalize and differentiate. In response, brands are pushing the envelope to uncover how consumption can align with a new Chinese cultural identity.

The real movers and shakers are young Chinese who are leading the way to push past dated assertions to develop more intimate interpretations of Chineseness. In this forward-facing experiment, youth are looking to combine new values and symbols infused with personal meaning. And they are asking brands to do the same.

Although the modern Chinese identity may not be clear yet, the pot is bubbling and original voices are emerging. In this dialogue, Chinese youth have found a platform to judge, broadcast, and fine-tune based on their beliefs.

Playing with what they are, have been, and will be, youth are creating smaller communities separate from the larger conversation of Chineseness. They are reclaiming their own memories, symbols, and icons that are not yet recognized by the world outside. There can no longer be one overarching conversation about Chinese identity; multiple conversations are brewing. The mere existence of this debate signals a change in what the world can expect from China, what Chinese can expect from themselves, and what they will come to expect from brands.

CURATING NEW SYMBOLS

The classic 1920s Chinese dress (the cheongsam or *qi pao*), Beijing opera, Chinese calligraphy, martial arts, and green tea are all traditional emblems that signal Chinese culture. Some of these symbols have maintained their domestic popularity, and some have been exported out of China to take on new incarnations overseas. But as youth come of age, they are mixing new tokens, international concepts, and forgotten memories to reflect fresh ideas about modern Chinese culture within their own communities. They are dipping their toes into the next era of Chinese identity.

Although retro styles have been commonly applied abroad, Chinese have stepped cautiously in bringing up the past. The Cultural Revolution in particular has been an uncomfortable period for reflection, and has, until recently, been skipped over. "Old Chinese" meant prerevolution, and "new Chinese" signaled the postrevolutionary period.

But Chinese youth are leading the way back to repatriate forgotten or ignored elements. By opening the conversation to not only what is Chinese in an old sense or foreign in a modern sense, young people are looking to build a new model. Confident in the value of their own experiences, youth are also looking to connect their personal histories to the larger conversation. They are resurrecting common memories around domestic and international media (television, music, movies, and books) and snagging souvenirs from student life to create a more intimate meeting ground. These youth are paving the way to a new discourse, asking questions about who they are and how they are connected.[4] They are subconsciously stewarding their own version of Chinese identity.

TRANSFORMING THEN TO NOW

The movie *Transformers* was a hit among post-80s generation youth who remember growing up with the television show. The film's combination of nostalgia for childhood and transformation resonated deeply with audiences at a cross roads in their own lives.

Youth were eager to use Transformers iconography to symbolize their kinship with the franchise's theme. The most basic application was Transformers-inspired stickers plastered onto cars, bikes, and scooters. But the revival also inspired more creative and committed do-it-yourself (DIY) efforts. For example, enthusiastic youth in Nanjing built their own Bumblebee replica. Brands followed suit hoping to connect with these now largely white-collar fans. Hewlett-Packard launched an online campaign empowering daring youth to "Be Your Own Transformer," and China Construction Bank issued a Transformers credit card.[5]

GRADUATING SYMBOLS

Feeling increasing pressure from society to perform as they enter adulthood, young people are looking back to childhood memories in search of refuge. For many, the most universal point of commonality is student life. This formative time bonded lonely single kids to schoolmates, who later would become like a second family. More often than not, the post-80s are still linked with alumni on social networking sites and may even participate in regular reunions to relive old memories and keep in touch with current happenings.

But it is not just the personal friendships that keep them connected. Post-80s generation youth are bonded by characters and symbols from their school days. One example of such characters' revival is Li Lei and Han Meimei, two well-known figures from English-language textbooks. A play and online song, "Li Lei and Han Meimei," allowed youth to speculate about what could have become of these childhood characters. Giordano, a Hong Kong-based fashion brand, released a limited edition T-shirt with a graphic of the characters to feed young consumers' appetite for the past. Revived enthusiasm for Li Lei and Han Meimei has opened the door for other period characters such as Black Cat Sergeant (aka Hei Mao Jing Zhang) and Calabash Boys (aka Hu Lu Wa) to return to popularity again.[6]

The desire of the post-80s to revisit their childhoods has even evolved into commercial spaces dedicated to recreating a shared memory. A hot pot restaurant in Beijing's Xicheng district is a meeting place for a generation keen on reliving its past. Upon walking through a gate (much like they would at school), patrons step into an environment designed to stimulate nostalgia. To enter, customers must present ID cards proving that they are members of the post-80s generation. They receive their schedule—study hall from 5:30 to 7:00 p.m., Chinese language class from 7:15 to 8:45 p.m., History from 9:00 to 10:30 p.m.—and are seated at desks fashioned as tables to enjoy a meal with friends. Chalkboards line the front and back of the classroom-styled dining room, and textbooks serve as table decorations.[7] By looking back into their own recent past, young Chinese are remembering common ground and making room for past sentiment to develop commercial value.

My Party

At two years old, Huang Yibo showed an interest in watching state-run China Central Television (CCTV) evening news. When he could read, this wunderkind turned to the official news source, *People's Daily*, to get information. At 13 years old, Huang became an Internet sensation.

As a top-ranking student in the Young Pioneers of China (a primary and middle school branch of the Communist Youth League), photos of Huang performing good deeds were published online to promote the group's activities. Initially, Huang's earnest, adult-like expression drew applause for its approximation to older party members. But accolades quickly turned to criticism when netizens noticed a very big fashion faux pas. In these photos, young Huang was pictured wearing a red scarf and a five-stripe badge—a two-stripe departure from the organization's charter. It was common knowledge that the highest-ranking leaders were limited to three stripes. But this was not the case in Huang's hometown of Wuhan. A special sub-branch of Young Pioneers had been established and decided to go rogue, bestowing the honor of two additional stripes on its young stars.

When youth first noticed the serious-looking teen sporting additional stripes, there was much ado about the chubby-faced Young Pioneer. Many suggested he was acting as a propaganda tool of the Chinese Communist Party.[8]

The incident sparked a fashion trend of five- (and even seven-) striped T-shirts and armbands, which made the rounds among trendy youth eager to get in on the joke. One Taobao shop, calling itself "Five Stripes Shopping Street," expanded the graphic's application to everything from sneakers to sofa covers.[9]

Wearing the overloaded badge signaled a mocking of little Huang and the old system that supported his rise to fame. By sporting a five-star badge of their own volition (self-designated and for sale), youth were poking fun at an old version of state-regulated success. In repossessing this celebrated symbol, they were sending a sarcastic but defiant message that they were the new up-and-comers. They too were superstars who could achieve more than anyone imagined possible—but they would do it in their own way, following their own rules.

OUTFITTING ROCK REBELS

The red neckerchief is ubiquitous in student uniforms, and is the only accessory that is standardized for members of the Communist Youth League. In fact, the official group is referred to simply as the "Red Scarves." Often bestowed the first time a student pledges allegiance to the Communist Party, the scarf is tied emblematically by an existing member onto a fresh inductee.

The scarf took a rebellious turn in 1994 when renegade rocker, He Yong, adopted the look.[10] He paired it with a blue-striped sailor shirt, a statement that had revolutionary undertones. The striped shirt, worn by sailors for decades as an undershirt, became a symbol of fashion rebellion during the Cultural Revolution. While most young people stuck to the uniform of black, white, grey, and dark blue, a small number of daring rule-breakers co-opted the shirts. At the time, although the striped shirt was readily available, few chose to brave being in the minority.[11] When He Yong took the stage in this look, he recreated the redirected the significance of the red scarf and striped shirt and gave China's new breed of rockers a fitting

Figure 7.1 A mannequin wearing a bunny mask, sailor-striped shirt and red scarf. Photo by Wang Yipeng

uniform. Back in fashion again, these tokens have been resurrected by contemporary alternative culture and are common sights today at music festivals and other non-mainstream group hang-outs.[12]

FASHIONABLY CORRECT

Today, counterculturalists are more fashion minded than politically motivated. Real estate companies, nightclubs, and restaurants have used old propaganda-style communications to grab youth's attention. Although employing Mao's image in a literal way carries heavy legal and social implications, small shops have co-opted his likeness to sell outside the mainstream. Mao Livehouse, a live music venue with locations in Shanghai and Beijing, references the chairman in its brand name and visual identity. The club's logo skirts the line with a cheeky reference to the outline of Mao's head.

Without much regard for politics, totems have been plucked and repackaged for modern consumption. For youth, embracing symbols from the Cultural Revolution is just part of the hunt for new experiences and a refreshed nationalism.

Figure 7.2   Mao Livehouse's logo subtly references Chairman Mao. Photo by Fan Yiying

LEARNING FROM LEI FENG

Lei Feng, a young orphaned soldier, was transformed into a mascot of the Cultural Revolution after his death in 1962. He was packaged as an icon to sell the values of selflessness, modesty, and dedication. In reverence, his birthplace changed its name to Leifeng, and a national holiday was entered into the books (March 5 is celebrated as "Learn From Lei Feng Day").

To pass on this righteous icon to modern youth, a video game called *Learn from Lei Feng Online* was developed by Shanda Interactive Entertainment, a NASDAQ-listed Chinese software company. Although the medium is modern, the game is classic political training; the ultimate goal is to get Mao's autograph.[13] For most young Chinese, old school politics (even when couched in entertainment) is unappealing. Pushing fashion not politics, Li Ning took a different approach that proved more popular with youth. The brand's execution better understood why and how retro symbols were important to modern consumers. The Lei Feng 001, a modified replica shoe, was neatly packaged in a vintage-style Army bag.

Figure 7.3 Classic Chinese sneaker brand Feiyue is reborn. Photo by Toni Young

A modification was made available only to Li Ning employees; the embroidered phrase was changed from "to serve the people" to a tongue-in-cheek interoffice memo "to serve Li Ning."[14] Playing with icons updated their relevance among young audiences in a way that a straight-faced game never could.

WHO OWNS NATIONAL STYLE?

When modern sneaker culture met up with classic Chinese revolutionary-era athletic shoes, a new movement was given a life all its own. The brand Feiyue was the focus of the trend, an exciting and exotic export for international sneaker fans to uncover and a surprising hero for China to rediscover. Feiyue was born in Shanghai in 1931 and became the "go-to" national sneaker brand, worn by workers, athletes, and politicians. The simple shoe worked for Chinese—until it was upstaged by the style, marketing, and status imported by foreign sports brands such as Nike and Adidas.

Today, few brand stories can match the twists and turns that Feiyue has taken since the mid-2000s. Like Shang Xia, its story poses questions about national identity against a still-evolving narrative on the subject. It speaks to how Chinese symbols are affected by international exposure and gives an example of how multiple interpretations can coexist.

The challenge started in Shanghai in 2005, when French sneaker fan Patrice Bastian was struck by the unique look of a pair of Feiyue. Bastian probably found them in a local family-run odds-and-ends shop parked beside mops and luggage. Has-been shoes being sold for around 15–30 RMB, Feiyue sneakers seemed in no shape to contend with global brands for a spot in trendy youth's closets. But Bastian saw potential in the simple shoe with a retro look and determined to find a new home for the discarded classic in France. Bastian and his team modified the sneaker, fattening the shoe's sole and giving it a thicker canvas. Their modifications transformed Feiyue from a classic martial-arts shoe into a modern, general-purpose lifestyle kick. The makeover unveiled a fresh perspective on quality and design. Feiyue debuted in France with an updated mold, new color combinations, and a much more boutique-friendly price of about 50 Euro.

The reborn Feiyue's reputation took off when actor Orlando Bloom was caught on film sporting a pair. When news traveled back to China that the discarded sneaker brand had found a hip audience abroad, trendy young Chinese were surprised—and flattered.[15] China's cool, youth-oriented magazines and websites became aware of the revival and helped build a local audience for the brand. Fashion-conscious kids eagerly picked up the trend that had the magic combination of Chinese roots and foreign approval.

In China, Feiyue has helped to push retro Chinese cool forward. While corner stores still sell Feiyue shoes (both real and fake versions), today they are also sold online and in specialty boutiques. These new distribution channels cater to shoppers who want a retail environment that more closely matches the brand's image.

Meanwhile, in France, Feiyue is taking root in its adopted home and even embarking on collaborations with other brands. The French children's concept store Bonton and Feiyue created a special limited-edition version of the Delta Mid Kid shoe. The shoes, available in red or blue, have the words Feiyue ♥ Bonton embroidered on the tongue. The insoles are printed with "keep your dreams" and "keep your smile," certainly not values that most Chinese youth experienced in their own childhoods. It seems the brand has left the nest so to speak, finding a completely new life and mission away from home.

It is hard to imagine a more dynamic trajectory. Two fraternal twins have come from Feiyue, each with its own design, distribution, price point, and citizenship. One has a very Europeanized identity outside of China, and another struts a fresh nationalism inside the Middle Kingdom. The elasticity of Feiyue's story provides food for thought about the nature, meaning, and application of Chinese identity.

But this is not the end of the story. While Chinese youth repatriated the brand and foreign sneaker enthusiasts enjoyed raising the new baby, yet another sibling emerged. In 2009, a Belgian brother and sister team set out to sell the original version of Feiyue shoes outside of China. Although prohibited from using the Feiyue name, they christened the old design Sudu, meaning "speed addict." The brand launched with three color waves, then added five more—mindful not to change the sole and shape, key differentiators from its French cousin.

In the mainland where ideas and rules are flexible, all three brands (the Chinese Feiyue, the French Feiyue, and Belgian Sudu) are available, often displayed right next to each other, with other historical brands yet to be publicized. They can be bought in their authentic branded form and also found, perhaps more readily, as fakes.

Transporting Cool

Feiyue is not the only brand exploring how to modernize without losing its national identity. Forever bicycle brand (aka Yongjiu) was another classic brand that fell out of favor until 23-year-old Chen Shan (the son of the chairman of the brand's parent company) took over. Chen, with help from a design team with international experience, created the sub-brand Forever C with an updated product line and marketing. Vintage-style 1970s and 1980s models were brought back to life with bright pastel colors and named after streets in hip Chinese cities. But unlike many other contemporary, youth-led Chinese brands, Forever C is about more than short-term design tricks. It is a brand leveraging its roots to appeal to a new audience. Forever C has steered the conversation from transportation to lifestyle. It communicates its brand values as "Classic, Chic Life, Clean, and China."[16]

The parent company has also launched a bicycle rental scheme with outposts in popular spots, allowing riders to pick up and drop off as needed. Like other similar programs in Europe and Hangzhou, Forever C's Shanghai program is a step forward in thinking about how bicycles can find a place in China's booming car culture.

Hyping at Home

Although foreign competitors initially imported prestige, mainland consumers have become more conscious nationalist consumers.

Buying local is no longer seen as just an issue of not having the money or the exposure to buy foreign; rather, it is gaining respect as an educated choice. Movements have bubbled up that support Chinese brands for what they mean to the nation and its people. Frank Chen, the former chief executive officer of Interbrand China, suggests that nationalism is a result of both government intervention and the population's growing self-confidence. "People are proud of themselves and of the GDP miracle we created. This is why people now prefer—and are more involved in—local brands. This nationalism is its own kind of culture."[17] This pride in local consumption pushes a cycle forward that helps to support more innovative products, better brands, and a revised image for China as more than a manufacturer.

Nationalism has a social value that has spread among consumers. The fashionable social networking site Douban, for instance, hosts more than a hundred groups organized around supporting national brands. Memberships range from single digits to over fifty thousand, and group names usually include the words "national brands," such as "Classic Nationals Brands Group," "Supporting National Brands Group," and "We All Love National Brands Group." Most posts share positive personal experiences that users have had with local options.

While these examples are loosely organized and primarily social, other online efforts have taken a more dedicated stance toward promoting national brands. iWallChina is a website that aims to promote domestic brand consumption by sharing information and allowing users to vote for their favorites. The site divides products into three categories: "National brands in my heart" (currently successful Chinese brands), "Classic brands for nostalgia" (brands that have the lineage but may have fallen out of favor), and the "The top 20 money-saving Chinese brands" (bargain brands). The site is the brainchild of an ambitious 20-something who is hoping to turn a profit and help cultivate preferences for local offerings.[18]

In promoting domestic brands, a political "us versus them" conversation is to be expected, but a new breed of nationalistic cheerleader is betting that substance is ready to meet style. Hung Huang, the chief executive of China Interactive Media Group, opened Brand

New China (BNC) in Beijing's Sanlitun Village with a purpose: to help build a stylish platform for developing local fashion designers. The popular figure is loaning her reputation to help push these brands forward, and her efforts may pay off in more ways than one. First, as local design becomes more popular, BNC will become an important "go-to" outlet. Second, as the next generation of local brands becomes more viable, they will be able to spend on advertising in Hung's magazine *iLOOK*. More shops like BNC have opened in China's higher-tier cities, betting that Chinese identity is ready for a fashionable makeover.[19]

While consumers a few years ago may have lacked the confidence to choose national brands, China's rise as a superpower has made going local more appealing. Chen notes the about-face in perception: "Now China is one of the best nations in the world.... If I [as a trendy person] use this product, I don't lose face. But ten years ago, people didn't have that kind of confidence. If I used local brands, it meant I was poor."[20] This association that local brands were a lesser option in terms of quality and cost has changed drastically in the last decade as consumers have gained confidence and local companies have dared to push into high-end and luxury categories.

LOOKING IN FROM THE OUTSIDE

When the Ralph Lauren team got down to designing its Fall/Winter 2011 collection, China was front and center. Ralph Lauren himself had taken his first trip to the Middle Kingdom and had come back with China clearly on his mind. With plans to open the brand's first company-owned stores in the mainland, Ralph Lauren was making an aggressive push to align itself with increasingly powerful Chinese consumers. In its strategy and design, the brand reflected its embrace of China as an epicenter and Consumers as the new movers and shakers.

When the collection went down the runway, the audience saw an updated version of an American classic. The show was a bold departure from previous collections and a far cry from the near-literal draping of the American flag that the Polo Ralph Lauren line was once known for. The new Ralph Lauren collection showcased classic Chinese references, including mandarin collars, dragons, and embroidery. Like earlier Americana collections, the ode was by no means subtle; jade jewelry swung against models on the catwalk to the tune of David Bowie's "China Girl." The show opened with Chinese model He Sui (aka Sui He) followed by other Chinese walkers behind her, including Liu Wen, Ma Jing (aka Jing Ma), and Xi Mengyao (aka Ming Xi).

When Karl Lagerfeld made history using the Great Wall as the world's longest runway in 2007, he was commenting on more than just the length of the catwalk. He was making a striking move to conquer barriers and conquer the Middle Kingdom. Other foreign brands had come before and surely many more will follow in trying to stake their claim.

What these examples demonstrate are attempts by foreigners to customize for and cater to the world's most promising market. But modern Chinese are not looking for an easy, superficial version of China to be reflected back to them; they are looking for inspirational ideas and relevant values. To be memorable and differentiate themselves, brands must thoughtfully link their own core values to corresponding tenets of Chinese culture. This requires more than generic decoration; it demands that brands thoughtfully consider who they are and how their values can connect with specific symbols and clear ideas.

THE CHINESE SUIT

As domestic brands have become more competitive and Chinese consumers more nationalistic, international brands have been forced to do more than just peacock their tried and true identities in the market. They have had to localize. Using the color red to court Chinese consumers has become almost a standard (perhaps clichéd) practice for foreign brands hoping to show their China friendliness. I call this donning the "Chinese suit." While superficial decorations were expected in the first stage, the next phase of localization demands that foreign brands and Chinese symbols relate and add value to each other.

In many cases, the Chinese calendar has been borrowed by brands to launch special editions. Nike Air Jordan 2011 Year of the Rabbit is one of the more intricately designed examples. The box and shoes themselves are red and gold, reminiscent of the traditional *hong bao,* a red envelope containing money given at holidays. Graphics mix Air Jordan brand elements with Chinese references; the box's cherry blossom border uses the word "Air" as petals and repeats Michael Jordan's Chicago Bulls' jersey number 23 in the design. The product's packaging makes a statement that could be interpreted as being directed at the consumer, or the brand itself: "Say goodbye to the past and welcome the future."

Microsoft has played with the Chinese zodiac by creating a mouse for the Lunar New Year that looks like it is made from blue and white (also available in red and white) Chinese porcelain. These examples show how contemporary brands can incorporate traditional elements of Chinese culture into modern products, but few are more than superficial executions. The real question is how brands can partner with Chinese symbols to distinguish themselves.

BUILDING BRAND HERITAGE

As brands develop their own histories in the Middle Kingdom, many are eager to leverage their accomplishment in consumer-facing ways. Companies often celebrate the anniversary of their launch in China as a way to engage on a different level with consumers. Chloé for example, celebrated its fifth year in the market with a limited edition Marcie sold only in China. The red leather bag announced the event on a bronze plate, "China 5th Anniversary Limited Edition." Faded metal accents gave the new product an aged look and feel.

Porsche also released a limited edition 911 Turbo S for its tenth anniversary. Unlike Chloé, Porsche was not looking to communicate heritage; its message was about flash—the body was metallic gold, after all. Inside, the glove compartment's plaque commemorated the company's tenth anniversary in simple terms: "Porsche China 2001–2011." Producing these kinds of limited-edition anniversary products helps brands develop their own local heritage in

China but also serves as a potent reminder of the real infancy of the market.

LOCALIZING WITHOUT LOSING OUT

Localization is a delicate balance between leveraging brand values and catering to a new locale. In the Middle Kingdom, brand rules often do not correspond to those that exist outside. Chinese consumers have been known to embrace differences that consumers with a longer history with brands might outright refuse. One poignant example of localization operating outside of current global branding principles is the well-reported case of the red Pepsi can. Pepsi tipped its hat to China in 2008, celebrating national athletes in the upcoming Olympics by turning its cans from iconic blue to red. When consumers went into stores to grab their favorite cola, they were met with two options: Coke and Pepsi, both dressed in red and sporting images of Chinese athletes.[21] While brand strategists in the West may have gasped, consumers did not seem to confuse the promotion with the brand. In fact, Pepsi sales in China saw a bump. As Tim Minges, the chairman of PepsiCo China, explains, "The red can was about noise value...It's always been in our PepsiCo mojo to be a little bit edgy because that's what youth expect. They don't want you to be stodgy or predictable. They want you to have a little bit of edge and the red can was just that, it was all about noise value."[22]

The idea of "going red" is an obvious play for brands looking to cater to the Chinese market. Apple employees traded in their customary blue T-shirts for red ones to celebrate store openings in Shanghai. But Apple went a step further by reconstructing its brand message. The first five thousand shoppers received free T-shirts heralding, "designed in California, made for China." In this revised slogan, Apple slyly changed the conversation from local manufacturing to American design, especially for China. They backed up the claim with limited-edition products sold only in Shanghai stores. Laptop sleeves and iPhone cases decorated with pop graphics of the Oriental Pearl Tower, Shanghai's most recognizable and futuristic structure, flew off the shelves.

LEVERAGING "SEE AND BE SEEN"

Perhaps the most eye-catching examples of localization to date come from food and beverage brands. Häagen-Dazs went way beyond the category's original footprint when it launched its retail presence in China. While it may have done so out of necessity (the price point for freezer hard-packs was too high to generate necessary volume), General Mills' decision to make ice cream a dine-in experience was a smart capitalization on consumers' desire to "see and be seen." The company chose restaurant locations to attract young couples and business people looking for a more sophisticated (and public) atmosphere for meetings. When customers move past the line of other waiting patrons (often queued neatly behind a ceremonious red rope) to be seated by the hostess, they are treated to a feeling of exclusivity. Patrons can enjoy traditional Häagen-Dazs favorites or indulge in a Chinese-inspired hot-pot concept product. The execution marries traditional culture (hot pot), new Chinese values ("see and be seen"), and the Häagen-Dazs brand image (indulgence) in a memorable and differentiated way.

Figure 7.4   Lay's chips localized flavors. Photo by Toni Young

Going Native

Lay's potato chips have so embraced the Chinese palate that youth I interviewed in 2007 mistook Lay's for a domestic brand. Their confusion is a compliment to the brand's efforts to achieve local relevance. In many ways, Lay's has localized enough in China to warrant a new degree of hybrid nationality. As the brand continues on its journey to increase its share of the booming packaged food industry in China, it balances the demands of the market and its own brand value in ways it never would—or could—on the outside. As Minges explains, "It's this recognition that China is a different market and if you're going to be locally relevant, you really do need to be in China, with China, and for China."[23] The company's willingness to experiment and to lead with innovations specifically for the market has surely helped Lay's become China's largest snack brand.

In 1994, Lay's (its Mandarin name means "happy things") moved into China with Cheetos and followed with Lay's potato chips in flavors that mirrored the brand's nationality, including classic American, barbecue, and sour cream and onion. At that time, international brands were highly aspirational, and playing up an American passport was an obvious advantage. But as the shimmer of foreign novelty diminished among consumers, Lay's recognized that to enhance its position, the brand would need to localize.

The next phase in Lay's development marked a departure in palate, adding flavors inspired by famous Chinese dishes. They did well, but they only engaged with existing chip fans. To penetrate deeper, Lay's needed to understand why some consumers were avoiding the chip aisle all together. Leveraging consumer research, Lay's realized that chips were being rejected for their health value—in a Chinese sense.

Unlike Westerners' preoccupation with trans fats and carbohydrates, Chinese are influenced by traditional Chinese medicine (TCM) and traditional Chinese ingredients (TCI). In Chinese culture, foods are a key means of achieving and maintaining equilibrium. Relationships with food and eating patterns are largely informed by a food's value in creating balance with other foods, individual health concerns, and the environment. Minges explains, "In the West, consumers live whatever lifestyle they want, they eat what they want and fall back on medicines to intervene in health. In China, people eat for health. Chinese believe it's better to be cured by food than by medicine, which explains why TCM and TCI—remain so prevalent today—even with youth.... It's beyond grandmother's logic or kitchen logic, it is ingrained so it's not just about selling our global range of products, they need to be locally relevant."[24]

Eating foods that are seen to have heating or cooling properties is an innate part of this balance. Lay's undertook a consumer investigation, in which the brand found that chips were perceived to have a heating property. While this worked to Lay's advantage in cooler seasons, the perception presented a block for chip consumption in the summer. Based on this insight, Lay's opened a new door and launched a cooling line in 2003. The first flavor incarnation was lemon, but the follow-up, cucumber, in 2004, was the real breakthrough. Other flavors with cooling properties followed, including little tomato and lemon tea. From a packaging design perspective, consumers can easily spot the white matte bag with pastel accents; it is an obvious move away from the glossy, primary colors standard in the category. The heating line also got a makeover of its own, adding hyper-hot flavors such as numb and spicy and hot-and-sour fish soup. Although available year round, the cooling chips are emphasized in summer months, while heating chips take their turn when the weather cools.

Adding to its growing flavor repertoire, the brand stepped away from the potato in 2011. Wheat and rice chips were launched with locally relevant flavors like black sesame and seaweed. To deliver the brand to consumers at a lower price point, Lay's has since used a wheat pellet base to create a line that is less expensive than other varieties.

Another barrier that Lay's encountered in China was a cultural bias against snacking in public or on the go. To work with (not against) cultural behaviors, Lay's adapted its packaging to encourage clean and easy "sneaky" snacking. Bite-sized chips were delivered in a more convenient, resealable canister that holds the chips in a tray for easy, no-mess grabbing and storage.

For many consumer brands, China is clearly the most dynamic market. To secure its place, Lay's is putting aside assumptions about how it has been successful in the past to discover how it will be successful in the future. In the brand's journey, it has listened to consumers' opinions about how they eat, what they eat, and who they want feeding them.

On its way, Lay's has held onto its roots, but not tightly. It has remained flexible and open-minded about the evolution of its business in the mainland. China has been a daring experiment; it is the only country in the world where Lay's operates as an umbrella brand. This distinct choice allows Lay's to leverage its reputation against multiple products and help control challenges posed by costs, competition, and distribution. Although this overarching strategy might be counterintuitive outside, it works in China, where consumer expectations demand constant innovation and flexibility.

Lay's strategy embraces Chinese palates, consumers' developing wallets, and attitudes about health and balance with open arms. As Minges points out, "The Chinese consumer market is really only a single generation old. It was not that long ago that food coupons, rations and friendship stores were the consumer economy in China. So this whole idea of marketing and consumption is very, very new and the rules are yet to be written.... Who knows what's going to evolve from it? But you have to be here, you have to be agile and you have to be risk taking. If you can do that, you can succeed. But you'll have to play by local rules."[25] This sage advice can be applied across categories and price points.

REVERSING CURRENTS

The idea of localization and innovation for China becomes critical as consumers gain confidence in preferring domestic alternatives and as Chinese brands becoming increasingly competitive. In 2009, research and consulting firm Frost & Sullivan reported that, for the first time, a domestic sports brand's sales had beat out a global brand.[26] After the buzz of the Olympics subsided, Nike had managed to maintain its #1 spot, but Li Ning had jumped to overtake Adidas's #2 position. This had implications for Adidas and Li Ning—and also for Nike, which had a new challenger nipping at its sporty heels. But the real eye-opener in this finding was that a new paradigm was possible; it was no longer a foregone conclusion that Chinese consumers would secure global players' position at the top and relegate domestic brands to the bottom.

For global brands in China, the question of localization is complicated by local brands' moving up the value chain. While global brands look to expand their reach from tier-one entry points into lower-tier markets, lower-tier players are implementing the marketing strategies that they have learned from global players to gain new ground. Regional brands from Fujian province (known as the center of China's sports brands) are looking to make big moves. Brands like 361 Degrees, Xtep, and Erke have leveraged multinational advertising agencies and sponsored teams and events outside of China to enhance their image. Anta has not only signed Kevin Garnett, but it has also acquired the rights to the Fila brand to help pump up the company's higher-end strategy.

While lower-tier brands move into higher-tier cities, many global competitors are concentrating their efforts to push further in. Adidas, for example, has stated that it will add more than 2,500 stores by 2015 to its lower-tier presence. Adidas' teen-focused casual line NEO is being sold at a fraction of the price of the brand's other lines. For now, Nike does not embrace the philosophy of meeting consumers where they are at; it sees its place squarely as an aspirational brand in the Middle Kingdom.[27]

CHINESE SPORTINESS

While working up a sweat at the gym recently, I flipped on Channel Young to watch some youth-targeted television. The discussion topic was how to exercise while sitting in front of a computer. The hosts were not building up a sweat, and there was no need for them to change out of office attire to work out. No one was aspiring in any shape or form to become an "athlete"; they were simply incorporating stretches into their sedentary lifestyle.

The show reminded me of numerous conversations I have had with global sports brands and their agencies about weak sports participation in China. While there are, of course, some moderate to hardcore athletes, there are many more lifestyle enthusiasts. These youth will happily consume parts of the culture, but certainly not the bits that require a lot of commitment or physical effort. To connect with these consumers, brands are having to redefine their message and build new products to help youth explore their sport-ish sides. For now, the game is not about performance. The ratio of fashion/lifestyle consumers to sports enthusiasts is forcing a reconceptualization of what a sports brand can be in the mainland.

Li Ning sees this disconnect between Western and Chinese attitudes about sports as a competitive advantage. The brand recognizes that sport in China is not as aggressive or individualistic as it is in the West, and it aims to present a thinking man's approach that incorporates mind and body. As Frank Chen, the chief marketing officer of Li Ning, explains, "[Sport in China] is not about the brute force like it is in the West. . . . Chinese wisdom, it's all about mind and body, agility, balance, and precision. This is the point of difference between Li Ning and global competitors; nobody can own that better than an Asian brand."[28] And perhaps no Chinese brand can own that better than Li Ning, whose founder was China's first modern sports hero, bringing home China's first gold medal from the 1984 Olympics.

Beyond differentiating its expression of sports, Li Ning has also reconsidered the motivation for youth to participate. Unlike global competitors that present athletics as an idealized release mechanism disengaged from the demands of everyday life, Li Ning's ethos translates the value of athletics into the classroom and workplace. As Chen posits, "Participating in sports, there are certain things you can apply to daily life—teamwork, discipline, respect for authority. These are the things that allow you to change who you are as a person. . . . by participating in sports, these attributes that you learn can apply to your studies."[29] For Chen, the role of sports in China is not as a diversion or a release, but rather acts as a friendly tutor to help young people get ahead.

Despite having a clearly differentiated point of view, Li Ning knows that sports culture is evolving in China and is hedging its bets. To remain flexible in an immature market, it has cobbled together strategies against multiple scenarios. In addition to its seven thousand or so Li Ning retail stores, its parent company also distributes products under the Z-DO brand to hypermarkets. To develop a specialty offering, Li Ning acquired the Chinese table tennis brand Double Happiness. Additionally, it entered into an exclusive 20-year licensing agreement to distribute and sell products from the Italian sports fashion brand Lotto in China.[30] Across these channels, the brand is hoping to provide coverage for any direction youth may want to move.

To help it stand up against global giants, homegrown favorite Li Ning has instigated a retail makeover. The design strategy, led by Portland, Oregon, shop Ziba, aimed to help the brand differentiate and compete. Choosing Ziba was not haphazard. Surely, Li Ning hoped that being from Nike's hometown would allow the agency to channel some of Nike's magic. Ziba's retail recommendations for Li Ning were thoughtful and multidimensional. Inspired by the traditional Chinese garden, store designs also incorporated icons from gymnasiums to reference the brand founder's own history as a gymnast.[31] The result is a mix that is at once cool enough for the category, steeped in traditional Chinese culture, and personal to the brand. The new in-store experience (although not rolled out to all doors) is more competitive with global brands' storytelling than consumers have been trained to expect from a local brand.

But the formula is not an investment meant only for the Chinese market; Li Ning's retail makeover, revised logo, and tag line are being used globally to represent the "ready for prime time" version of the brand. Besides developing its marketing and design, Li Ning has spent years accumulating the necessary star power to position itself as an up-and-coming global sports leader outside of China. The brand has beefed up connections to international teams and athletes by outfitting Spain's Olympic athletes in 2008 and sponsoring teams such as the Swedish and Argentine national basketball teams, American table tennis team, and Spanish soccer club Sevilla FC.

MOVING ON OUT

Cracking the US market would perhaps be Li Ning's biggest coup, with aftershocks that would undoubtedly benefit the brand's reputation in other international markets, but especially in China. To this end, the brand has already accumulated a roster of sponsored American athletes such as Shaquille O'Neal, Damon Jones, Chuck Hayes, and Baron Davis. Taking its message on the road, the mark was also associated with the NBA Jam Van tour.[32]

To stand apart in America, Li Ning is pushing its Chinese heritage front and center as a key differentiator. Heralding its arrival, Li Ning launched a tongue-in-cheek commercial. The focal point of the spot is two customs officers who cannot believe such cool kicks with great dunk-nology could come from China.

The store's Portland, Oregon, flagship opening event had a mix of global, local, and Chinese dignitaries, including Baron Davis and Portland's mayor, as well as a supply of Chinese beer—but the brand is looking for more than one good night. The current product mix offers badminton, table tennis, kung fu, and taichi gear alongside the requisite selection of basketball-related and limited-edition, athlete-inspired merchandise.[33] But, like foreign brands in China, Li Ning is acting on an awareness that localization is critical to court consumers in the new territory. It has already produced running shoes specifically for the US market. Hiring more US-focused designers to deliver products specifically for American body types and tastes is slated next. Chen is optimistic about the brand's move into the American market and suggests "[US consumers] are open; they welcome something new. You have to tell them who you are and what you represent and how you connect emotionally with what their values and priorities are in life."[34] This counsel could be equally applied to foreign brands in China.

Crossing Cultural Assumptions

As China gains power and platform, Chinese culture is finding the confidence and audience necessary to add to larger conversations taking place inside and outside the mainland. Its influence is bound to inspire new conceptions as acceptance of the value of Chinese culture ticks upward. Both at home and abroad, Chinese are confidently speaking up to reimagine sport, leisure, and lifestyle.

As cultural icons have crisscrossed borders, they have led a new wave of third-culture phenomena and attracted both fans and cocreators. As part of this movement, Chinese sports are finding new homes and incarnations in the United States. Portland, Oregon, for example, now hosts a badminton club, and table tennis is getting a hip makeover in New York City. American actress Susan Sarandon, co-owner of Manhattan table tennis club "SPiN," brought an Americanized understanding of the sport back to the mainland. Her US-based team took part in a friendly match in Shanghai as part of the Volkswagen 2011 China versus World Team Challenge table tennis tournament. The match marked the growing internationalism of the sport but also showcased a new interpretation of a local classic. For Chinese, table tennis was a leisure activity as well as a highly competitive sport. For Americans, leisure clearly led the sport. The two camps mingled different interpretations—but there was no need to determine whether there was a right or wrong approach. Increasingly, Chinese culture is finding multiple expressions and adaptations, adding value to consumers both at home and abroad.

Looking Back

As mainland consumers become more confident, they are increasingly embracing symbols of Chineseness. Youth are not only celebrating the past, they are handpicking indicators to design a more modern and intimate nationalism. Moving swiftly away from the idea that foreign brands are innately better, they are recasting local brands as stylish and relevant choices. Equally, foreign brands are pushing for greater local relevance. As Chinese brands move outside the Middle Kingdom, they will export their new and improved Chineseness—backed by the lessons of flexibility, efficiency, and constant evolution that they have mastered at home.

LOOKING FORWARD

This chapter is meant to help you think more deeply about connecting to youth. How could the information be leveraged in these scenarios?

1. How can brand values and new symbols of Chinese identity be combined for mutual benefit?
2. How can barriers to adoption be recast as opportunities for localization?
3. What can foreign brands learn from local competitors?

NOTES

INTRODUCTION

1. "Pan Ni De Yi Shu Shao Nv Su Zi Zi: Zai Wo De Shen Shang Xie Xia Ni Men Zi Ji" [Rebellious artsy girl Su Zizi: express yourself on my body], *Legal Weekly*, May 5, 2011, accessed May 5, 2011, http://www.chinanews.com/cul/2011/05-05/3017601.shtml

2. "Su Zi Zi Yi Shu Zhan Zheng Yi Sheng Zhong Kai Mu Tang Jia Li Peng Chang" [Su Zizi art exhibition opens to controversy], *Chinanews.com*, April 28, 2011, accessed April 28, 2011, http://www.chinanews.com/life/2011/04-28/3004265.shtml

3. "Su Zi Zi Yi Shu Zhan Zheng Yi Sheng Zhong Kai Mu Tang Jia Li Peng Chang" [Su Zizi art exhibition opens to controversy].

1 THE NEW (R)EVOLUTIONARIES: THE POST-70s, POST-80s, AND POST-90s GENERATIONS

1. "Han Han: 80 Hou Ya Li Zui Da" [Han Han: post-80s has the most pressures], *Today Morning Express*, April 3, 2010, http://news.163.com/10/0403/05/63ASJGQJ000146BB.html, accessed April 3, 2010

2. David Hole, Le Zhong, and Jeff Schwartz, "Talking about Whose Generation?" *Deloitte Review*, no. 6, 2010, accessed November 21, 2011, http://www.deloitte.com/view/en_US/us/Insights/Browse-by-Content-Type/deloitte-review/5d6e2bb18ef26210VgnVCM100000ba42f00aRCRD.htm

3. FengKe, "Zai Qu Zhi Yuan Zhe 80% Shi 80 Hou: Xing Dong Zheng Ming Bu Shi 'Kua Diao De Yi Dai'" [Eighty percent of the Wenchuan earthquake volunteers are post-80s: they are not the Beat generation], *Farmers' Daily*, June 13, 2008, accessed June 13, 2008, http://news.xinhuanet.com/society/2008-06/13/content_8361571.htm

4. "The War between Post-80s and Post-90s in China." *Shanghai Daily*, July 8, 2008, accessed July 8, 2008, http://www.chinadaily.com.cn/china/2008-07/08/content_6827911_2.htm

5. "Fei Zhu Liu Chao Ji Xin Wen Lian Bo" [Non-Mainstream super news], *Tudou.com,* July 15, 2011, accessed July 15, 2011, http://www.tudou.com/programs/view/6OTWdNCzB-0/

6. Farrer, James, *Opening Up: Youth Sex Culture and Market Reform in Shanghai* (Chicago: The University of Chicago Press, 2002).

7. Telephone interview with James Farrer, June 22, 2011.

8. Valerie Blanco and Ellen Feberwee, *In China, My Name Is,* (New York: Mark Batty Publisher, 2009).

9. "Shanghai Stock Exchange," *China Daily,* October 17, 2006, accessed October 17, 2006, http://www.chinadaily.com.cn/bizchina/2006-10/17/content_791456.htm

10. Sun Zhenyu, "Joining WTO Was a Positive Move," *China Daily,* June 1, 2011, accessed June 1, 2001, http://www.chinadaily.com.cn/cndy/2011-06/01/content_12619259.htm

11. "Challenges and Opportunities," *Department of Finance Canada,* accessed September 1, 2011, http://www.fin.gc.ca/ec2005/agenda/agc3-eng.asp

12. Xu Anqi, "Hai Zi De Jing Ji Cheng Ben: Zhuan Xing Qi De Jie Gou Bian Hua He You Hua" [The economic cost of a child: changes and optimization during the transformation period], *Youth Studies* 12 (2004), 1–9

13. Liu Jie, "McDonald's Growing in China," *China Daily,* September 8, 2008, accessed September 8, 2008, http://www.chinadaily.com.cn/business/2008-09/08/content_7007412.htm

14. "Nv Da Xue Sheng Su Zi Zi Zuo Luo Mo Zhuan Qian Shang Xue" [Female university student Su Zizi works as a nude model to earn tuition fee], *City Express,* January 7, 2011, accessed January 7, 2011, http://news.ifeng.com/gundong/detail_2011_01/07/4070692_0.shtml

15. "Ren Ti Mo Te Su Zi Zi" [Nude model Su Zizi], *Youku.com,* January 18, 2011, accessed January 18, 2011, http://video.soso.com/play/%E4%BA%BA%E4%BD%93%E6%A8%A1%E7%89%B9%E8%8B%8F%E7%B4%AB%E7%B4%AB/?zd=0&i=6&start=0&ch=v.res.play

16. "We Can't Escape," *Neocha.com,* July 13, 2009, accessed July 13, 2009 http://edge.neocha.com/zh/animation/we-cant-escape/

17. Interview with Joan Ren, September 6, 2011, Shanghai.

18. Interview with Joan Ren, September 6, 2011, Shanghai.

19. Interview with Joan Ren, September 6, 2011, Shanghai.

20. Interview with Joan Ren, September 6, 2011, Shanghai.

21. Interview with Joan Ren, September 6, 2011, Shanghai.

22. Interview with Joan Ren, September 6, 2011, Shanghai.

23. Interview with Joan Ren, September 6, 2011, Shanghai.
24. Interview with Frank Chen, August 27, 2011, Shanghai.
25. Interview with Frank Chen, August 27, 2011, Shanghai.
26. Interview with Frank Chen, August 27, 2011, Shanghai.

2   PROGRESS: MAPPING NEW ROADS TO SUCCESS

1. Li Kaiyu, "Nu Li Bu Yi Ding Cheng Gong, Dan Fang Qi Yi Ding Shi Bai" [You may not always succeed even if you work hard, but you will fail if you give up], *Qianjiang Evening Post*, April 15, 2011, accessed April 16, 2011, http://cbachina.163.com/11/0415/05/71LJ09O600052UUC.html
2. Yu Tianyu, "China's Post-80s Get Businesslike," *China Daily*, June 7, 2010, accessed June 7, 2010, http://www.chinadaily.com.cn/video/focus/2010-06/07/content_12269445.htm
3. "Shou Fen 'Fu Er Dai' Qun Ti Diao Yan Bao Gao Fa Bu" [The first 'rich 2 generation' group research report published], *China Youth Daily*, October 19, 2009, accessed October 19, 2009, http://zqb.cyol.com/content/2009-10/19/content_2892236.htm
4. Nandani Lynton and Kirsten Høgh Thøgersen, "Reckoning with Chinese Gen Y," *Businessweek*, January 25, 2010, accessed January 25, 2010, http://www.businessweek.com/globalbiz/content/jan2010/gb20100125_065225.htm
5. Tom Doctoroff, *Billions: Selling to the New Chinese Consumer* (New York: Palgrave Macmillan, 2005). Tom Doctoroff, *What Chinese Want: Culture, Communism and China's Modern Consumer* (New York: Palgrave Macmillan, 2012).
6. Interview with Tom Doctoroff, August 3, 2011, Shanghai.
7. Richard Nisbett, *The Geography of Thought: How Asians and Westerners Think Differently… and Why* (New York: Free Press, 2004).
8. Carey Goldberg, "Differences between East and West Discovered in People's Brain Activity," *The Tech,* March 4, 2008, accessed March 4, 2008, http://tech.mit.edu/V128/N9/culture.html
9. Carey Goldberg, "East and West: Seeing the World through Different Lenses," *New York Times*, March 4, 2008, accessed March 4, 2008, http://www.nytimes.com/2008/03/04/health/04iht-6sncult.1.10695876.html
10. Telephone interview with Nandani Lynton, November 11, 2010.
11. Zhao Xia, Zhu Song, and Ma Guodong, "Zhong Ri Han Mei Si Guo Gao Zhong Sheng Quan Yi Zhuang Kuang Bi Jiao Yan Jiu Bao Gao" [Comparative investigation report of high school students' right condition in China, Japan, Korea, and America], *The China Youth*

and Children Research Center, April, 2010, accessed April, 2010, http://sunyunxiao.youth.cn/jygd/xsbg/201004/t20100409_1193480.htm

12. Lynton, Nandani, and Kurt April, "Generation Y in Cross-Cultural Comparison: Results from China and South Africa," 2011, under review.

13. Telephone interview with Nandani Lynton, November 11, 2010.

14. Cao Hongbei, "Zhong Guo Xin Wen Zhou Kan: Tou Shi Zai Zhong Fu Xia Qian Xing De Zhong Guo Bai Ling Sheng Huo" [White-collar workers' life under huge pressure], *China News Week*, June 23, 2005, accessed June 23, 2005, http://news.sina.com.cn/s/2005-06-23/12357026135.shtml

15. Cao Hongbei, "Zhong Guo Xin Wen Zhou Kan: Tou Shi Zai Zhong Fu Xia Qian Xing De Zhong Guo Bai Ling Sheng Huo" [White-collar workers' life under huge pressure].

16. Li Ke, *Du La La Sheng Zhi Ji* [A story of Lala's promotion] (Shaanxi: Shaanxi Normal University Press, 2007).

17. Anita Chang, "Young Migrants Changing the Face of China's Cities," *Washington Post*, March 13, 2011, accessed March 13, 2011, http://www.washingtonpost.com/wp-dyn/content/article/2011/03/12/AR2011031203054.html

18. Ralph Jennings, "China's 'Ant Tribe' Poses Policy Challenge for Beijing," *Reuters*, February 17, 2010, accessed February 17, 2010, http://www.reuters.com/article/2010/02/18/us-china-middleclass-idUSTRE61H01220100218

19. Lian Si, *Yi Zu*, [Ant tribe] (Guilin: Guangxi Normal University Press, 2009).

20. Lian Si, *Yi Zu II: Shei De Shi Dai*, [Ant tribe II: whose era is it] (Beijing: Citic Press, 2010).

21. Chen Siwu and Li Yahong, "China's 'Ant Tribe' Searches for Better Future," *Xinhuanet.com*, January 16, 2010, accessed January 16, 2010, http://news.xinhuanet.com/english/2010-01/16/content_12819010.htm

22. Anita Chang, "Young Migrants Changing the Face of China's Cities."

23. Joel Johnson, "1 Million Workers. 90 Million iPhones. 17 Suicides. Who's to Blame?" *Wired*, February 28, 2011, accessed March 28, 2011, http://www.wired.com/magazine/2011/02/ff_joelinchina/all/1

24. David Barboza, "After Suicides, Scrutiny of China's Grim Factories," *New York Times*, June 6, 2010, accessed June 6, 2010, http://www.nytimes.com/2010/06/07/business/global/07suicide.html?pagewanted=all

25. Li Li, "Zhong Ri Han Mei Si Guo Gao Zhong Sheng Diao Cha Xian Shi Zhong Guo Xue Sheng Xue Xi Ya Li Zui Da," [Comparative

investigation report of high school students in China, Japan, Korea, and America: Chinese students have the most pressure to study], *Beijing Evening News,* April 8, 2010, accessed April 8, 2010, http://www.chinanews.com/edu/edu-jygg/news/2010/04-08/2214528.shtml

26. Cao Hongbei, "Zhong Guo Xin Wen Zhou Kan: Tou Shi Zai Zhong Fu Xia Qian Xing De Zhong Guo Bai Ling Sheng Huo" [White-collar workers' life under huge pressure].

27. "China Consumer Market Strategies 2011," *Booz & Company,* http://www.booz.com/media/file/China_Consumer_Market_Strategies_2011.pdf

28. "Gu Zhu, Shei Shi Da Xue Sheng De Zui Ai—Jie Du '2008 Zhong Guo Da Xue Sheng Zui Jia Gu Zhu Diao Cha Bao Gao'" [Who's university graduates' favorite employer?], *ChinaHR.com,* August 5, 2008, accessed August 5, 2008, http://content.chinahr.com/jobs_test/Article(52243)ArticleInfo.view

29. "Zhong Hua Ying Cai Wang Di Ba Jie Da Xue Sheng Zui Jia Gu Zhu Diao Cha Bao Gao," [ChinaHR.com publishes the eighth survey report on best employers among Chinese university students], *ChinaHR.com,* July 2010, accessed July 30, 2010, http://www.chinahr.com/promotion/mkt/2010bestemployer/images/2010report.pdf

30. Ruo Chen, "Da Xue Sheng Jiu Ye 'Qiu Wen' Zheng Chang Hai Shi Zhang Ai" [University graduates career motivation: stableness first], *China Youth Daily,* January 20, 2011, accessed January 20, 2011, http://zqb.cyol.com/html/2011-01/20/nw.D110000zgqnb_20110120_7-02.htm?div=-1

31. Michael Tighe, "China Jobs Slump Makes Graduates Swap Dreams for Civil Service," *Bloomberg,* May 14, 2009, accessed May 14, 2009, http://www.bloomberg.com/apps/news?pid=newsarchive&sid=aUtH5xTy1zB0&refer=home

32. Ian Ransom, "Jobless China Graduates Mired in Gloom amid Slowdown," *Reuters,* March 12, 2009, accessed March 12, 2009, http://in.reuters.com/article/2009/03/12/idINIndia-38466120090312

33. Liang Fei, "College Graduate Salaries Down, Migrant Worker Pay Up," *Global Times,* November 24, 2010, accessed November 24, 2010, http://business.globaltimes.cn/china-economy/2010-11/596020.html

34. Wang Yan, "Employment Pressure to Peak in June," *China Daily,* February 18, 2010, accessed February 18, 2010, http://www.chinadaily.com.cn/china/2010-02/18/content_9473273.htm

35. Cheng Mei, "Min Diao Xian Shi: 'Shai Gong Zi' Rang San Cheng Ren Gan Tan Shou Ru Cha Ju Tai Da" [Online exposing salary makes thirty percent of people feel great income gap], *China Youth Daily,* February 5, 2007, accessed February 5, 2007, http://news.xinhuanet.com/employment/2007-02/05/content_5698256.htm

36. Cao Hongbei, "Zhong Guo Xin Wen Zhou Kan: Tou Shi Zai Zhong Fu Xia Qian Xing De Zhong Guo Bai Ling Sheng Huo" [White-collar workers' life under huge pressure].

37. Cao Hongbei, "Zhong Guo Xin Wen Zhou Kan: Tou Shi Zai Zhong Fu Xia Qian Xing De Zhong Guo Bai Ling Sheng Huo" [White-collar workers' life under huge pressure].

38. Zhang Tingting, "Are You 'Working Poor?'" *China.org.cn*, May 12, 2008, accessed May 12, 2008, http://www.china.org.cn/china/national /2008-05/12/content_15165616.htm

39. Interview with Christine Xu, August 29, 2011, Shanghai.

40. Interview with Christine Xu, August 29, 2011, Shanghai.

41. Interview with Christine Xu, August 29, 2011, Shanghai.

42. Interview with Christine Xu, August 29, 2011, Shanghai.

43. Marianne Hurstel, "The Chinese Prosumer: Different Perspective, Same Values," *EURO RSCG*, June 30, 2010, accessed June 30, 2010, http://www.thenewconsumer.com/2010/06/30/the-chinese-prosumer -different-perspective-same-values/

44. Mary Bergstrom, "Ten Trends Driving Sales in China's Retail Industry," *Ad Age China*, October 27, 2010, accessed October 27, 2010, http://adage.com/china/article/viewpoint/mary-bergstrom-identifies -ten-trends-driving-sales-in-chinas-retail-industry/146700/

45. Mary Bergstrom, "Ten Trends Driving Sales in China's Retail Industry."

46. "Cong '80 Hou' Qing Nian De Zhi Chang Zhuang Kuang Kan Wo Guo De Ji Chu Jiao Yu" [Understanding China's basic education from the post-80s' career performance], *The China Youth and Children Research Center,* 2008, accessed 2008, http://sunyunxiao.youth.cn /jygd/xsbg/200812/t20081226_842534.htm

47. Interview with Tom Doctoroff, August 3, 2011, Shanghai.

48. "Zhong Hua Ying Cai Wang Di Jiu Jie Da Xue Sheng Zui Jia Gu Zhu Diao Cha Bao Gao" [ChinaHR.com publishes the ninth survey report on best employers among Chinese university students], *ChinaHR.com,* July 2011, accessed July 2011, http://image.chinahr .com/market/2011bestemployer01/images/2011report.pdf

49. "Zhong Hua Ying Cai Wang Di Jiu Jie Da Xue Sheng Zui Jia Gu Zhu Diao Cha Bao Gao" [ChinaHR.com publishes the ninth survey report on best employers among Chinese university students].

50. Yu Tianyu, "China's Post-80s Get Businesslike."

51. Xu Junqian, "L'Oréal Finances Young Entrepreneurs," *China Daily*, December 28, 2009, accessed December 28, 2009, 10, http://www .chinadaily.com.cn/bw/2009-12/28/content_9235127.htm

52. Huang Daohen, "Vancl Tries Out E-Commerce 2.0," *Beijing Today*, March 25, 2011, accessed March 25, 2011, http://www.beijingtoday .com.cn/business/vancl-tries-out-e-commerce-2-0

53. "New-Gen Workers in India & China: Reshaping Their Workplaces & the World," *Steelcase*, November 2010, accessed April 5, 2011, http:// www.steelcase.com/en/Resources/Research/360%20white%20 papers/Documents/Steelcase%20360Whitepaper_Gen%20Y%20 China-India_dec2010.pdf

54. Telephone interview with Nandani Lynton, November 11, 2010.

3 TIPPING GENDER SCALES: FROM BOYS RULE TO GIRL POWER

1. Justin Bergman, "China's TV Dating Shows: For Love or Money?" *Time,* June 30, 2010, accessed June 30, 2010, http://www.time.com /time/world/article/0,8599,2000558,00.html

2. "Xiamen Merchant Cashes In on Controversial 'Sister Feng,'" *What's on Xiamen*, November 5, 2010, accessed November 5, 2010, http:// www.whatsonxiamen.com/news15573.html

3. Isaac Stone Fish, "Chinese Women Go Shopping," *Newsweek*, August 27, 2010, accessed August 27, 2010, http://www.newsweek .com/2010/08/27/chinese-women-go-shopping.html

4. Shaun Rein, "How to Tap China's Super Spending Women," *CNBC*, June 6, 2011, accessed June 6, 2011, http://www.cnbc.com /id/43290845/How_to_Tap_China_s_Super_Spending_Women

5. R. M. Schneiderman and Alexandra A. Seno, "The Women Who Want to Run the World," *Newsweek*, August 27, 2010, accessed August 27, 2010, http://www.newsweek.com/2010/08/27/chinese -women-are-more-ambitious-than-americans.html

6. Allan Walker and Clive Dimmock, *School Leadership and Administration: Adopting A Cultural Perspective* (New York: RoutledgeFalmer, 2002), 183.

7. Niall Ferguson, "Men without Women," *Newsweek*, March 6, 2011, accessed March 6, 2011, http://www.newsweek.com/2011/03/06/men -without-women.html

8. Ferguson, "Men Without Women."

9. Ferguson, "Men Without Women."

10. Ferguson, "Men Without Women."

11. Ferguson, "Men Without Women."

12. David Eimer, "Bride-Trafficking Grows as the Number of Single Men Soars," *China Daily*, August 1, 2005, accessed August 1, 2005,

http://www.chinadaily.com.cn/english/doc/2005-08/01/content_465222.htm

13. Mitch Moxley, "Men Becoming More Suicide-Prone," *Inter Press Service*, February 20, 2011, accessed February 20, 2011, http://ipsnews.net/news.asp?idnews=54545

14. Moxley, "Men Becoming More Suicide-Prone."

15. Shang-Jin Wei and Xiaobo Zhang, "The Competitive Saving Motive: Evidence from Rising Sex Ratios and Savings Rates in China", *National Bureau of Economic Research,* June 2009, http://www.nber.org/papers/w15093.pdf

16. Telephone interview with James Farrer, June 22, 2011.

17. "80 Hou Cheng Hun Fang Zhu Li 70 Hou Yi Mai 90 Hou Bu Zhao Ji" [The post-80s become primary home buyers, buying houses for marriage; the post-70s already bought while the post-90s don't care], *Wuhan Evening News,* March 9, 2010, accessed November 28, 2010, http://sh.house.163.com/10/0309/09/61ATT3PI00073SDJ.html

18. Li Ying, "'80 Hou' De Hun Yin Zhen Hui Si Zai Fang Zi Shang Ma" [Are post-80s' marriages broken because of housing problems?], *China Youth Daily*, May 5, 2009, accessed May 5, 2009, http://zqb.cyol.com/content/2009-05/05/content_2651051.htm

19. Zhang Tiankan, "Mai Fang Zu Fang Dou Bu Xing Fu" [Neither buying nor renting a house is happy], *China Youth Daily*, November 27, 2009, accessed November 27, 2009, http://zqb.cyol.com/content/2009-11/27/content_2956416.htm

20. Liu Liu, "Ren Zhi Qiang Jian Yan 'Wo Ju' 80 Hou: Zhong Guo Nian Qing Ren Jiu Gai Mai Bu Qi Fang" [Ren Zhiqiang said: Chinese post-80s should not be able to afford to buy a house], *China Economic Net*, December 2, 2009, accessed December 2, 2009, http://www.ce.cn/macro/more/200912/01/t20091201_20536193.shtml

21. Wang Di, "Du Jia Diao Cha: Chao 9 Cheng Wang You Zheng Zuo Fang Nu, Jin 4 Cheng Yin Mai Fang Shi Qu Kuai Le" [Investigation: over ninety percent netizens try to be house slaves and about forty percent feel unhappy because of buying houses], *Sina.com*, December 3, 2009, accessed December 3, 2009, http://www.cnstock.com/test/node4/node102/200912/288800.htm

22. Alice Xin Liu, "Narrow Dwellings: A TV Series That Slipped through SARFT's Guidelines," *Danwei.org,* December 11, 2009, accessed December 11, 2009, http://www.danwei.org/tv/narrow_dwellings.php

23. Alice Xin Liu, "Narrow Dwellings: A TV Series That Slipped through SARFT's Guidelines," *Danwei.org,* December 11, 2009, accessed December 11, 2009, http://www.danwei.org/tv/narrow_dwellings.php

24. Yu Ying, "Bai Ling Hai Shi Yi Zu: *Wo Ju* Huan Xing Shi Dai Yin Tong" [White-collar workers or ant tribes: *Narrow Dwellings* reflects sorrows

of the time], *Time Weekly*, November 26, 2009, accessed November 26, 2009, http://money.hexun.com/2009-11-26/121821421.html

25. Yu Tianyu, "Chinese Women Top Self-Made Rich List," *China Daily*, October 13, 2010, accessed October 13, 2010, http://www.chinadaily.com.cn/cndy/2010-10/13/content_11402225.htm

26. "2005 Nian Fen Di Qu Ping Jun Chu Hun Nian Ling" [National area average age at first marriage in 2005], *National Bureau of Statistics of China*, http://www.stats.gov.cn/tjsj/ndsj/renkou/2005/html/0604.htm

27. Tao Ningning, "08 Hun Yin Deng Ji Bao Gao Chu Lu 'Liang Di Hun' Duo Chu Hun Nian Ling Jiang" [2008 marriage registration report: trans-regional marriages increase while average age at first marriage decrease], *Dongfang Daily*, January 13, 2009, accessed January 13, 2009, http://old.jfdaily.com/news/xwsh/200901/t20090113_507285.htm

28. Telephone interview with James Farrer, June 22, 2011.

29. Zhou Zhou, "Zhong Guo Cheng Shi Nian Qing Nv Xing Geng Jia Zhu Zhong Shi Ye Fa Zhan" [Chinese urban young women put more emphasis on career development], *Xinhuanet.com*, March 6, 2010, accessed March 6, 2010, http://news.xinhuanet.com/politics/2010-03/06/content_13112011.htm

30. Xie Chuanjiao, "Matchmakers to Be Put under Regulation," *China Daily*, November 10, 2007, http://www.chinadaily.com.cn/cndy/2007-11/10/content_6244681.htm

31. "Matchmaking Changes in China," *CRI ENGLISH*, February 16, 2009, accessed February 16, 2009, http://english.cri.cn/4406/2009/02/16/2062s454316.htm

32. "'Money for Love' a Growing Trend," *CRI*, September 1, 2010, accessed September 1, 2010, http://www.china.org.cn/china/2010-09/01/content_20843343.htm

33. Han Hao and Ling Zi, "Hun Lian Guan Nian Diao Cha: Hun Qian Tong Ju Huo Jie Shou, Xiang Qin Bu Zai Lao Tu" [Marriage values survey: premarital cohabitation is acceptable and blind dating is fashionable again], *Nanfang Daily*, October 24, 2009, accessed October 24, 2009, http://www.chinanews.com/sh/news/2009/10-24/1928453.shtml

34. Hewitt Duncan, *Getting Rich First: Life in a Changing China* (London: Chatto & Windus 2007), 220.

35. Telephone interview with James Farrer, Shanghai, China, June 22, 2011.

36. Han Hao and Ling Zi, "Hun Lian Guan NianDiao Cha: Hun Qian Tong Ju Huo Jie Shou, Xiang Qin Bu Zai Lao Tu" [Marriage values survey: premarital cohabitation is acceptable and blind dating is fashionable again].

37. Zhang Hao, "Guo Ban Shu Qing Shao Nian Sheng Zhi Jian Kang Zhi Shi Kao 'Zi Xue'" [Over half of youth learn reproductive health knowledge on their own], *Jian Kang Bao*, May 5, 2010, accessed May 5, 2010, http://kids.youth.cn/xzbb/yw/201005/t20100505_1221959.htm

38. Zhang, "Guo Ban Shu Qing Shao Nian Sheng Zhi Jian Kang Zhi Shi Kao 'ZiXue'" [Over half of youth learn reproductive health knowledge on their own].

39. Alexa Olesen, "Young Women Tied to Abortion Rise in China," *MSNBC*, January 9, 2011, accessed January 9, 2011, http://www.msnbc.msn.com/id/40967081/ns/health-womens_health/t/young-women-tied-abortion-rise-china/

40. Zhang Peng, "Bei Jing Min Ying Yi Yuan Tui Ren Liu Xue Sheng Tao Can, Zao Yun Shao Nv Zeng Jia" [A Beijing private hospital launches abortion sets for students, number of young pregnant girls rises], *Beijing Evening Post*, November 9, 2010, accessed November 9, 2010, http://news.sohu.com/20101109/n277489989.shtml

41. Zhang, "Bei Jing Min Ying Yi Yuan Ren Liu Xue Sheng Tao Can, Zao Yun Shao Nv Zeng Jia" [A Beijing private hospital launches abortion sets for students, number of young pregnant girls rises].

42. Rob, "Sex in Society: A New Culture War amongst China's Post-90's," *Enovate China*, November 30, 2010, accessed November 30, 2010, http://blog.enovatechina.com/sex-in-society-a-new-culture-war-amongst-chinas-post-90s/

43. Zhang, "Bei Jing Min Ying Yi Yuan Ren Liu Xue Sheng Tao Can, Zao Yun Shao Nv Zeng Jia" [A Beijing private hospital launches abortion sets for students, number of young pregnant girls rises].

44. Telephone interview with James Farrer, June 22, 2011.

45. Han Hao and LingZi, "Hun Lian Guan NianDiao Cha: Hun Qian Tong Ju Huo Jie Shou, Xiang Qin Bu Zai Lao Tu" [Marriage values survey: premarital cohabitation is acceptable and blind dating is fashionable again].

46. Han Hao and LingZi, "Hun Lian Guan NianDiao Cha: Hun Qian Tong JuHuoJieShou, Xiang Qin Bu Zai Lao Tu" [Marriage values survey: premarital cohabitation is acceptable and blind dating is fashionable again].

47. Tao Ningning, "Shang Hai Zhong Gao Duan Hun Li Ping Jun Hua Fei 39 Wan Yuan, Bi Mei Guo Gui Liang Bei" [Average wedding cost in Shanghai is 390 thousand, three times as in America], *Dongfang Daily*, March 31, 2011, accessed March 31, 2011, http://finance.people.com.cn/GB/42877/14281806.html

48. "Diao Cha: 'Luo Hun,' Nan Nv Tai Du Da Bu Tong" [About naked wedding: great differences between men and women], *NetEase.com*,

accessed February 5, 2010, http://lady.163.com/special/00261MPK /luohun.html

49. Jiang Xiaochuan and Liu Haijian, "'80 Hou' Gan Jue Jia Ban Xiang Liu Tang, '70 Hou' Shi Zhi Chang Pin Ming San Lang" [Post-80s think of overtime work as detention, while post-70s are workaholics], *Guangzhou Daily*, May 4, 2010, accessed May 4, 2010, http://gzdaily .dayoo.com/html/2010-05/04/content_952210.htm

50. Qi Xianghao, "Fen Xi 80 Hou Nv Xing Li Hun Guan Si, Qi Cheng Li Hun Su Song You Nv Fang Ti Qi" [Post-80s divorce analysis: seventy percent are issued by women], *Zhejiang Online*, September 8, 2010, http://zjnews.zjol.com.cn/05zjnews/system/2010/09/08/016913804.shtml

51. Wang Qing, "Wu Han 80 Hou Li Hun Qi Cheng Shi 'Nv Xiu Nan'" [Wu Han post-80s divorces: seventy percent are required by women], *Changjiang Times*, January 7, 2011, accessed January 7, 2011, http:// news.163.com/11/0107/05/6PP6HFMG00014AED.html

52. Chen Jia, "'Child's Slave' Is Media Hype, Survey Shows," *China Daily*, February 11, 2010, accessed February 11, 2010, http://www .chinadaily.com.cn/china/2010-02/11/content_9459594.htm

53. Huang Haiying and Teng Yang, "Diao Cha Xian Shi: Zhi Chang Nv Xing 'Ding Ke' Zu 3 Nian Zeng Jia 5 Bei" [Survey: career women DINCs increase five times in three years], *Chengdu Evening News*, March 11, 2008, accessed March 11, 2008, http://news.163 .com/08/0311/09/46OCDQUK000120GU.html

54. Xu Lin, "Sharing The Burden," *China Daily*, March 15, 2011, accessed March 15, 2011, http://www.chinadaily.com.cn/usa/life/2011-03/15 /content_12174672.htm

4 ABOUT FACE: SEEING NEW BEAUTY CODES

1. "Li Yu Chun Ai Zhong Xing Da Ban Zi Cheng You Ren Xi Huan Jiu Bu Cuo Le" [Li Yuchun likes neutral dressing style and says few guys will love her], *Sina.com*, March 16, 2009, accessed November 22, 2011, http://ent.cqnews.net/ylove/200903/t20090316_3099216.htm

2. Clifford Coonan, "Handsome Chinese Vagrant Draws Fans of 'Homeless Chic,'" *The Independent*, March 4, 2010, accessed March 4, 2010, http://www.independent.co.uk/news/world/asia/handsome -chinese-vagrant-draws-fans-of-homeless-chic-1915812.html

3. "Brother Sharp," *Know Your Mem.com*, April 18, 2010, accessed March 28, 2010, http://knowyourmeme.com/memes/brother-sharp -%E7%8A%80%E5%88%A9%E5%93%A5

4. Carrie Lennard and Euromonitor International, "BRIC: Continued Domination of Global Beauty Sales," GCI Magazine, July 13, 2011,

accessed July 13, 2011, http://www.gcimagazine.com/marketstrends
/regions/bric/125481838.html?page=1

5. Email interview with Tom Doctoroff, August 22, 2011.

6. Li Ai, "Bei Jing Ao Yun Li Yi Xiao Jie Yao Kuai Zi Xun Lian Wei
Xiao" [Beijing Olympics girls are trained to smile better by biting
chopsticks], *Beijing Times*, January 10, 2008, accessed January 10,
2008, http://epaper.jinghua.cn/html/2008-01/10/content_201153
.htm

7. "'Iron Girl' of Mao Era Regaining Feminine Self," *Beijing Times*,
March 8, 2003, accessed March 8, 2003, http://english.peopledaily
.com.cn/200303/08/eng20030308_112946.shtml

8. Mao Zedong, *Mao Zedong Poems* (Beijing: Foreign Languages Press,
1976).

9. Chen Nan, "A Versatile 'Flower Vase,'" *China Daily*, September 12, 2008,
http://www.chinadaily.com.cn/cndy/2008-09/12/content_7021150.htm

10. Attilio Jesús, "China's New Faces," *Le Monde Diplomatique*, June 2005,
accessed June 2005, http://mondediplo.com/2005/06/17beauty

11. Saga McFarland, "Once Rejected, China Embraces Beauty Pageants,"
CNN.com, October 18, 2011, accessed November 28, 2011, http://
articles.cnn.com/2011-10-18/asia/world_asia_china-beauty
-pageant_1_pageants-contestants-outer-beauty/3?_s=PM:ASIA

12. "Timeline," *China Daily*, October 4, 2011, accessed November 28,
2011, http://www.chinadaily.com.cn/cndy/2011-10/04/content
_13835839.htm

13. Email interview with Tom Doctoroff, August 22, 2011.

14. Yuval Atsmon, Vinay Dixit, Glenn Leibowitz, and Cathy Wu,
"Understanding China's Growing Love for Luxury," *McKinsey*, March
2011, accessed March 2011, http://www.mckinsey.com/locations
/greaterchina/InsightsChina_LuxuryGoods.pdf

15. Phone interview with Charles de Brabant, July 27, 2011.

16. Chen Hong, "Beauty Queen Sparks Ugly Debate in Shenzhen," *China
Daily*, November 24, 2005, accessed November 24, 2005, http://www
.chinadaily.com.cn/english/doc/2005-11/24/content_497425.htm

17. Tania Branigan, "Chinese City Wardens Wanted: Must Be Young,
Female and Pretty," *Guardian*, October 28, 2010, accessed March 16,
2011, http://www.guardian.co.uk/world/2010/oct/28/chinese-city
-wardens-women

18. Chen Yangkai, An Xiaoqing, and Zhong Huixian, "60% De Nv Xing
Bu Ru Qi Nei Gong Zuo Nan Zhao" [Sixty percent of female workers
feel it is difficult to find a job while breastfeeding], *Southern Metropolis
Daily*, March 2, 2011, FA02, accessed March 2, 2011, http://gcontent
.oeeee.com/c/08/c0826819636026dd/Blog/448/17aca0.html

19. Bridget Lee, "Plastic Surgery and Attitudes of Beauty and Success," *China Daily*, July 5, 2004, accessed July 5, 2004, http://www.chinadaily.com.cn/english/doc/2004-07/05/content_345598.htm

20. Wen Hua, "'Being Good-Looking Is Capital': Cosmetic Surgery in China Today," *The Chinese University of Hong Kong*, Asian Anthropology 8 (2009), accessed August 1, 2011, http://cup.cuhk.edu.hk/ojs/index.php/AsianAnthropology/article/viewArticle/2163/2920

21. "Insight: Ever-Increasing Plastic Surgery Market," *China Network Television*, November 29, 2010, accessed November 29, 2010, http://english.cntv.cn/program/china24/20101129/102227.shtml

22. Wang Zhenghua, "Men in Shanghai Go under Knife for Beauty," *China Daily*, September 26, 2006, 3, accessed September 26, 2006, http://www.chinadaily.com.cn/china/2006-09/26/content_696993.htm

23. Email interview with Tom Doctoroff, August 22, 2011.

24. "72% in Survey Say Society Created Plastic Surgery Fad," *China Daily*, December 10, 2010, accessed December 10 , 2010, http://www.chinadaily.com.cn/2010-12/10/content_11684479.htm

25. Phone interview wih James Farrer, Jun 22, 2011.

26. Yu Tianyu, "Males Turn to Cosmetic Appearance,"*China Daily*, January 6, 2011, accessed January 6, 2011, http://www.chinadaily.com.cn/usa/2011-01/06/content_11802981.htm

27. Yu Tianyu, "Males Turn to Cosmetic Appearance."

28. Yu Tianyu, "Males Turn to Cosmetic Appearance."

29. Frederik Balfour, "China's 'City Jade Men' Indulge in Mud Masks, L'Oreal Creams," *Bloomberg*, December 13, 2010, accessed December 13, 2010, http://www.bloomberg.com/news/2010-12-12/china-s-city-jade-men-indulge-in-mud-masks-l-oreal-creams.html

30. Yu Tianyu, "Males Turn to Cosmetic Appearance."

31. David Pierson, "In China, Alpha Males Carry Designer Purses," *Los Angeles Times*, February 7, 2011, accessed February 7, 2011, http://articles.latimes.com/2011/feb/07/business/la-fi-china-man-purse-20110207

32. David Barboza, "The People's Republic of Sex Kittens and Metrosexuals," *New York Times*, March 4, 2007, WK3, accessed March 4, 2007, http://www.nytimes.com/2007/03/04/weekinreview/04barboza.html

33. Yu Tianyu, "Males Turn to Cosmetic Appearance."

34. Phone interview with Charles de Brabant, July 27, 2011.

35. Adaline Lau, "Lenovo Continues Youth Focus with Xiao Ben," *Marketing Magazine*, February 10, 2010, accessed February 10, 2010, http://www.marketing-interactive.com/news/17625

36. "Health, Beauty & Personal Grooming: A Global Nielsen Consumer Report," *Nielsen*, March, 2007, http://pt.nielsen.com /documents/0705_PersonalGrooming.pdf

37. Du Xiaodan, "Lv Yan: From Ugly Duckling to Super Model," CCTV. com, January 15, 2007, accessed January 15, 2007, http://www.cctv .com/program/cultureexpress/20070115/104026_10.shtml

38. Susan Jakes, "Li Yuchun," *Time*, October 3, 2005, accessed October 3, 2005, http://www.time.com/time/world/article/0,8599,2054304,00 .html

39. Xiang Nan, "Zhong Qing Zai Xian: 65% De Ren Dan Xin 'Zhong Xing Feng' Shi Ren Xing Wei Pian Cha" [Sixty-five percent of informants worry 'neutral style' induces behavior peculiarity] *China Youth Daily*, December 30, 2010, accessed December 30, 2010, http://news .xinhuanet.com/newmedia/2010-12/30/c_12933631_3.htm

40. Shi Xi, "Report Shows Healthy Outlook for China's Children," *People's Daily*, June 1, 2011, accessed June 1, 2011, http://english.peopledaily .com.cn/90001/90776/90882/7397862.html

41. Shi Xi, "Report Shows Healthy Outlook for China's Children."

5 SPEAKING UP: THE SEEDS OF ACTIVISM

1. "Ma Yun Chuang Ye Zhen Jing: Nian Qing Ren Chuang Ye De San Da Yuan Ze" [Ma Yun entrepreneurial tips: three principles for young entrepreneurs], *Umiwi.com,* November 17, 2011, accessed November 24, 2011, http://chuangye.umiwi.com/2011/1117/48770_2.shtml

2. Interview with Christine Xu, August 29, 2011, Shanghai.

3. Interview with Christine Xu, August 29, 2011, Shanghai.

4. Phone interview wih Duncan Hewitt, June 17, 2011.

5. Phone interview wih Duncan Hewitt, June 17, 2011.

6. Edward Wong, "An Online Scandal Underscores Chinese Distrust of State Charities," *New York Times,* July 3, 2011, accessed July 3, 2011, http://www.nytimes.com/2011/07/04/world/asia/04china.html? ref=philanthropy

7. Edward Wong, "An Online Scandal Underscores Chinese Distrust of State Charities."

8. Peter Walker, "Chinese Faked Photograph Leaves Officials on Street of Shame," *Guardian,* June 29, 2011, accessed July 30, 2011, http:// www.guardian.co.uk/world/2011/jun/29/chinese-county-ridicule -doctored-photograph

9. "The Coming of Age," *McKinsey,* June 2010, accessed June 10, 2010, http://www.mckinsey.com/locations/greaterchina/mckonchina /reports/mcKinsey_wealthy_consumer_report.pdf

10. Interview with Tim Minges, August 22, 2011, Shanghai.

11. Interview with Tim Minges, August 22, 2011, Shanghai.

12. Interview with Tim Minges, August 22, 2011, Shanghai.

13. "Over 12,000 Chinese Children Sick from Tainted Milk," *China Daily,* September 22, 2008, accessed September 22, 2008, http://www.chinadaily.com.cn/china/2008-09/22/content_7046709.htm

14. Austin Ramzy and Lin Yang, "Tainted Baby-Milk Scandal in China," *Times,* September 16, 2008, accessed September 16, 2008, http://www.time.com/time/world/article/0,8599,1841535,00.html

15. "Mengniu Milk Sickens Shaanxi Schoolchildren," *Global Times,* April 23 2011, accessed April 23 2011, http://china.globaltimes.cn/society/2011-04/647836.html

16. "China Detains 483 in Three-Day Fake Booze Crackdown," *Xinhuanet.com,* April 14, 2011, accessed April 14, 2011, http://www.chinaipr.gov.cn/newsarticle/news/government/201104/1216177_1.html

17. "China Police Crack Down on Fake Booze in Capital," *The China Post,* May 17, 2011, accessed May 17, 2011, http://www.chinapost.com.tw/china/local-news/beijing/2011/05/17/302674/China-police.htm

18. Joseph Tsai, "Conflict between Japan and China May Benefit Taiwan Notebook Brands, Says Paper," *DIGITIMES,* October 1, 2010, accessed October 1, 2010, http://www.digitimes.com/news/a20101001PB201.html

19. Lionel Laurent, "LVMH Boss Shrugs Off Beijing Boycott," *Forbes,* April 19, 2008, accessed April 19, 2008, http://www.forbes.com/2008/04/19/arnault-lvmh-china-face-markets-cx_ll_0417autofacescan02.html

20. Zhang, Keen. "Carrefour Boycott and Sophisticated CNN." *China.org.cn,* April 16, 2008, accessed April 16, 2008, http://www.china.org.cn/china/Lhasa_Unrest/2008 04/16/content_14966297.htm

21. Wang Xiaoqiao and Pan Xiaoling, "Kua Guo Gong Si Bu Man 'Guo Ji Tie Zhong Ji Pai Hang Bang' Qiu Jiu Shang Wu Bu" [International firms object the international iron rooster list and ask help from ministry of commerce of the People's Republic of China], *South Weekend,* May 29, 2008, accessed May 29, 2008, http://finance.ifeng.com/news/hgjj/200805/0529_2201_568825_1.shtml

22. John Garnaut and Maya Li, "Loyal Citizens Take Heart," *The Age,* April 23, 2008, accessed April 23, 2008, http://www.theage.com.au/news/national/loyal-citizens-take-heart/2008/04/22/1208742941505.html

23. "Nv Tong Xing Lian Diao Cha: Duo Wei Yan Jiu Sheng Gong Wu Yuan, Ju Hui Duo Zai Jiu Ba" [Lesbian investigation: they mainly consist of postgraduates and civil servants and have parties in bars],

Du Shi Nv Bao, June 22, 2011, accessed June 22, 2011, http://news
.sohu.com/20110622/n311262399.shtml

24. QianYanfeng, "Shanghai Hosts First Gay Pride Festival," *China Daily,*
    June 10, 2009, accessed June 10, 2009, http://www.chinadaily.com
    .cn/china/2009-06/10/content_8265878.htm
25. Andrew Jacobs, "Chinese Gay Pageant Is Shut Down," *New York
    Times,* January 15, 2010, accessed January 15, 2010, http://www
    .nytimes.com/2010/01/16/world/asia/16beijing.html
26. Shijiu Yin, LinhaiWu, Lili Dub, and Mo Chena, "Consumers'
    Purchase Intention of Organic Food in China," *Wiley Interscience,* 13
    April 2010, DOI 10.1002/jsfa.3936
27. "Get Going with Green: Closing the Sustainability Gap,"
    OgilvyEarth, April 22, 2011, accessed April 22, 2011, http://www
    .ogilvyearth.com/wp-content/uploads/2011/05/Get_Going_with
    _Green_Chinese.pdf
28. Wang Xiaojie, "LOHAS Concept Enters into China," *Xinhua.org,*
    July 18, 2006, accessed November 25, 2011, http://news.qq.com
    /a/20060718/001599.htm
29. "LOHAS in Beijing," *Global Times,* December 15, 2009, accessed
    December 15, 2009, http://english.people.com.cn/90001/90782
    /6842186.html
30. Kai Lukoff, "Chinese SNS Kaixin001's Open Platform Experiment,"
    China Social Games, August 18, 2010, accessed August 18, 2010,
    http://www.chinasocialgames.com/?p=602
31. Phone interview wih Duncan Hewitt, June 17, 2011.
32. Phone interview wih Duncan Hewitt, June 17, 2011.

6 DRIVING SUBCULTURES:
BUILDING A CENTER ON THE EDGE

1. Interview with Denya, February 13, 2009, Shenzhen, China.
2. Louise Edwards and Elaine Jeffreys, *Celebrity in China* (Hong Kong:
   Hong Kong University Press, 2010), 222–223.
3. Edward Cody, "In Chinese Cyberspace, A Blossoming Passion,"
   The Washington Post, July 19, 2005, accessed July 19, 2005, http://
   www.washingtonpost.com/wp-dyn/content/article/2005/07/18
   /AR2005071801561.html
4. Louise Edwards and Elaine Jeffreys, *Celebrity in China* (Hong Kong:
   Hong Kong University Press, 2010), 217–218.
5. Raymond Zhou, "Hibiscus Blooms and Creates a Buzz on the Net,"
   China Daily, July 1, 2005, accessed July 1, 2005, http://www2.chinadaily
   .com.cn/english/doc/2005-07/01/content_456357.htm

6. "China Leads the US in Digital Self-Expression: IAC and JWT Study Reveals New Means of Expression for China's Tech-Savvy Youth," *IAC*, November 23, 2007, accessed November 23, 2007, http://iac.mediaroom.com/index.php?s=43&item=1455

7. Interview with Tom Doctoroff, August 3, 2011, Shanghai.

8. "China's Flagship Blog Site Loses Lawsuit, Stirs Debate," *Xinhuanet.com*, August 5, 2006, accessed August 5, 2006, http://www.china.org.cn/english/China/177046.htm

9. Interview with Isaac Mao, August 29, 2011, Shanghai.

10. Tania Branigan, "Chinese Sex Workers Protest against Crackdown," *The Guardian,* August 3, 2010, accessed August 3, 2010, http://www.guardian.co.uk/world/2010/aug/03/china-prostitution-sex-workers-protest

11. Josh Bernoff and Jacqueline Anderson, "Social Technographics Defined," *Forrester*, August 2, 2010, accessed August 2, 2010, http://www.forrester.com/empowered/ladder2010

12. Forrester Research"s North American Technographics® Online Benchmark Survey, *Forrester,* Q2 2010 (US); Forrester Research"s Asia Pacific Technographics® Survey, *Forrester,* Q4 2009 (Asia Pacific) http://www.forrester.com/empowered/tool_consumer.html

13. Xan Brooks, "Forget Harry Potter, Here's Harry Fatter," *The Guardian*, November 16, 2006, accessed November 16, 2006, http://www.guardian.co.uk/film/filmblog/2006/nov/16/forgetharrypotterheresharr

14. David Pierson, "China's favorite Internet craze: 'Jia Junpeng, your mom is calling you to come home and eat,'" *Los Angeles Times*, September 05, 2009, http://articles.latimes.com/2009/sep/05/business/fi-china-internet-fad5.

15. Juliet Ye and Jason Dean, "China Blogger Conference Is Canceled under Pressure," *The Wall Street Journal*, November 21, 2010, accessed November 21, 2010, http://online.wsj.com/article/SB1000142405274870444430457562841067022643.0.html

16. Shepherd Laughlin, "2011 Tudou Video Festival Awards: The Best of China's Online Films," *CNNGo*, May 17, 2011, accessed May 17, 2011, http://www.cnngo.com/shanghai/life/2011-tudou-video-festival-awards-best-chinas-online-films-629109

17. "How Will China's Tech-Savvy, Post-90s Generation Shape the Nation?," *CNN*, July 18, 2010, accessed July 18, 2010, http://articles.cnn.com/2010-07-18/tech/china.post90s.generation_1_internet-analyst-wild-card-generation-tencent?_s=PM:TECH

18. Ogreenworld, "囧," *Know Your Meme*, October, 2010, accessed October, 2010, http://knowyourmeme.com/memes/%E5%9B%A7

19. Wan Li and Wu Yang, "Kong Da Ren, Yin Wei Chi Ai Suo Yi Tao Kong Qian Bao" [Spending money on obsessions], *Chongqing Evening News,* March 10, 2011, accessed March 10, 2011, http://www.cqwb.com.cn /cqwb/html/2011-03/10/content_258585.htm

20. "The Rise of Net Buzzword 'Gelivable,'" *Shanghai Daily,* November 12, 2010, accessed November 12, 2010, http://www.china.org.cn /china/2010-11/12/content_21327924.htm

21. Michelle Dai, "Holiday Live Music Roundup: Blonde Redhead, Brett Anderson," *The Beijinger,* September 30, 2010, accessed September 30, 2010, http://www.thebeijinger.com/blog/2010/09/30/Holiday-Live -Music-Roundup-Blonde-Redhead-Brett-Anderson

22. Uking Sun, "Midi Music Festival Rocks Costal City," *China Daily,* May 30, 2011, accessed May 30, 2011, http://www.chinadaily.com .cn/slides/2011-05/30/content_12605165.htm

23. Mao Xiubing, Shi Yue, and Tang Ming, "Yin Yue Jie Shi Chang Ji Su Sheng Wen De Bei Hou" [What's behind music festival development], *China Culture Daily*, December 14, 2010, accessed December 14, 2010, http://fashion.ifeng.com/news/detail_2010_12/14/3496817_0 .shtml

24. Mao Xiubing, Shi Yue, and Tang Min, "Yin Yue Jie Shi Chang Ji Su Sheng Wen De Bei Hou" [What's behind music festival development]

25. Jordan Small, "Zebra Music Festival," *That's Shanghai,* August 11, 2011, accessed August 11, 2011, http://www.thatsmags.com/shanghai /index.php/article/detail/818/zebra-music-festival

26. Interview with Ian Stewart, August 17, 2011, Shanghai

27. "Kuang Wei He Hou Hai Da Sha Yu: Dao Ni Le" [Converse and Queen Sea Big Shark: let's play], *Neocha.com,* September 1, 2009, accessed September 1, 2009, http://edge.neocha.com/zh/brands-agencies -companies/converse/converse-new-campaign/

28. Interview with Ian Stewart, August 17, 2011, Shanghai.

29. Interview with Ian Stewart, August 17, 2011, Shanghai.

30. Interview with Ian Stewart, August 17, 2011, Shanghai.

31. Interview with Ian Stewart, August 17, 2011, Shanghai.

7　REBRANDING CHINESENESS:
NEW CHINA, NEW IDENTITY

1. Robb Young, "Jiang Qionger, Shang Xia's CEO & Artistic Director," luxurysociety.com, January 5, 2011, accessed January 5, 2011, http:// luxurysociety.com/articles/2011/01/jiang-qiong-er-shang-xias-ceo -artistic-director

2. Interview with Tom Doctoroff, August 3, 2011, Shanghai, China.

3. "Marketing to the New Chinese Consumer," Forbes, 2011, accessed 2011, http://images.forbes.com/forbesinsights/StudyPDFs /Marketing_to_the_Chinese_Consumer.pdf

4. Jerry Clode, "Marketers Play on Nostalgia to Reach China's Post-1980s Generation," *Ad Age China,* February 16, 2011, accessed February 16, 2011, http://adage.com/article/global-news/marketers-play-nostalgia -reach-china-s-post-1980s-generation/148906/

5. Jerry Clode, "Marketers Play on Nostalgia to Reach China's Post-1980s Generation."

6. Betty Bei Chen, "Nostalgia a Strong Draw for China's 'Post-80s' Consumers," *Jing Daily,* March 9, 2011, accessed May 12, 2011, http://www.jingdaily.com/en/culture/nostalgia-a-strong-draw-for -chinas-post-80s-consumers/

7. "Generation-Specific Restaurant in Beijing Entices 80s VIPs," *The Bergstrom Group,* September 3, 2010, accessed September 3, 2011, http://bergstromtrends.com/generation-specific-restaurant-in -beijing-entices-80s-vips/

8. Shen Hong, "Five Stripes: Rise and Fall of China's Youngest Political Star," *Wall Street Journal,* May 5, 2011, accessed May 5, 2011, http:// blogs.wsj.com/chinarealtime/2011/05/05/five-stripes-rise-and-fall-of -china%E2%80%99s-youngest-political-star/

9. Key, "Brother Scorn Becomes Famous on the Internet, Following Five-Stripe Boy," *China Hush,* May 9, 2011, accessed May 10, 2011, http://www.chinahush.com/2011/05/09/brother-scorn-becomes -famous-on-the-internet-following-five-stripe-boy/

10. Alice Xin Liu, "Beijing Rock Scene Is Inspired by Western Hipster Chic Rather Than the Search for a Deeper Soul," *Huffington Post,* May 6, 2010, accessed May 6, 2010, http://www.huffingtonpost .com/alice-xin-liu/beijing-rock-scene-is-ins_b_566874.html

11. Jimi, "China's Classic Haihun Shan," Neocha, July 23, 2009, accessed July 23, 2009, http://edge.neocha.com/culture/chinas-classic-haihun -shan/

12. Alice Xin Liu, "Beijing Rock Scene Is Inspired by Western Hipster Chic Rather Than the Search for a Deeper Soul."

13. "Lei Feng Becomes Online Game Hero," *Shanghai Daily,* March 15, 2006, accessed March 16, 2006, http://news.xinhuanet.com /english/2006-03/16/content_4308138.htm

14. Xiao Du, "Li Ning X Lei Feng Trainers", 56minus1, May 14, 2009, accessed May 14, 2009, http://56minus1.com/2009/05/chic-but-not -cheap-lei-feng-has-a-new-pair-of-shoes/

15. Xiao Changyan, "Taking Giant Strides," *China Daily,* August 22, 2008, accessed August 22, 2008, http://www.chinadaily.com.cn /bizchina/2008-08/22/content_6961265.htm

16. Rebecca Kanthor, "Cycle City: Shanghai Ramps Up Its Bike-share Schemes," *CNNGo,* April 22, 2010, accessed April 30, 2010, http://www.cnngo.com/shanghai/shop/forever-c-shanghai-traditional-brand-revive-cycling-culture-060028

17. Interview with Frank Chen, July 1, 2011, Shanghai.

18. "New Web Site's Mission: Popularity Contest for Chinese Brands," *Wall Street Journal,* January 11, 2009, accessed January 11, 2009, http://blogs.wsj.com/chinarealtime/2009/01/11/new-web-sites-mission-popularity-contest-for-chinese-brands/?mod=rss_WSJBlog

19. Li Yuan, "The Godmother of Chinese Designers," *Wall Street Journal,* August 5, 2010, accessed August 5, 2010, http://online.wsj.com/article/SB10001424052748703960004575426852614702026.html?mod=googlenews_wsj

20. Interview with Frank Chen, July 1, 2011, Shanghai, China.

21. Loretta Chao and Betsy McKay, "Pepsi Steps into Coke Realm: Red, China," *Wall Street Journal,* September 12, 2007, accessed September 12, 2007, http://online.wsj.com/article/SB118953841749624079-email.html

22. Interview with Tim Minges, August 22, 2011, Shanghai.

23. Interview with Tim Minges, August 22, 2011, Shanghai.

24. Interview with Tim Minges, August 22, 2011, Shanghai.

25. Interview with Tim Minges, August 22, 2011, Shanghai.

26. Glenn Smith, "Sportswear in China—How Local Brands Challenged the Might of Nike and Adidas," *Warc Exclusive,* December 2010, Accessed April 6, 2010, http://www.warc.com/Samples/93120.pdf

27. Glenn Smith, "Sportswear in China—How Local Brands Challenged the Might of Nike and Adidas."

28. Phone interview with Frank Chen, August 27, 2011.

29. Phone interview with Frank Chen, August 27, 2011.

30. Vivian Wai-yin Kwok, "Chinese Sports Brand Takes On Nike," *Forbes,* January 13, 2010, accessed January 13, 2010, http://www.forbes.com/2010/01/13/li-ning-us-expansion-markets-business-sportsgear.html

31. Jonathan Birchall, "Li Ning's Bid to Brand China," *Financial Times,* January 11, 2011, accessed January 11, 2011, http://blogs.ft.com/beyond-brics/2011/01/11/li-nings-bid-to-brand-china/#axzz1QYcDXnTu

32. Frederik Balfour, "China's Li Ning Toe-to-Toe Against Nike and Adidas," *Business Week,* May 1, 2008, accessed May 1, 2008, http://www.businessweek.com/magazine/content/08_19/b4083051446468.htm

33. Vivian Wai-yin Kwok, "Chinese Sports Brand Takes On Nike."

34. Phone interview with Frank Chen, August 27, 2011.

INDEX